Can We Know Better?

Praise for this book

'T.S. Eliot famously asked, "Where is the wisdom we have lost in knowledge? Where is the knowledge we have lost in information?" The answer: it is here, in this book, in the accumulated knowledge of Robert Chambers' six decades of experience and thinking about development, and in the great wisdom he brings to bear on the fantasies and foibles of practitioners, academics and funders. All of them should take time to read this important book and to think hard about what it means when they go back to their work.'

*Ian Smillie, President of the Canadian Association
for the Study of International Development, 2015–17*

'Robert Chambers is a global public good, a true development guru that all should follow. In his latest work, he explores our claims to be able to distinguish between what is true and false – what do we "know" and why do we so often get it wrong? Drawing on almost 60 years of relentlessly questioning orthodoxies and standing up for those excluded from power and decisions, Robert Chambers asks us to fundamentally question the nature of such "knowledge", its biases and blind spots. Then with his customary energy and optimism, he shows how we can "know better" and thus "do better". An indispensable book.'

Dr Duncan Green, Strategic Adviser, Oxfam and author of
How Change Happens

'This book is a salvo against development smugness, much needed at a time when the Sustainable Development Goals are beginning to gain traction. Taking head-on the central question of how we know, and how that shapes what we do through development policy, Chambers employs his clear eye and gently acerbic tongue to show why development professionals need to be more humble, more self-reflexive, and more passionate about our mission.'

*Gita Sen, Distinguished Professor & Director, Ramalingaswami
Centre on Equity & Social Determinants of Health,
Public Health Foundation of India*

'Always prescient and always wise, Robert Chambers has given development scholars and practitioners yet another gift with this provocative call for "a revolution in development knowing, thinking, and practice". But what a commentary on development in practice, that the supposed beneficiaries of development continue to be marginalized and dispossessed. Weep for them and their needless suffering – but read Chambers' new book and get into action!'

*Professor Robin Broad, International
Development Program, American University*

'Robert Chambers once again demonstrates that assessing both the intractable and the emerging development challenges of today is fundamentally about values – from the personal to the socio-economic and political – and the courage to affirm them.'

Ricardo Wilson-Grau, Independent international evaluator with Ricardo Wilson-Grau Consultoria, Rio de Janeiro, Brazil

'In *Can We Know Better?* Robert Chambers provides a stark exposition of the errors of power, and their depressing frequency in development practice. Exposing the tendency of all of us to seek comfort in the myths and misperceptions of our professions with wit, compelling stories and evidence, he lays out the challenge to shift development thinking to a truly universal framing. At the heart is a personal challenge to recognize when we are misled by interests, biases and tricks of memory into ignoring or misrepresenting the realities of change. He shows how, without a commitment to reflecting on ourselves, we run the real risk of getting both the big and small things completely wrong.'

Andrew Norton, Director of the International Institute for Environment and Development

'Robert Chambers' *Can We Know Better*? is a powerful and timely call for those working in development to stand back and reflect critically on how we know and how we might know better. In this book, Chambers exhaustively categorizes manifestations of personal, political and methodological error, bias and privileging. Drawing from a wealth of case study material he illustrates the dramatic and even catastrophic developmental impact of error. He challenges us to know better by recognizing and resisting – through critical reflection tied to "inclusive rigour" and a "revolutionary professionalism" – all forms of bias and ignorance. For all those development professionals and practitioners – we who are "not last" but who claim to act for those who are last – this is a profoundly important book.'

Jeremy Holland, Associate, Social Development, Oxford Policy Management

About the author

Professor Robert Chambers is a research associate of the Institute of Development Studies, at the University of Sussex, UK, which has been his base since 1969 with periods in other countries. His educational background is in natural sciences, history and public administration. His main administrative and research experience in development has been in East Africa and South Asia. Among other work he has been a field administrator and trainer of administrators in Kenya and East Africa, a field researcher in Kenya, India and Sri Lanka, an evaluation officer with UNHCR and a project specialist with the Ford Foundation in India.

Books he has written include *Rural Development: Putting the Last First* (1983), *Challenging the Professions* (1993), *Whose Reality Counts? Putting the First Last* (1997), *Participatory Workshops* (2002), *Ideas for Development* (2005), *Revolutions in Development Inquiry* (2008), *Provocations for Development* (2012) and *Into the Unknown: Explorations in development practice*. His current work and interests include participatory methodologies; participation, power and complexity; professional perceptions and the realities of poverty and well-being; and going to scale with community-led total sanitation.

Can We Know Better?
Reflections for Development

Robert Chambers

PRACTICAL ACTION
Publishing

Practical Action Publishing Ltd
The Schumacher Centre,
Bourton on Dunsmore, Rugby,
Warwickshire, CV23 9QZ, UK
www.practicalactionpublishing.org

A catalogue record for this book is available from the British Library.
A catalogue record for this book has been requested from the Library of Congress.

ISBN 9781853399442 Hardback
ISBN 9781853399459 Paperback
ISBN 9781780449449 Library Ebook
ISBN 9781780449456 Ebook

Citation: Chambers, R. (2017) *Can We Know Better? Reflections for Development,* Rugby, UK: Practical Action Publishing, <http://dx.doi.org/10.3362/9781780449449>.

Since 1974, Practical Action Publishing has published and disseminated books and information in support of international development work throughout the world. Practical Action Publishing is a trading name of Practical Action Publishing Ltd (Company Reg. No. 1159018), the wholly owned publishing company of Practical Action. Practical Action Publishing trades only in support of its parent charity objectives and any profits are covenanted back to Practical Action (Charity Reg. No. 247257, Group VAT Registration No. 880 9924 76).

The views and opinions in this publication are those of the author and do not represent those of Practical Action Publishing Ltd or its parent charity Practical Action. Reasonable efforts have been made to publish reliable data and information, but the authors and publisher cannot assume responsibility for the validity of all materials or for the consequences of their use.

Cover design by Mercer Design
Typeset by Allzone Digital Services
Printed in the UK

FSC

Contents

List of Tables, Figures and Boxes   x
Preface   xi
Acknowledgements   xvii
Abbreviations   xix

1. Error and myth   1
  Prologue   1
  Being wrong: clusters of errors and myths   3
    Policies and programmes   3
    Professionals' beliefs about rural realities   4
    Rejection of heresies   5
  Defences against dissonance   7
  Sources of error and myth   9
    Relational and personal   9
    Data-related   11
    Behavioural and experiential   14
  Coda   19
  Agenda for reflection and action   20
  Notes   21
  References   23

2. Biases and blind spots   27
  Overview and purpose   27
  Strategic ignorance   28
  Biased experience: development tourism revisited   30
  Past blind spots: a selection reviewed   31
    Gender, cultural, social, and space   31
    Backwaters of research   33
    Out of the closet: blind spots of WASH   37
  Recurring dimensions of blind spots   43
  Biases and blind spots: past and present   45
  Biases and blind spots: the future   46
  The blind spot of ourselves   49
  Agenda for reflection and action   50
  Notes   51
  References   53

3. Lenses and lock-ins   57
  Basic framing   58
  Limited by lenses   58

http://dx.doi.org/10.3362/9781780449449.000

Epistemic relativism: views of poverty   58
Economists: quantitative, reductionist, and non-contextual   60
Anthropological particularism: qualitative,
inclusive, and contextual   61
Disciplinary convergence   61
Findings as artefacts of methodology   62
Relativism and realism: the Rashomon effect   63
Locked in by mechanistic methodologies   63
Randomized control trials   64
Systematic reviews   69
Cost-effective alternatives to RCTs and SRs   71
Locked in by mechanistic procedures   72
Logframes and beyond   72
Competitive bidding   75
Shared characteristics   77
Trends, irreversibility, and alternatives   80
Agenda for reflection and action   82
Notes   82
References   85

4. **Rigour for complexity**   **91**
Exploring: an invitation   91
The paradigmatic context   92
Inclusive rigour for complexity   94
Meanings and forms of 'rigour'   94
The personal dimension   98
Canons of methodological rigour   98
Rigour from plural synergies   101
Rigour from participation   101
Rigour from reflexivity   103
The rigour of responsible relevance   104
Pioneering rigour at scale   105
PIALA in Ghana   105
Rigour from systemic approaches   107
Rigour for wicked mess and gridlock   109
The sugar industry in Kenya   109
Rural sanitation in India   111
Contrasts, commonalities, and concluding   112
Agenda for reflection and action   115
Notes   115
References   116

5. **Power, participation, and knowledge: knowing better together**   **119**
Springboard for this chapter   119
Fundamentals: power, knowledge, and who? Whose?   120
Participatory methodologies   122

A brief history and overview 123
The nature and life cycles of participatory methodologies 125
The proliferation of participatory methods 127
Eclectic methodological pluralism: a new space 128
Participatory pluralism within organizations 131
Three methodologies for transformative revolutions 131
Participatory ICTs 131
Participatory statistics: a win–win 133
The Reality Check Approach 134
Empowerment and the realities of those who are last 136
Co-generating and sharing knowledges 138
The future of participatory approaches and methods 139
Agenda for reflection and action 139
Notes 140
References 141

6. Knowing for a better future 149
Knowing better in our unforeseeable 21st century 150
Accelerating social change 150
Redefining development 151
To know better in the new context 152
For a new professionalism of knowing: five fundamentals 153
Words and concepts 154
Ground-truthing: a participatory rigour of realism 156
Facilitation: behaviours attitudes, relationships, and being 156
Reflexivity 158
Principles, values, and passion 161
Practical transformations 162
Revolutionary professionalism 162
Participatory management and institutions 164
The primacy of the personal 165
Collective passionate communities 166
The transformative power of funding 167
To make it happen: vision, guts, and passion 169
Notes 171
References 173

Glossary of meanings 177
Index 183

List of Tables, Figures and Boxes

Tables

1.1	An example of misleading 'findings'	13
2.1	Number of psychology articles with shame and disgust in their titles	37
2.2	Contrasting characteristics of diarrhoeas and EED	40
2.3	Professional values and preferences as perceived in 1983	47
2.4	Professional and personal biases and preferences to review and offset when making choices for research and action	48
3.1	Two methodological paradigms	59
4.1	Characteristics of Newtonian and Complexity paradigms	96
5.1	Changes in gender responsibilities over 10 years	127
5.2	Verbal, visual, and digital compared	129
6.1	Contrasting lexicons of the mid-1990s and mid-2010s	155
6.2	What is SMART?	155

Figures

1.1	Toilet coverage in India	12
4.1	Basic elements in a paradigm	93
4.2	Elements in a paradigm of Newtonian practice	94
4.3	Elements in a paradigm of adaptive pluralism	95
4.4	Group-visual synergy	103
4.5	Causal linkages in the sugar industry in Kenya	110

Boxes

3.1	Payment by results experience from an INGO working in an African country, 14 November 2014	76
5.1	Monitoring and measuring empowerment and social change: the case of a social movement in Bangladesh	137

Preface

'Certainty is the greatest of all illusions...it is what the ancients meant by *hubris*. The only certainty, it seems to me, is that those who believe they are certainly right are certainly wrong.'

Iain McGilchrist, *The Master and his Emissary* (2009: 460)

'Now, *here*, you see, it takes all the running *you* can do, to keep in the same place. If you want to get somewhere else, you must run at least twice as fast as that!'

Lewis Carroll, *Alice Through the Looking Glass*

'Start, stumble, self-correct, share.'

Precept from participatory rural appraisal in the 1990s

Context and direction

This is a challenging and thrilling time to be alive, active, and engaged with development. So much has changed and is changing so fast. Potentials for making a difference grow. Rapid change and communication mean that small strategic actions can have big impacts later. Negatively, the worse things are, and since drafting this preface in 2016 they have become much worse, the greater can be the scope for making them less bad. Positively, it is a galvanizing opportunity to be confronted by so much to keep up with, so much to learn and unlearn, and so many new domains of knowledge continuously opening up. At the same time, many of us are so bombarded and overstimulated by digital information and demands that little time is left to stand back and reflect critically on how we know and how we might know better. This has made it a privilege to have had the time and support to write this book.

It is thrilling too because meanings of 'development' continuously evolve and diversify. I use it to mean 'good change', applying this to humankind universally. Past is the time when it referred just to developing countries. The 17 Sustainable Development Goals (SDGs) apply everywhere. All countries have signed up to them. The old dichotomies and mindsets of donor–recipient, North–South, developed–developing are superseded. In the spirit of the SDGs, *Can We Know Better?* is for all in all countries who work on or wish to contribute to the goals and what they stand for, and to achieve justice, equality, sustainability, security, and a better life for all now and in the future. For the present, we have the wonderful opportunities of living and working in new ways in new spaces of reciprocity, and mutual learning and sharing.

In this context, I question and challenge much in prevailing professionalism. I have been struck by the scale and depth of what I have found: that error, myth, biases, and blind spots are deeply endemic; that widely accepted and required procedures, approaches, and concepts of rigour distort vision and diminish effectiveness; that the power of funding often carries conditions that misfit complex realities and incur high hidden costs. There are successes to celebrate, not least the explosion of participatory methodologies. But many well-intended actions in the name of development miss the mark. I present evidence that development practice has been driven further and further in a damaging direction. The issues here are at once epistemological, paradigmatic, and practical.

Those whose lives much of the rhetoric of development aims to improve – those who are poor, vulnerable, marginalized, weak, displaced, insecure, stigmatized, excluded, powerless, those left out and left behind – in sum, all those who are 'last' – deserve that those of us who are not last learn to know better and be more in touch and up to date with their realities, and more committed and fired with passion to know the truth and to do better. Those who are last, and those of us who are not last, are to be found in all countries. To make our rhetoric real cries out for a revolution in development knowing, thinking, and practice everywhere. We have to transform how we see things, how we behave, how we interact, how we learn and know, and what we do.

Self-critical reflexivity

Self-critical reflexivity is at the core of knowing better. So I must start with myself and explain the drivers behind this book. Let me warn you about biases, predispositions, and errors that I recognize in myself and in the origins and content of this book. I mention others in the text and yet more you will notice in your reading.

As I perceive it, writing this book has been driven (and no doubt distorted) by a mix of anger, frustration, curiosity, and enthusiasm. The anger verging on disbelief is at the grotesque and growing inequalities of our world, the ideology of greed and the stupidity and short-sightedness that so widely prevail, the dishonesty, fake news and lies glossed as 'alternative facts' that are now widespread, reminiscent of Ribbentrop and Orwell's Ministry of Truth, and the mean xenophobia that has spread in a world with an unimaginable scale of suffering from wars, famine, and injustice. I am angry too with myself for the hypocrisy of my life and feeble responses. The frustration is with the dead hand of professional conservatism and its academic and bureaucratic reproduction through values, incentives, procedures, habits, and mindsets that condition, constrain, distort, and blinker perceptions and practice, so often leading to blindness, errors, and bad ways of doing things.

My curiosity and enthusiasm stem from a fascination with evidence, which allows me the fond delusion that I have a passion for truth, tracing this to a background in natural sciences and history. In university I studied the unification of Italy where evidence conflicted, some had been forged, myths had been generated, and actors' motivations were complex and inscrutable. It was fascinating trying to get closer to elusive realities. At times the only reasonable conclusion was that we did not know and could never know. Which now may apply to more of this book than I care to recognize. But again and again it has been exciting to explore how we 'know' and how we get things wrong. It has been enthralling to search, drawing on others' experience, for better ways of knowing and doing and getting closer to truth, and to know eureka moments of ah-ha!

In none of this am I 'holier than thou'. Looking back at almost six decades of personal engagement with 'development', I recognize that I have often and for long periods been seriously wrong while sure that I was right (see Chambers, 2014). Experience as a decolonizing administrator and trainer in Kenya left me with top-down attitudes and behaviours and a mindset which took long to recognize and unlearn. My authoritarian and unreflective management contributed to the failure of an evaluation I was in charge of in Kenya. The first books I wrote saw things and prescribed actions from the perspectives of managers, not those of the managed. Participation was little on my map. There is much in those earlier books that I now see as biased; and if I was wrong then, I am surely still wrong now, if in other ways.

In the first three chapters you may detect unjustified dogmatism: in gleefully detecting errors and myths in Chapter 1, identifying biases and blind spots in Chapter 2, and exposing deficiencies of mechanistic processes and procedures in Chapter 3. You may sense that I am vulnerable to enjoying the sport of Bank- and donor-baiting. I pose as balanced but have caught myself cherry picking evidence to support the case I wish to make. I have made corrections, for instance in qualifying my critique of mechanistic practices and procedures in Chapter 3, but errors of fact and judgement will surely remain. That said, I live in hope that readers will take on board the major points and perspectives.

The more positive and forward-looking second half of the book is infused with an optimism which negative academics may find naïve and those embedded in bureaucracies difficult to put into practice. As this goes to press events have unfolded which introduce new nastiness, irresponsibility, and danger into our world. This book should support all who stand for the human values of inclusiveness, honesty, respect, and love. I make no apologies for my hope and optimism. I am hard-wired to look for win–win solutions. This can lead me to underplay conflict situations which are zero sum. But I cannot help being thrilled by what I see as vast potentials for practical realism: for knowing and doing better in development through rigour for complexity (Chapter 4), participatory approaches and methods (Chapter 5), and reflexivity and facilitation (Chapter 6).

Despite my dogmatic style of writing, I remain full of doubts. The question mark in the title signals that the assertions throughout the book are provisional. Many sentences should end with question marks. My analysis of errors, myths, biases, and blind spots surely suffers from errors, myths, biases, and blind spots itself. These pages are the stumbling steps of one traveller on our collective journey in search of practical realism and what I dare to call truth. But realities and the truths about them continuously evolve. There is no final arrival. The future becomes ever less predictable. None of the conclusions here can be set in stone. All must be open to challenge. In our troubled and turbulent world, there will for ever be new constellations of being wrong and new ways of being right, of being in touch, up to date, and realistic. We will always need to go on learning how to know better, and through knowing better, doing better.

About this book

Writing this book has not been easy. It tries to cover a range of knowledges and practices, to critique mainstream conventions, and to propose practical alternatives. In the 15 years since I began it, our universe of knowing has transformed with astonishing speed. The explosion of digital and other technologies and their applications (Ramalingam et al., 2016) has been hard to keep up with, and the future of knowing has itself become less and less knowable. In the proverbial painting of the Forth Bridge, by the time one end was reached, the other needed repainting. In this case, the bridge has not only got longer and longer but has also all needed repainting all the time. Or as in Alice's world, to keep in touch and up to date I have needed to run ever faster and faster, updating and rewriting version after version of each of the chapters.

There is much this book is not. It is not primarily about how change happens: that is well covered in Duncan Green's book of that title, *How Change Happens* (2016). Nor is it primarily about foreign aid: a magisterial overview of the state of play with that is David Hulme's *Should Rich Nations Help the Poor?* (2016). Both these books are readable, engaging and accessible. Nor is it a handbook or manual of approaches and methods, though some of these are noted in Chapter 5. Neither is it a balanced review for development studies: for that, see Andy Sumner and Michael Tribe, *International Development Studies: theories and methods in research and practice* (2008). Nor does it deal directly with some of the great issues of our time such as climate change, sustainability, insecurity, population growth, migration, refugees and displaced people, disarmament, xenophobia, archaic electoral systems, democratic and international governance, tax evasion, avoidance and havens, obscene and growing inequalities of wealth and income, or the many dimensions of injustice and abuses of human rights; and that is no more than a partial list. What it does seek to do is raise questions about what we believe we know, what we do not know, and how we might come to know more and better and so see better what to do.

The original title was *Knowing in Development* but this was too passive. A eureka breakthrough was when Clare Tawney of Practical Action Publishing suggested *Knowing Better*. This was more purposive and impelled me to rethink and rewrite with a more active orientation. This included adding *agenda for action and reflection* to each of the first five chapters. But the title still carried overtones of certainty and authority. Others helped with suggestions finally leading to *Can We Know Better?* The question invites you to reflect critically and to suggest yourself what can be done to take us closer to realities and truth.

Who this is for

I have written this ambitiously hoping it will be of interest and help to those who want to confront and correct the injustices and inequalities of our world and make it a better place for all. It is for development professionals, policy-makers, politicians, officials, scientists, students, academics, religious leaders, freelancers, service providers, those who work in many departments and at many levels in many organisations, and all who are concerned and engaged with change for the better in all countries. We are people in government organizations, international agencies, NGOs, social movements, universities, colleges and schools, research and training institutes, faith organizations of all religions, the private sector, the media, and members of the general public from all walks of life and of all political persuasions. In the world we now live in, we are all in this together, interconnected as a new class. We cannot hide. We cannot escape responsibility. And with embarrassment I also address this to myself, and my own hubris and hypocrisy.

Let me now invite you into the book. The abstracts at the head of each chapter give a quick overview. The index and the chapter titles in the table of contents are to help you be selective. My hope is to shock, provoke, convince, and incite you to see and do things differently. The organization into six stand-alone chapters may lend itself to university, college and other courses, with six sessions, say one a week. Being open access, anyone can read or download these without cost.

A 'revolutionary new professionalism' may be hyperbole. Dream on, you may say. Well, I do dream. So if words like *normal, conventional, pedestrian, business as usual* or *nothing new* come to mind as you read, I shall have failed. I want this book, however modestly, to help us to know better how to make our world a fairer, more equal, more secure, and fulfilling place, for all of us but mostly for those who are last. As long as our human race survives, there should be no end to knowing and doing and thrilling adventures of reflexive ground-truthing and exploration. Please read, criticize, improve on what is here, and enjoy.

References

Chambers, R. (2014) 'Critical reflections of a development nomad,' in my book *Into the Unknown*, Rugby, UK: Practical Action Publishing, 3–21.
Green, D. (2016) *How Change Happens*, Oxford University Press.

Hulme, D. (2016) *Should Rich Nations Help the Poor?*, Wiley.
McGilchrist, I. (2009) *The Master and his Emissary: The Divided Brain and the Making of the Western World*, New Haven, CT and London: Yale University Press.
Ramalingam, B., Hernandez, K., Prieto Martin, P. and Faith, B. (2016) *Ten Frontier Technologies for International Development*, Brighton, UK: Institute of Development Studies.
Sumner, A. and Tribe, M. (2008) *International Development Studies: Theories and Methods in Research and Practice*, Sage Books.

Acknowledgements

I thank Practical Action Publishing for combining patience with persistence, and an anonymous reviewer for perceptive and helpful comments. Almost all of *Can We Know Better?* is new writing. It builds on and moves forward from earlier books. To avoid repeating what is already accessible in print, I refer to these where appropriate, with perhaps excessive self-referencing. Other sources by chapter are as follows. Chapter 1 has evolved through many iterations and updates from an unpublished paper to the 2002 Costa Rica conference of the CGIAR on 'Why has impact evaluation had so little impact?' In Chapter 2 the section on the biases of rural development tourism draws on *Revolutions in Development Inquiry* (2008). The discussion of the blind spot of faecally transmitted infections follows on from joint work with Gregor von Medeazza published as *IDS Working Paper* 450, 'Reframing undernutrition: faecally transmitted infections and the 5 As' (2014). Chapter 4 has evolved from 'Inclusive rigour for complexity', *Journal of Development Effectiveness*, vol. 7, no. 2 (2015). I have tried to acknowledge sources of ideas but I do not always know where they came from and have a deplorable tendency to think that those of others are mine. Any plagiarism is inadvertent and I apologize.

Many who have helped and contributed over my working life, cannot be acknowledged, but colleagues, friends and family I thank them all. I must give special mention to those who founded the Institutional Learning and Change (ILAC) network of the CGIAR following the 2002 Costa Rica conference and who informed and encouraged me in the early stages of writing. Over many years, Norman Uphoff has been an inspiration and a source of new perspectives. Far too many others have contributed directly and indirectly to this book for me to acknowledge them personally. But let me thank them all. They will know who they are. I have a special debt to Richard Douglass for his ideas and advice, and his patient, painstaking and good humoured work on the text, references and diagrams. For comments, corrections and additions to chapters which have saved me from errors and added to insight and content I thank Marina Apgar, Lu Caizhen, Max Friedrich and Cathy Shutt for Chapter 3, Adinda van Hemelrijck for Chapter 4, Dee Jupp, Esse Nilsson, Tony Roberts and Jane Stevens for Chapter 5 and Jenny Chambers for Chapter 6. To Ashish Shah I am grateful for the case of the complexity of the sugar industry in Kenya in Chapter 4 and for his influence on other chapters. I have a debt to many in India and elsewhere for the experiences of working on rural sanitation. None of the above necessarily agree with the views I have expressed and responsibility for judgements, errors and omissions is mine alone. It has been a privilege over the years to be based at the Institute of Development Studies, Sussex. IDS and my colleagues there have provided stimulation, advice, opportunities to keep in closer touch with many topics, and the freedom to choose how to use my time. And throughout all this, my very special thanks are to Jenny for our life together and her ideas and insights. It was she who challenged me and turned me round when I still believed in trickle down, a turnaround which led to *Putting the Last First* in 1983. She has an unerring sense of what matters, and has often been right when I have been wrong. There is no way I could have reached this point, or this book could have been written, without her.

Abbreviations

AAI	ActionAid International
ADB	Asian Development Bank
aka	also known as
BMGF	Bill and Melinda Gates Foundation, Seattle
BRAC	originally the Bangladesh Rural Advancement Committee, now an INGO known simply as BRAC
CGIAR	Consultative Group for International Agricultural Research
CIFOR	Centre for International Forestry Research
CLTS	community-led total sanitation
DHS	Demographic Health Survey
DFID	Department for International Development (UK)
EED	environmental enteric dysfunction (aka environmental enteropathy)
ESOL	English for speakers of other languages
FGM/C	female genital mutilation/cutting
FTI	faecally transmitted infection
GIS	geographical information system
GM	genetic modification, genetically modified
GPS	global positioning system
HYM	high-yielding methodology
HYV	high-yielding variety (of a crop)
IAS	Indian Administrative Service
ICRISAT	International Crops Research Institute for the Semi-Arid Tropics, Hyderabad, India
ICDDR,B	International Centre for Diarrhoeal Disease Research, Bangladesh
ICT	information and communication technology
IDS	Institute of Development Studies, Sussex
IFAD	International Fund for Agricultural Development, Rome
INGO	international non-governmental organization
IPCC	Intergovernmental Panel on Climate Change
IRRI	International Rice Research Institute, Los Banos, Philippines
J-PAL	Poverty Action Laboratory (at MIT)
K	potassium
LGBT	lesbian, gay, bisexual, transsexual
MDG	Millennium Development Goal (1990–2015)
MDWS	Ministry of Drinking Water and Sanitation (India)

M&E	monitoring and evaluation
MIT	Massachusetts Institute of Technology
MSU	Michigan State University
N	nitrogen
NGO	non-governmental organization
OD	open defecation
ODF	open defecation-free
P	phosphorus
PbR	payment by results
PDA	Participatory Development Associates, Ghana
PIALA	Participatory Impact Assessment and Learning Approach
PM	participatory methodology
PPA	participatory poverty assessment
PRA	participatory rural appraisal
PRRP	Participatory Review and Reflection (ActionAid International)
RALU	Rapid Action Learning Unit (India, rural sanitation)
RBM	results-based management
RCT	randomized control trial
RNA	ribonucleic acid
RRA	rapid rural appraisal
RTIMP	Root and Tuber Improvement and Marketing Programme, Ghana
SDG	Sustainable Development Goal. There are 17 SDGs, with a target date of 2030
SEWA	Self-Employed Women's Association, an Indian trade union now international
SG 2000	Sasakawa Global 2000, a programme for smallholder agriculture in Africa
Sida	Swedish International Development Cooperation Agency
SMS	short message service (text messages)
SR	systematic review
SRI	System of Rice Intensification
T and V	Training and Visit, a system for agricultural extension
ToC	theory of change
TSC	Total Sanitation Campaign (India)
USAID	United States Agency for International Development
VSO	Voluntary Service Overseas
WARDA	West African Rice Development Association
WASH	water, sanitation and hygiene
WSP	Water and Sanitation Programme of the World Bank

CHAPTER 1
Error and myth

Abstract

The history of international development is replete with errors of knowledge and practice and self-sustaining myths to which they have given rise. Often these are generated, propagated with passion, and acted on in good faith, by people who mean well, only later to be recognized as wrong. Examples are presented from policies and programmes, beliefs about rural realities, supposed and asserted scientific and medical 'facts', and heresies which later proved to be true. Analysis of these and other evidence identifies three clusters of actors and forces which alone or in combination generate and sustain error and myth. These are, first, relational and personal (power, interests, mindsets, and ego); second, data-related (misleading data, extrapolating out of context, and overlooking history); and third, behavioural and experiential (embedding narratives and beliefs; distance and insulation; selective experiences through visits, presentations and perceptions; repeating narratives, stories and statistics; repetitive confirmation bias; public relations, soundbites and speeches; and reimagining and rewriting history assisted by the self-serving malleability of memory). Combined variously in different contexts, these factors and forces stand in the way of knowing better. To confront them, an agenda is proposed for reflection and action.

Keywords: error, myth, beliefs, heresies, mindsets, data, narratives, repetition, memory, ego, self-delusion

> To err is human. (Seneca, Roman stoic philosopher, *c.* 4 BC–AD 65)
>
> Anyone who has never made a mistake has never tried anything new. (Albert Einstein)
>
> Adults are obsolete children. (Dr Seuss, psychologist and cartoonist)

Prologue

International development is replete with errors, myths, and omissions.[1] To know better, we need first to understand how these come about and are sustained and to reflect on what can be done. In this chapter I describe some errors and myths and try to tease out some of their common characteristics.

We all make mistakes. We can all learn from them. But whether we actually do learn from them, and our speed of learning, are things that decline with age. As infants and children, our trial, error, and correction are continuous: falling

http://dx.doi.org/10.3362/9781780449449.001

over or mispronouncing words are ways we learn. But as we grow older, know more, and are more in control of our actions, we become more responsible for what we do and do not do, and errors of commission or omission become increasingly matters of shame to be hidden or denied. Learning is less instantaneous and automatic: the time between actions and effects extends with longer causal chains. We know much more, and it is more embedded. Feedback from which we can learn takes longer and may be distorted or rejected. Power, social relations, and ego more and more influence how and what we learn, mislearn, and do not learn. From a learning point of view, we can ask ourselves, do we become, have we become, as in Dr Seuss's aphorism, obsolete children?

What has this to do with development? I ask this question both for development in the sense of 'good change' everywhere, and for international development in its past usual sense. For these, as I shall illustrate in later chapters, changes are accelerating in the conditions we experience, in what we need to know, what we need to learn and unlearn, and how we do that. One major shift is reflected in the Sustainable Development Goals (SDGs). In the past development and international development referred to less developed and developing countries, but in 2016 the SDGs have made development objectives universal. SDG 10, for instance, to reduce inequality between and within countries, applies to the USA, UK, and Russia as much as to Afghanistan, the Philippines, or Zimbabwe. The old distinctions of North and South, of developed and developing countries, make less sense than ever as we all recognize that we have much to learn collegially from each other.

On the positive side, enormous progress has been made with outstanding contributions to understanding and action. Among scholars, Amartya Sen stands out for his revolutionary insights and thinking, and among international organizations, UNICEF for its leadership and contributions to the welfare of children and women. And across the board, innumerable past errors have been corrected.

So learning, learning to learn better, and learning from each other become opportunities and priorities for us all. We cannot return to childhood: the causal chains between actions and effects are often uncertain and feedback missing or misleading. But what we can do is ask how we 'know', and how we learn, and how we can know and learn better. Can we 'embrace error', to use David Korten's phrase from the 1980s? What can we learn from failure, from what has not worked, and what lessons can we draw that are applicable across countries and contexts? And what can we learn from the resilience of myths, of beliefs that are false?

In searching for answers to these questions, I have chosen to focus on examples and evidence with which I have some familiarity. This gives a bias towards rural development, agriculture, and sanitation. The reader will make her own judgement whether this distorts the inferences and conclusions I draw, or whether and to what extent they have general validity.

The costs of errors and myths to those who are 'last', those who are poorer, weaker, and more vulnerable, have been horrendous. The environmental, social, economic, and other costs in damage done and resources misallocated have been beyond counting. These errors and myths have often been generated and propagated with passion and acted on in good faith by people who meant well, only later to be revealed as ill-founded and wrong. Like others, I have myself been seriously wrong (see, for example, chapter 1 in Chambers, 2014) and have done harm when believing that I was doing good. This has led me to wonder how I and others could have been so misguided and made me curious about error and myth, how we know and do not know, and how and why we so often get it wrong. So in what follows there is no 'holier than thou'. My hope is that if we can understand how and why we – the collective development professional 'we' – have been so wrong so often and for so long, perhaps we can learn to do better.

With this in mind, this first chapter is empirically based on cases of error and myth (for more detail on the examples, see Chambers, 1997: 15–32). If we accept that all knowledge is contingent and provisional, this applies also to 'corrected' versions. There is no simple, final or complete truth and there will always remain the residual question of who debunks the debunker.

Being wrong: clusters of errors and myths

The errors and myths I shall consider cluster into three domains: policies and programmes; professionals' beliefs about rural realities; and rejected heresies which have later been recognized as well founded. I draw on these for insights. I describe some of these briefly. The impatient reader may wish to skim or skip to the analysis which starts on page 7.

Policies and programmes

Policies and programmes are conspicuous because of the vast scale of their impacts and the many deficiencies of feedback to those responsible.

Internationally, the most conspicuous is structural adjustment. This was imperiously forced on indebted countries in the 1980s, requiring them to cut budgets to education, health, infrastructure, and other services.[2] Many millions of children were denied education and many millions will have suffered and died younger than they otherwise would have done. The costs to poor and vulnerable people were unseen by those responsible for the policy. Later debt relief reduced the burden but only after irreparable harm had been done on a vast scale.

Two other international policy errors imposed by the World Bank compounded countries' debts. For Integrated Rural Development Projects the Bank lent poor countries $19 bn over 13 years. These untested projects were driven rapidly to scale. Top-down, conceived and planned without participation, most of them especially in Africa, the projects were disastrous failures which, to its credit, the World Bank itself exposed (World Bank, 1988). Another disaster promoted by the World Bank in the latter 1970s and much of the 1980s was the Training and Visit (T and V) System of Agricultural Extension (Benor and Harrison, 1977). This rigid, routinized, top-down system of agricultural extension was a paradigmatic misfit for agriculture. As Asian countries saw this and rejected T and V, its proponents moved on to Africa.[3] Hailed as a breakthrough, it was a catastrophic and expensive failure with the costs borne by the countries at the receiving end.

Passing to national policies and programmes, three catastrophic failures are sources of lessons that I shall draw out later. First, the village collective farming of the *Ujamaa* programme in Nyerere's Tanzania was believed nationally and internationally to be widespread. Research by political science students at the University of Dar es Salaam on vacation, edited by Proctor and published with the ironic but diplomatic title *Building Ujamaa Villages in Tanzania* (1971), revealed that it was deeply unpopular, with extensive coercion, resistance, and non-implementation. A second massive failure was the attempt in India to spread the *warabandi* system of irrigation water distribution from north-west India to the rest of the country. But the *warabandi* system of fixed, timed rotation of canal irrigation water is only feasible in the special physical, climatic, and social conditions of north-west India (Chambers, 1988: 92–102). The Seventh Five-Year Plan (1980–1985) set a target of 8 million hectares to be covered, all over India. The programme was an almost total failure, littering rural India with metal boards listing distribution times, remaining rusting for the delight only of scrap metal merchants and archaeologists of error. Third, the Indian Government's rural sanitation programmes were comprehensive and sustained failures over some three decades to 2014, to an extent and on a scale to which there may be no equivalent examples outside totalitarian regimes. For instance, the Total Sanitation Campaign (TSC) launched in 1999 had a target date for an open defecation-free rural India of 2012. In 2011 the Ministry of Drinking Water and Sanitation reported rural sanitation coverage of 68 per cent. The census of 2011 found 31 per cent, indicating that over 8 million more households were defecating in the open than 10 years earlier (see p. 12).

Professionals' beliefs about rural realities

Here by way of illustration are four:

Woodfuel gap theory led to predictions of acute fuel shortages in rural Africa. In the 1970s and 1980s it was believed that much of sub-Saharan Africa faced a severe fuel crisis and that in many areas fuelwood would run out. The pattern varied but in general the crisis did not happen, and in quite extensive areas woody biomass became more plentiful, for example on farms in much of Kenya (Tiffen et al., 1993).

Post-harvest losses of harvested crops were for many years cited as 30 per cent. A major source of this figure was not farmers' fields and practices, but a time-of-harvesting trial for rice on the International Rice Research Institute (IRRI) research station (De Padua, 1976, cited in Greeley, 1987). At least 10 projects of careful field research showed these post-harvest losses to lie most often in the range of 4 to 7 per cent.

People destroy trees. Through colonial times and into the 1990s, scientists and administrators in Guinea and latterly also donors believed that the forest islands in the forest-savanna transition zone in West Africa were relics of a much more extensive forest. Human activity, including burning, had turned forest into savanna. Sustained and meticulous field research drawing on many sources, including travellers' journals, oral histories, time series aerial photographs, and analysis of forest species composition and age, showed the reverse to be true. Through cultivation, judicious burning, and planting and protecting trees, people extended the forests around their settlements (Fairhead and Leach, 1996a, b). This was also the case in the same eco-zone elsewhere in West Africa (Fairhead and Leach, 2003).

Desertification: the Sahara is marching south. The mainstream desertification narrative flourished in the 1970s and 1980s. A standard statement was that each year 6 million hectares of land were being 'irretrievably lost through various forms of desertification or destroyed to desert-like conditions' and 21 million hectares annually were being reduced to zero or even negative productivity (UNEP, 1984, cited in Swift, 1997: 81, and repeated in the Brundtland Report [WCED, 1987: 128] and elsewhere). Human activity was deemed responsible, but later research found it overwhelmingly related to rainfall.

Rejection of heresies

The third cluster of errors is the out of hand rejection of heresies which later come to be accepted.

These are best known in science and medicine with a roll of honour of scientists, medical researchers, and others who have been the first to make a discovery and see a new truth, or who have questioned a conventional dogma, mindset, or shibboleth, and have been disbelieved, ridiculed, and penalized. They have faced entrenched received wisdom[4] often wielding powerful sanctions against apostates. Historical cases like Giordano Bruno and Galileo are well known. Others are more recent, for instance:

- Alfred Wegener, a meteorologist, set out the theory of continental drift in 1912. Despite geographical and geological evidence, his theory was ridiculed and not taken seriously for six decades until evidence of magma convection currents provided a causal force that could explain it.
- Barry Marshall, following up on a discovery by J.R. Warren in 1979 of a bacterium *Helicobacter pylori* in the stomach (which was believed to be too acidic for bacteria), had eventually to infect himself to persuade a sceptical establishment that peptic ulcers were caused by bacteria and could be treated with antibiotics. Before that they had been attributed to stress and sometimes part of the stomach was removed (Uphoff and Coombs, 2001).
- Kilmer McCully observed in the mid-1960s that arteriosclerosis was associated with high levels of the amino acid homocysteine, counter to

the prevailing belief that it was caused by high blood levels of cholesterol. Unable to obtain research grants, he had to leave Harvard Medical School and Massachusetts General Hospital. Eventually other researchers confirmed his results, and his research was widely praised for being correct decades before its time (Uphoff and Coombs, 2001).

- In 1949, three years before the development of the Salk polio vaccine in 1952, Frederick Klenner reported having cured 60 out of 60 polio patients, including some who were already showing symptoms of paralysis, with massive intravenous doses of vitamin C. Klenner presented his findings to an annual session of the American Medical Association but the medical establishment took no notice, although at the time polio was a worldwide scourge and there was no effective treatment (Levy, 2002: 19–30). The Salk vaccine later became the universal treatment.[5]

- Howard Temin, whose finding that non-genetic changes in RNA could be inherited confronted orthodox neo-Darwinian genetic reductionism, was condemned for heresy before later being recognized with a Nobel prize (Lipton, 2008: 58).

- *Umami*, the fifth taste after sweet, sour, salt, and bitter, was finally accepted 90 years after its discovery by the Japanese chemist Kikunae Ikeda. The acceptance came when in 2000 and 2002 receptors were finally found on the tongue that were specific to it! Lehrer (2008: 59) writes that 'science had persisted in its naïve and unscientific belief in four, and only four, tastes'.

And these are but a few in a long and growing list.

Similar rejection and ridicule have been evident in rural development:

- In the late 1980s, N.C. Saxena, a senior Indian bureaucrat, recognized that contrary to the universal professional view, prohibiting small farmers from harvesting trees on their land had the perverse effect that they would cut them to realize their value while they could, and then not plant or protect others, whereas if they were free to harvest and sell them at any time they would do the opposite – plant and protect trees. He found himself a lone voice among a dozen foresters and others in arguing for abolishing the restrictions. The Minister for the Environment was vehemently against abolishing restrictions. It was years before it was generally accepted that Saxena was right and that farmers who can cut their trees any time they wish normally preserve them as savings until they need to cash them.

- Rickets was reported in part of rural Bangladesh. Rickets was known to be associated with lack of vitamin D or of sunlight. There was plenty of sunlight in rural Bangladesh. The reports were met with 'a bewildering array of rebuttals' (Uphoff and Coombs, 2001). Yet it was there, with nearly a third of the children in one community affected by it. It had been overlooked for 15 years. The subsequent explanation was calcium deficiency, and its occurrence was recognized as an unseen epidemic (Uphoff and Coombs, 2001).

- SRI, the System of Rice Intensification, is a rich case for deriving lessons (see SRI-Rice, 2015a). It has revolutionized much rice growing. It was evolved in Madagascar by Father Henri de Laulanié in the early 1980s. It entails simultaneous radical changes in the traditional cultivation practices of both farmers and scientists worldwide, especially flooding. It involves very early transplanting of single seedlings rather than clumps, wide spacing, aeration of roots, and weeding with a roller. With these practices, plant architecture above and below ground is dramatically different, tillers proliferate, and yields rise sharply, often by a half or more, sometimes doubling or trebling. On occasion these have reached over 20 tons/hectare, beyond what scientists had believed to be the biological maximum potential. SRI also reduces water use by up to 50 per cent. SRI attracted professional denial and rejection by scientists, especially at IRRI. Articles published in refereed international scientific journals denied the evidence and provoked what were characterized as the 'rice wars'. SRI was publicly rubbished at international conferences. Meanwhile governments were promoting SRI based on their own research findings. And hundreds of thousands, and then millions of farmers could hardly have been wrong, whatever some scientists said and published in peer-reviewed international journals. The number of countries in which SRI was known to have been adopted and to be spreading rose from 15 in 2003 to over 50 in 2016, by which time it had become very widespread in Bangladesh, Cambodia, China, India, Indonesia, Pakistan, and Vietnam, countries where two-thirds of the world's rice is grown. In China the area under SRI rose from 200,000 hectares in 2007 to 700,000 hectares in 2011. And the principles of SRI have been extended successfully to other crops including millet, wheat, sugarcane, and teff (SRI-Rice, 2015b). Eventually, in 2012, IRRI set up a website on SRI.

These examples of heresies which have been rejected, often vehemently, and whose originators were often vilified and discriminated against, do not mean that new theories and ideas should not be carefully examined and debated. What they do indicate, taken together, is a need for open-mindedness, understanding, and offsetting tendencies for knee-jerk collective dismissal.

Defences against dissonance

Conventional views and embedded errors and myths can be strenuously defended and robustly resilient. Challenges to them by discordant evidence or heresies can be threatening. Moreover, confronting and disputing errors can be to expose oneself or one's organization. Careers, egos, institutions, funding, research programmes, and institutional and personal reputations and prestige can be put at risk or believed to be endangered. Defences come into play. These take many forms.

The threats posed by findings or ideas which are discordant, unwelcome, or potentially damaging may be personal or institutional or both. The history of science is well provided with examples of rejection, denial, or disparaging the discordant when a paradigm is threatened by new evidence or ideas. It is reinforced when governments, departments, organizations, or individuals have commitments of funding and prestige in high-profile programmes, such as *warabandi* and a succession of sanitation programmes in India, IRRI's research to produce a 'golden rice', and Tanzania's programme of *ujamaa*. Those concerned deserve understanding and even sympathy, given their personal and institutional investments, if they seek dissonance reduction. And admitting error or changing course is more difficult when the alternatives, as is often the case, are less clear cut, more diverse, and harder to 'sell'.

Denial, disparagement, and denigration have a wide-ranging and versatile repertoire, engaging human inventiveness and creativity. Strategic ignorance (pp. 28–30) is the most basic: simply taking no notice of a heretic and heresy or of discordant information. Klenner was ignored. His dramatic claims for massive doses of intravenous vitamin C, which if substantiated could have attacked polio on a wide front, were never tested. Denying resources for research is another. Marshall had to infect himself to prove that bacteria were responsible for duodenal ulcers. McCully could not obtain research grants to test his findings which challenged the established view of the causes of arteriosclerosis. IRRI did not test SRI, and when there was to be a large-scale trial comparing SRI with IRRI's 'best management practices', at a late stage funding was withdrawn. Whether consciously strategic or not, denying research resources sustains ignorance.

Career discrimination, sidelining, and even termination of appointments, from which all the medical heretics suffered to different degrees, is another defence. Yet another is disparagement, whether in public or in print. The lexicon of phrases of denial, dismissal, and ridicule that can be deployed is impressive: 'a local phenomenon', 'anecdotal', 'unverified', 'not replicated', 'unrigorous', 'unhelpful', 'unsubstantiated', 'unconfirmed', 'needs expert diagnosis', 'not supported in the literature', 'not peer-reviewed', and even with SRI 'alchemy'. Some yields with SRI were so high that they were dismissed as 'beyond the biological maximum'. As with Wegener (a meteorologist by training) and Uphoff (a political scientist), an unspoken reason for not taking heretics seriously may be that they have no business outside the proper confines or silos of their disciplines and cannot know what they are talking about. Again and again, the pioneers suffer discrimination and denigration before their new truth is recognized, though with Wegener that happened only long after he had died.

'Shooting the messenger' who bears unwelcome news is another response. Consultants or researchers with 'unhelpful' findings find they are not approached or funded again. Sasakawa Global 2000, a programme for small farmer agricultural development in African countries, sought collaboration with agricultural economists from Michigan State University (MSU) to analyse and evaluate field realities. In Ethiopia MSU were kicked out of the country because of a report that was critical of food distribution. In Mozambique, the MSU collaboration was terminated when local objection was taken to their finding that at current farmer management levels, and depending on when the maize was sold, one-third to two-thirds of the plots were not profitable for the farmer.

Confidentiality and secrecy are also part of the repertoire. While rejection and denial do at least sometimes allow scope for progress through debate, secrecy can be very damaging. Hugh Lamprey's influential 1975 report on desertification (see later) 'remained unpublished – indeed was treated as confidential – for at least a decade after it was written, but its conclusions were widely cited' (Swift, 1997: 78). One is reminded of the refusal of access to the skull of Piltdown man as a result of which it was many years before it was exposed as a hoax. Lamprey's report was not a hoax, but it seems likely that had access to it been open, the weakness of the desertification narrative would have been appreciated much earlier.

Sources of error and myth

The many defences of conventional views against criticism and heresies go some way to explaining how error can be robustly resilient. Let us turn now, elaborating and drawing on these illustrations and adding other evidence, to considering ways in which error is generated in the first place and then sustained.

Besides the repertoire of defences, the factors and forces which generate and sustain error and myth are many, overlapping and intertwined. They include bad science and flawed methodology. Bad science is a vast subject which I will touch on only tangentially; flawed methodology is treated in Chapter 3. For purposes of description and illustration here, I disentangle causal factors and forces into those that are: relational and personal (power, interests, mind-sets, and ego); data-related (defects in data and overlooking history); and behavioural and experiential (selective visits, presentations and perceptions; overgeneralizing; repeating narratives, stories, and statistics; public relations, soundbites, and speeches; and distorting the past by the self-serving fallibility of memory rewriting history).

Relational and personal

Power. This refers especially to power to reward and recognize or to penalize and dismiss. It has manifestations which are interpersonal, institutional, and professional. In their seminal book *The Lie of the Land: Challenging Received Wisdom on the African Environment*, editors Melissa Leach and Robin Mearns conclude that it is 'hierarchical relations of power between various partici-pating actors, which lead to convergences of commitments that coalesce in certain dominant directions' and that these account for 'the remarkable con-tinuity in received wisdom about environmental change in Africa' (1996: 28).

The more powerful people or institutions are, the more likely they are to demand, receive, and believe distorted information, with incestuous reinforcement from acolytes, dependants, or colleagues. An extreme case is Bush, Blair, and the illegal and murderous invasion of Iraq where, as the prolonged and painstaking Chilcot Inquiry has found, 'there was an ingrained belief in UK policy and intelligence communities that Iraq had retained some chemical and biological capabilities' (Iraq Inquiry, 2016). Within the intelligence communities themselves, and between them and the politicians, it can now be seen that power relations, commitments, needing to believe, wishful thinking, and other drivers identified in this chapter (below) combined to sustain a grotesque myth leading to the deaths of hundreds of thousands and the sustained insecurity and suffering of many millions. With apologies to Lord Acton, all power deceives.[6]

Interests. This refers to institutional and personal motivations, benefits, and disbenefits. These include patronage and funding from foundations, governments, international agencies, or the private sector; institutional survival and growth; personal income, prestige, security, recognition, and international travel; and creative and moral satisfactions from good work and changing things for the better. Obvious examples of institutional interests can be found with multinationals dealing in fertilizers, pesticides, and genetically modified crops. Combinations of interests are especially potent. With desertification, for example, as Swift (1997: 86–9) persuasively argued, national governments in Africa, international aid bureaucracies, some bilateral donors, and some groups of scientists all had common interests in promoting the narrative. With SRI it is easy to interpret and understand the slow response of International Agricultural Research Centres[7] when they were professionally and institutionally committed to long-term funding for other approaches and lacked the resources for rapid changes of programme and priority. The political economy of research is further examined in Chapter 3.

Mindsets. This term is used to cover personal and professional orientations, ideologies, and predispositions, including ways of seeing and interpreting things. They are conditioned by professional training, for example through textbooks, lectures, and examinations in colleges and universities, by methods and the behaviours and findings which derive from using them, by professional norms and the policies of journal editors, and more generally through current beliefs, fashions, and ideologies. Neo-Marxist ideology and frames of analysis were in vogue at the time when radical political scientists and social anthropologists were looking for evidence of the green revolution turning red (see later). Modernism and a belief in the top-down transfer of technology were widely accepted at the time of the green revolution and the subsequent propagation of the Training and Visit system was supported by a belief that non-adopters of innovations were ignorant or irrational laggards. *Warabandi* with its appearance of order and strict irrigation timings and amounts could be expected to appeal to engineers for whom mathematical exactness was a professional value. African socialism and a desire to build on traditional African values of sharing and community predisposed Nyerere and other leaders and thinkers to advocate and promote *ujamaa*. In Swift's interpretation of the desertification narrative, national governments in Africa in the 1970s were seeking 'to rescue an ideology, already failing at that time, of authoritarian intervention in rural land use: "desertification" was the crisis scenario they used to claim rights to stewardship over resources previously outside their control' (Swift, 1997: 86). In these cases, ideologies and mindsets, often combined with interests, predisposed observers or policy-makers to promote the ideas, interpretations, and policies which were subsequently found to be misguided.

Ego. Ego is a pervasive manifestation of the personal. Pride, status, and the esteem in which one is held professionally are potent if normally unspoken motivators and determinants of behaviour. With policies, programmes, research projects, and even research findings, personal ego and reputation can be at stake. Ego can also be linked with ideology, which may be called into question if new evidence or ideas present a paradigmatic challenge.

To acknowledge error, and confront power, mindsets, and ego, requires confidence and courage. I remember with admiration the agricultural scientist who said that in his research on cotton in northern Nigeria he had wasted 20 years of his life. He had been planting cotton at the best time for the cotton but farmers planted their food crops then, and cash crops only later. He only realized this when David Norman, an agricultural economist, helped him to see that he should do the same as the farmers.

Data-related

Misleading data. Misleading statistics are notorious. Three examples from the case evidence described earlier illustrate how easy it is to be spectacularly wrong.

1. *Untested assumptions without ground-truthing:* Woodfuel gap theory projected consumption and production. One set of projections found that the last tree in Tanzania would disappear in 1990. The absurdity of these calculations was comprehensively exposed by Gerald Leach and Robin Mearns (1988). Demand had been overestimated and supply and substitutions underestimated. In fact, with increasing rural population density, tree cover on smallholder farms could increase, as it did in neighbouring Kenya. The Tanzanian projections were based on untested assumptions and ignorance of on the ground realities which could have been corrected by a sensitive afternoon in a village.

2. *Cumulative errors:* The Indian Government's Total Sanitation Campaign (TSC) launched in 1999 set a target date of 2012 for rural India to be open defecation-free.[8] Statistics for toilet coverage were based on disbursements. On this basis, in 2011 the Ministry of Drinking Water

and Sanitation reported rural sanitation coverage of 68 per cent (Hueso and Bell, 2013: 41), up from 22 per cent in 2001; but the 2011 national census (GOI, 2012) found only 31 per cent of households with sanitation (see Figure 1.1). Less than one in five toilets reportedly constructed in rural India between 2001 and 2011 were found on the ground, leaving some 57 million toilets 'missing'. Officials had known that the numbers were distorted but not the extent of the distortion. With population increase the census showed that there were nearly 8.3 million more rural households practising open defecation (Hueso and Bell, 2013: 41–2) at the end of the intercensal period.[9]

3. *Propagating 'findings' that conveniently confirm beliefs:* From its inception, community-led total sanitation (CLTS) stressed the importance of 'total', that is to say, that all members of a community must be safely confining their faeces for all to gain full benefits (see CLTS Knowledge Hub, 2011). Decline in diarrhoea was a preferred measure of benefits. To contribute to a manual, the World Bank's Water and Sanitation Program (WSP) in India commissioned formative research. Misleading findings reported in a published field note (WSP, 2007) are reproduced in Table 1.1.

The text summarized, 'Even villages with close to 100 per cent toilet coverage showed a significantly high recall of diarrhoea incidence. Only villages declared to be open defecation-free, with 100 per cent toilet usage, reported a significant drop in diarrhoea recall to 7 per cent'. However, it turned out that the villages reporting 95 per cent usage, were a sample of just 19 households in two villages, 18 of which had toilets and one of which did not. In addition to this tiny and unrepresentative sample, the table and note were weak on other counts: diarrhoea

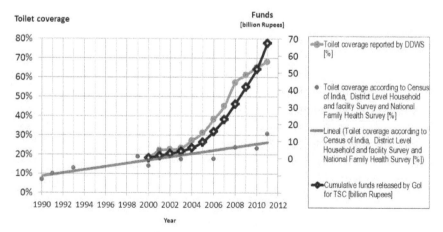

Figure 1.1 Toilet coverage in India
Note: The toilet coverage is as reported according to the TSC online monitoring system. The dots and straight trend line represent the actual toilet coverage as found by the census and other household surveys. The line which ends highest represents the cumulative funds spent by the TSC, closely related to the reported coverage.
Source: Hueso and Bell (2013)

Table 1.1 An example of misleading 'findings': 'Individual sanitation practices affect the whole community'

Category	Users of toilet (%)	Prevalence of diarrhoea (%)
Open-defecation-prevalent villages	29	38
Almost open defecation-free villages	95	26
Open defecation-free villages	100	7

Source: WSP (2007)

recall data can be very unreliable (Alam et al., 1989; de Melo et al., 2007)[10] and coverage was assumed to be the same as usage, when it is widespread practice in rural India for some members of households with functioning toilets to defecate in the open some or all of the time (Chambers and Myers, 2016).

Extrapolating out of context. Simple narratives and statistics are often derived by scaling up from local research.[11]

Good research scientists hedge their findings with caveats and qualifications. They can then be horrified when they find figures taken out of context, generalized for regions or even the globe, and repeatedly quoted to justify policies and programmes. In a section entitled 'Constructing facts: the emergence of a scientific case', Keeley and Scoones (2003) pointed out that in agriculture aggregated Africa-wide nutrient balance figures had been based on extrapolations from a limited amount of work carried out in small areas in a few African countries.[12] They quoted a 'widely-circulated special publication of the Bulletin of the American Soil Science Society on soil fertility' which announced:

> The magnitude of nutrient depletion in Africa's land is enormous. Calculations from Smaling's seminal work indicate that an average of 660 kg N per year, 75 kg P per year, and 450 kg K per year during the last 30 years has been lost from about 200 million ha of cultivated land in 37 African countries, excluding South Africa. (Sanchez et al., 1997: 4)

Yet Smaling et al. (1997: 50–2) commented on their work that, 'The studies were often done at the mini-plot level, the results of which cannot be linearly scaled up to the watershed' (let alone, one might add, to 200 million ha in 37 countries). One soil scientist said of a research study, 'When we wrote it we added umpteen footnotes and qualifications which seemed to get lost as the figures were taken up.'

A second example is the short air and ground ecological reconnaissance carried out by Hugh Lamprey in about three weeks in 1975 in the north-western Sudan. He compared the conditions he found with those reported in a botanical survey in 1958, and concluded that ecological boundaries had shifted south, the desert boundary by about 90–100 km in the 17 years. This was used by others to extrapolate for the whole southern fringe of the Sahara that there was a 6 kilometres per annum southward movement of desert. A later study found that, 'There was a severe drought impact on crop yield during the Sahelian drought 1965–74 in the Sudan followed by signifi-cant recovery as soon as the rains returned' and that, 'No major changes in vegetation cover and crop productivity was identified, which could not be explained by varying rainfall characteristics' (Hellden, 1991: 379, cited in Swift, 1997: 84).

Overlooking history. Ignorance of history is a widespread factor. The past is easily and often overlooked by outside observers, researchers, and visitors. Communities have much longer memories as well as incomparably more knowledge of local context and history than visiting professionals. Common-sense solutions to problems thought out by outsiders fail again and again through ignorance of what has already not worked. A typical example is the multi-donor Flood Action Plan in Bangladesh drawn up in 1989 and imple-mented at huge cost to build embankments to prevent floods, a 'solution' which had already failed, only to be abandoned after a few years (Lewis, 2013: 119–21). History was overlooked in the myth of 'the green revolution turning red'. As John Harriss pointed out (1977: 35), the much-cited Kilvenmani inci-dent in Thanjavur in 1968, in which 43 Harijans were massacred, was not a new phenomenon: such incidents had been described by a social anthropologist, Kathleen Gough, 20 years earlier. Leach and Mearns (1996), in their critique of received wisdom about the environment in Africa, stressed 'the exclusion of historical data from much ecological science' as a weakness. A variety of forms of historical evidence and insight were crucial in leading Fairhead and Leach (1996a, b) and their colleagues to overturn the deforestation myth of the forest-savanna transition zone in West Africa. A historical dimension was key to the findings of the research in Machakos District, Kenya, about popula-tion, soils, and degradation: it included dramatically contrasting photographs taken near the same points in 1937 and 1991, showing that a transformation from bad erosion to an intensive and sustainable agriculture with terracing and trees had occurred in parallel with a sixfold increase in population (Tiffen et al., 1993). A similar photographic contrast could be found in parts of Nepal (G. Gill, pers. comm., *c.* 1992).

Behavioural and experiential

Many sources of error and of the sustainability of myths are related to our behaviour and experiences from which we learn and which powerfully influ-ence our mindsets and actions.

Embedded narratives and beliefs. How deeply the dominant narrative of human damage to the environment is embedded can be illustrated from Nepal. Gerry Gill told me that he would show audiences two aerial photographs, taken 10 years apart, of the same land. One was covered in trees and vegetation, and the other bare. He would ask his audience which was earlier, which later. Invariably they chose the bare one as later. But the truth was the opposite (see Chambers, 1997: 29–30). There was a powerful deforestation narrative in Nepal that overpopulation was driving deforestation and erosion, buttressed and given authority by an Asian Development Bank report (NARC/ADB, 1991). The reality was that, as the forest fringes were depopulated by outmigration for employment in India and elsewhere, rice terraces were collapsing for lack of maintenance. The narrative was sustained by a regular annual increase in reported area under cultivation. But when Gill dug into the statistics he found that every year an agricultural resurvey was carried out in two or so districts. These increased the reported area under agriculture in each district by between two and eight times. These totals were then added each year to the national figure. The myth of erosion being caused by increasing population was maintained by a statistical artefact. The reality was the opposite: the cause of erosion was not too many people but too few.

Distance and insulation. Error and myth are protected from correction by distance and insulation from people and ground realities. Structural adjustment policies were determined in Washington, DC, and other capital cities by economists cocooned in their offices incestuously interacting and with virtually no contact with field realities, let alone actual people affected. Richard Jolly (2015) has recorded, in what may have been an exceptional degree of exposure and feedback, how:

> A young World Bank official once told me that as his aeroplane was taking off from a Caribbean Island for Washington he saw from the plane window people rioting in the streets. Having just negotiated and signed an adjustment programme with that country, he wondered how much he was responsible.

The dire and ridiculous predictions of woodfuel gap theory came from calculations made in an office far away from the reality they purported to represent. And so on, again and again.

Selective experiences through visits. The biases of 'rural development tourism' are not a new discovery (see, for example, Chambers, 1983: 10–23, and Chapter 2). The visitor is taken to a special place which has had special treatment, and is treated to special presentations by people who have been specially trained and briefed and who have often done it often before.[13] The storyline in each case is well rehearsed and guides have embedded it like a catechism, sometimes through almost daily repetition. The roll call of special projects visited around the world is lengthy: in India three used to stand out – Sukhomajri, Mohini, and Ralegaon Sindhi – all of which had received quite extraordinary attention.

A key moment in the history of the Sasakawa Global 2000[14] programme for smallholder agriculture in Ethiopia was an impromptu field visit in September 1994 by Meles Zenawi, already in power and subsequently prime minister, together with Jimmy Carter (Keeley and Scoones, 2003: Chapter 4). It is hardly likely that they were taken to farmers who were failing.[15] Biased brief rural visits by VIPs from which policy conclusions were drawn, were probably common in SG 2000. Following this visit the Ethiopian Government scaled up the programme to a national campaign.

In the national programme of *ujamaa* in Tanzania the intention was to move towards an ideal of collective agriculture in every village. The programme had a high political profile. For a time there was a common belief that it could and would achieve some success. Many villages cultivated a small common plot to show to party officials and visitors.

In the 1960s and 1970s, *Mbioni*, the influential journal of Kivukoni College in Dar es Salaam, published accounts of *ujamaa* based on repeated visits to three exceptional communities: Upper Kitete, Mbambara, and the Ruvuma Development Association (RDA) (Ibbott, 2015). With hindsight, these were probably almost the only instances of successful collective agriculture, and all three were idiosyncratically non-replicable: Upper Kitete was on a land frontier with economies of scale with wheat and cattle, and an exceptionally capable and committed manager; Mbambara was a sisal estate taken over by the workers when its owner abandoned it; and the RDA, in a very poor and isolated area, was unique for its two charismatic and ideologically committed leaders, Ralph Ibbott and Ntimbanjao Millinga, and for its communalism. Of all the thousands of supposed *ujamaa* villages in Tanzania he might have visited, Julius Nyerere went twice to the RDA. With such selective perceptions it is not surprising that it was some years before the widespread failure or non-existence of *ujamaa* was recognized and the programme abandoned.[16]

Repeating narratives, stories, and statistics. Simple, striking, and memorable narratives, stories, and statistics become powerful and persuasive through repetition.

Dominant narratives are reviewed by Keeley and Scoones (2003). An example is the neo-Malthusian vicious circle of population increase, environmental degradation, and a growing food gap. Narratives tend to embody simple relationships, occluding local complexities, qualifications, and exceptions. The linearity of sentences constrains expression and thought to simple cause–effect relationships which are then generalized. Unlike diagrams, words do not readily permit the presentation of multiple causality or local complexity and diversity. Syntax forces us to simplify and streamline concepts and relationships in ways which fail to represent realities adequately.

For their part, stories can be a powerful way of changing organizations and their cultures (Denning, 2000). They can also reinforce beliefs. 'Good' stories, whether true, representative, or not, get repeated and spread on their own. Much of the 'evidence' that the green revolution was turning red was the single Kilvenmani incident (cited, for example, in Wharton, 1969, and Frankel, 1971: 115–6). Much was made of this. But as John Harriss (1977: 35) observed, 'The Kilvenmanai incident...has been made the basis for optimistic predictions about the likelihood of "the green revolution turning red" by a kind of "rapportage overkill" which has used one incident many times over as evidence of the imminence of revolution'.

The same is true of sticky statistics – numbers which are simple, memorable, remembered, and embedded and believed through repetition. Two numbers have recurred in different contexts: 30 per cent and 6 million hectares. That post-harvest grain losses at the village level were of the order of 30 per cent was striking and shocking when the figure began to be quoted at conferences and workshops. Its frequent repetition then led to major misallocations of resources.[17] The main source for the figure was a rounding of the findings of a time-of-harvesting trial at the IRRI research station. Although careful field-level research showed only 4–7 per cent losses (e.g. Greeley, 1987), 30 per cent had a resilient life of its own and survived like a coelacanth into the 2010s. Now it has a reincarnation as 30 per cent global food losses including waste. This later 30 per cent may have been arrived at totally independently, or may have come to mind consciously or unconsciously for those making the estimate because it was already familiar from a related context.

As for 6 million hectares, this has cropped up in at least three contexts: the annual rate at which desertification was spreading in Africa; the irrigated area in India subject to waterlogging; and the area in India suffering erosion and degradation. That desertification in Africa was spreading at the rate of 6 million hectares a year was embedded in the environmental discourse through its use by the United Nations Environment Programme and the Brundtland Commission. The 6 million hectares waterlogged from canal irrigation, though almost certainly spurious, was endlessly repeated in India in the 1980s (Chambers, 1988: 21 and 27).[18]

Repeating narratives, stories, and statistics, or reading them in several sources, or seeing them on a video or PowerPoint several times, embeds them like rote learning. Catechists and teachers are well aware of the importance of repetition for internalizing knowledge and beliefs. Repeated often enough, or in enough places or media, they become simplified, losing their qualifications, and are then internalized and believed as truth. This may occur especially among those who speak in public about their subjects, and do this in a mode of advocacy: priests, preachers, politicians, passionate advocates of a cause, or guides who show a succession of visitors round a project. All these are liable to speak each time with more conviction. How profoundly disabling public repetition can be by drowning doubt and cementing dogma, is barely recognized, despite its many pathological manifestations whatever the persuasion of the speaker.

Nor are scientists or engineers immune as shown by Starkey's (1988) scholarly and sobering study of multi-purpose wheeled toolcarriers for agriculture. These received much publicity, not least from ICRISAT, which invested much professional time and resources in developing a model. Worldwide, Starkey found that over 45 designs had been made, but that of the 10,000 or so toolcarriers produced the number ever used by farmers was negligible. When he corresponded with those who were developing and testing toolcarriers a common reply was that they were facing difficulties but they knew they had succeeded elsewhere.

None of his correspondents appreciated the extent to which they were deceived. They were creators and victims of a self-sustaining collective fantasy.

Repetitive confirmation bias. Confirmation bias is the tendency to search for, favour, recall, and repeat information that confirms what one believes or wants to believe; with the corollary of discounting, dismissing, or denying whatever is contradictory. Vulnerability to confirmation bias is part of the human condition.

There is then a tendency for statistics that one would like to believe or which support a programme, to be repeated and internalized, and for this to continue long after they have been exposed as flawed. Like many others I wanted to believe the table (Table 1.1) that showed a dramatic drop in diarrhoea when a community moves from 95 per cent to 100 per cent toilet coverage. It reinforced the case for the focus of CLTS on *total* sanitation. I projected the table repeatedly in workshops and talks. It is now embedded in many PowerPoint presentations with their own repetitive inertia. But even though evidence on which it was based was flimsy, flawed, unreliable, and contradicted by other evidence, the field note which contained it (WSP, 2007) remained in circulation and was even distributed at the South Asia Conference on Sanitation in 2013. The table will no doubt continue to have a long life of its own.[19]

I have been horrified to catch myself out. In Participatory Rural Appraisal-related workshops for several years I recounted an example of participatory mapping, reported by Jules Pretty, in an Indian village. I said that four separate groups of villagers came up with populations of 312, 312, 316, and 321. When villagers checked the numbers they found that 316 was double-counting a household of four, and 321 included an outcast household of nine on the edge of the village. When I went back to the original source I was shocked to find that the actual figures (Chambers, 1997: 145) were 239, 239, 242, and 247. On some occasion I may have said 'the figures were something like...' and then it was what I had said that I remembered the next time, repeating them without the qualification. Also the extra people were three not four, and not in one household but divided between three households, and the extra family had five members not nine. The point is that I really believed 312, 312, 316, and 321 and the story I was telling. One wonders how widespread this phenomenon is. Politicians must be especially vulnerable.

Public relations, soundbites, and speeches. Myths are also established and reinforced through public relations activities. Annual reports, videos to introduce visitors to institutions, and activities of public relations firms all contribute. Professionally, the latter are concerned to please their clients by propagating whatever their message may be and establishing whatever image they wish. They also seek to minimize criticism. An SG 2000 meeting was convened in London and organized by a public relations consultant. Ambassadors and High Commissioners from African countries were invited. The programme was organized with only 15 minutes for questions and discussion, from 1300 to 1315, with lunch pending. This was so obviously inadequate for any serious discussion that I and another critic declined to go. Which made the public relations ploy that much more effective.

Soundbites, too, have their part to play. The green revolution turning red, the desert on the move, the food gap widening – these are phrases that catch on. Speechwriters play a part here. They need catchy and simple messages. They know what needs to be said, for whatever political or institutional reasons. And as asserted above, those who then read and speak the messages internalize, remember, and believe them.

Malleable memory: reimagining and rewriting history. Two illuminating books shed fascinating light on a pervasive but neglected source of error: the malleability of memory and how we reimagine and rewrite history.

Kathryn Schultz's *Being Wrong: Adventures in the Margin of Error* (2010) is a magisterial review of the psychology of human error. Schultz documents repeatedly how memory is 'notoriously unreliable'. For instance, students in USA were asked their recollection of the *Challenger* disaster the day after it happened and then again three years later. Less than 7 per cent of the later memories matched the earlier ones, 50 per cent were wrong in half their assertions, and 25 per cent were wrong in every major detail (Schultz, 2010: 72–3). But even when our memories are wrong, we 'feel' that they are right. Memories are malleable: they are moulded and remoulded. We recreate our past.

In *Fabulous Science: Fact and Fiction in the History of Scientific Discovery* (2002), John Waller examines the behaviour of several scientists of fame and distinction. He presents evidence of how they concealed or distorted the history of their discoveries and underplayed or ignored the part played by others. Waller notes (p. 285) 'the constructivist nature of memory'. Scientists, like others,[20] come to believe false and flattering versions of the past. Ego and self-delusion play their part. Ambitious scientists may be intensely tempted to claim as their own the ideas and discoveries of others. This can include when these have a complex and intertwined provenance with many significant actors. Events like Alexander Fleming's chance discovery of penicillin in 1926 make good stories. As they gain the aura of foundation myths, subsequent sequences and actions easily acquire an appearance of unbroken linearity with simplistic over-attribution. The wrong versions are sustained and reinforced by journalists, biographers, honours, and repetition and are less and less likely to be challenged or denied.[21] However human and understandable they may be, Waller is right to call these 'Sins against history'. Which leaves the uncomfortable questions: are we all sinners? And who can cast the first stone?

Coda

Alone, any one of these tendencies and influences might be difficult to overcome. When power, interests, mindsets, ego and self-esteem, errors in data, and behaviours and experiences variously combine with constructivist memory, the resulting errors can become difficult to dispel and correct. They can, as the cases cited illustrate, take off into robustly self-sustaining myth, resilient in the face of contrary evidence. Nor, as we shall see in later chapters, can professional groups who claim to be objective claim immunity. Compounding and reinforcing error and myth are the temptations of repeating and ease of remembering simple narratives and statistics which become embedded as unqualified beliefs. In Swift's (1997: 85) words, 'A simple idea, adorned with powerful slogans, proves remarkably hard to change, even when shown to be patently inaccurate'.

Agenda for reflection and action

The evidence and analysis of this chapter lead us to an agenda of questions for reflection and action. With all knowledge – and the assertions, beliefs, conclusions, ideas, policies, proposals, statements, statistics, and the like which express and reflect them – we can ask about origins, sources, and processes. These are questions that can be addressed to almost any context, institution, or person, including oneself:

- *Discordance and heresies.* Have contradictory, discordant, or heretical ideas, evidence, or sources of information been dismissed or have they received fair hearing and testing?
- *Power.* Have power relations distorted learning, communication, and perception?
- *Construction of knowledge.* How have the statements, statistics, assertions, ideas, beliefs and conclusions under review been shaped by sources, processes, and predispositions?
- *Ignorance.* Have the full realities been appreciated? What has been missed?
- *History.* Has historical experience been taken into account?
- *Selectivity.* Have evidence, presentations, visits, and perceptions been selective and biased?
- *Extrapolation.* Has the local been extrapolated erroneously to higher scales?
- *Repetition.* Have narratives, stories, statistics, or soundbites been repeated in writing, videos, PowerPoints, conversation, public relations exercises, or speeches, and distorted and believed?
- *Ego and interests.* Have special interests influenced the methodology and topics researched or investigated, and the outcomes and findings?
- *Predispositions and critical awareness.* To what conclusions or beliefs have those involved been predisposed? Have they been self-critically aware and transparent? Have they acknowledged and sought to offset distortions?

These questions point to two themes which thread through this book: the importance of ground-truthing, checking against empirical realities; and the universal relevance of reflexivity, of self-critical epistemological awareness, questioning how we know, how we learn and unlearn, and how we can learn to know better.

Notes

1. For a wide-ranging overview of error and myth in international development with much further evidence see Black, 2015. This is well-researched, replete with evidence and examples, radical, realistic, succinct, and comprehensive, the best short critical introduction I know.
2. For a succinct account of the origin and rationale of structural adjustment see Black, 2015: 24, 64–5.
3. Recognition of the failure of the T and V system was delayed by moving on from country to country and continent to continent, provoking me to write these lines:

   > If Asian countries throw you out
   > It's only they that have the clout
   > In Africa you can insist
   > They have no power to resist

4. I recommend the extended empirically based Chapter 1 of 'Challenging received wisdom in Africa' in Leach and Mearns, *The Lie of the Land*. Published in 1996, this deserves to be on reading lists of all who work on environmental issues for many years to come.
5. The point about Klenner's claim is not that it was necessarily valid, though it may well have been and still may be, but that despite enormous potential implications for human well-being in attacking polio, it was not taken seriously.
6. Lord Acton's aphorism 'All power tends to corrupt; and absolute power corrupts absolutely' is popularly shortened to 'All power corrupts...'. All power deceives is the title of Chapter 5 in *Whose Reality Counts?* (Chambers, 1997). Does absolute power deceive absolutely?
7. Since writing this in 2002 it has been paradoxically ICRISAT (the International Crops Research Centre for the Semi-Arid Tropics) not IRRI (the International Rice Research Institute) that picked up on SRI, conducted research and identified applications with other crops, including sugar cane, for which see Gujja et al., 2009.
8. For a comprehensive account of India's earlier sanitation programmes, see Alok, 2010.
9. By 2016 much attention had been given to improving monitoring, including the use of GPS with smartphones.
10. The Brazilian study (de Melo et al., 2007) found with visits every other day that over a four-week period, 33 out of 84 children under 40 months had diarrhoea but parental recall at the end of the period reported only 10. Issues included the understanding of what constituted diarrhoea.
11. It will not, and certainly should not, escape the reader that I repeatedly extrapolate from the particular to the general. We all do this. What matters is to struggle to be optimally aware of this, and to try

to strike a balance between uncritical generalization and over-cautious qualification.

12. This paragraph is based on Chapter 3 of Keeley and Scoones, 2003, which is also the source of the quotations.

13. One indicator is to ask a presenter how many times she or he has done it before. What 'it' is may itself have changed. A Nepali forester has told me that on approaching a village [probably near Kathmandu] a man came out to meet him with a piece of paper and at once began drawing a map. 'Have you done this before?' 'Oh at least a hundred times' (personal communication with Yam Malla).

14. Sasakawa Global 2000 is a programme for smallholder agriculture in Africa, founded in 1986 by Normal Borlaug, Ryoichi Sasakawa, and Jimmy Carter.

15. In an earlier version, I had included Norman Borlaug in this visit but I have since learned reliably that he did not take part. The next sentence was, 'An Ethiopian informant (who did not wish to be named) told me that one farmer visited had a magnificent crop which had received three times the recommended dose of fertiliser.' By repeating this hearsay story, I was doing precisely what I criticize. I am grateful to Christopher Dowswell for pointing out that Zinawi and Carter almost certainly visited wheat, not maize, and that wheat would lodge (fall over) with such high applications. The low-grade information I was repeating fitted my views about rural development tourism and my prejudices about SG 2000. It was what I wanted to believe.

16. There is a large literature on *ujamaa*. For a fascinating and insightful analysis see Chapter 7, 'Compulsory villagization in Tanzania: aesthetics and miniaturization' in Scott, 1998. For a revealing insider's account of the Ruvuma Development Association, the experiment that was closest to embodying the ideals of *ujamaa*, and of why and how it was disbanded by the TANU Party, see Ibbott, 2015.

17. For a summary of evidence for these statements, see Chambers, 1997: 19–21. Though comprehensively discredited 30 to 40 years earlier, the 30 to 40 per cent losses figure has been resiliently enduring. And it may not be an entirely trivial speculation to wonder why, when faced in this note with the need to give a vague past date, somehow 30–40 years came to my mind.

18. In the early 1980s the figure of 6 million hectares waterlogged as a result of irrigation was raised in a parliamentary question in Delhi. I could not hide my glee when, indulging in the fun of statistical archaeology, I traced it back through three sources, each citing an earlier one, to the *Report of the Irrigation Commission* (MOIP, 1972), which gave almost a third (1.85 million hectares) of the total in West Bengal, a state with less than 1 million hectares under canal irrigation. The likely explanation for the discrepancy is the flooding from rivers and rainfall to which West Bengal is vulnerable. The figure of 6 million hectares flooded because of irrigation appeared a gross overestimate (Chambers, 1988: 21, 27).

19. I hesitated to republish it here for fear it might be copied without the text being read and cited as evidence! For better or for worse, it is a very clear example of confirmation bias.

20. Social scientists may be more vulnerable than natural scientists, as revealed in Waller's scholarly, detailed, and devastating dissection and demolition of the famous Hawthorne effect (2002: 78–98). This is the finding of an experiment which purported to show that the productivity of workers rose whatever changes were made in their conditions. This was attributed to the effects of being observed by the experimentalist.

21. According to John Waller, by 1930 Alexander Fleming had only the most oblique interest in penicillin. It was only in 1941, by which time years of intense work by a team led by Howard Florey had tested penicillin on humans and found how to make it at scale that Fleming's interest revived to claim credit. Fleming received 25 honorary degrees, 26 medals, 13 decorations, the freedoms of 15 cities and boroughs, and membership of 89 academies and societies (Waller, 2002: 246–67).

References

Alam, N., Henry, F. and Rahaman, M. (1989) 'Reporting errors in one-week diarrhoea recall surveys: experience from a prospective study in rural Bangladesh', *International Journal of Epidemiology* 18(3): 697–700.

Alok, K. (2010) *Squatting with Dignity: Lessons from India*, Sage Publications.

Benor, D. and Harrison, J.Q. (1977) *Agricultural Extension: The Training and Visit System*, Washington, DC: World Bank.

Black, M. (2015) *International Development: Illusions and Realities*, Oxford, UK: New Internationalist Publications.

Chambers, R. (1983) *Rural Development: Putting the Last First*, Harlow, UK: Longman.

Chambers, R. (1988) *Managing Canal Irrigation: Practical Analysis from South Asia*, New Delhi: Oxford and IBH; Cambridge: Cambridge University Press.

Chambers, R. (1997) *Whose Reality Counts? Putting the First Last*, Rugby: ITDG Publishing.

Chambers, R. (2014) *Into the Unknown. Explorations in Development Practice*, Rugby, Practical Action Publishing.

Chambers, R. and Myers, J. (2016) *Norms, Knowledge and Usage*, Frontiers in CLTS No 7, Brighton: CLTS Knowledge Hub, IDS.

CLTS Knowledge Hub (2011) *Community-led total sanitation*, Institute of Development Studies, <http://www.communityledtotalsanitation.org/> [accessed 26 February 2017].

de Melo, C.N., de A C Taddei, J.A., Diniz-Santos, D.R., May, D.S., Carneiro, N.B. and Silva, L.R. (2007) 'Incidence of diarrhea: poor parental recall ability', *Brazilian Journal of Infectious Diseases* 11(6): 571–9 <http://dx.doi.org/10.1590/S1413-86702007000600009>.

Denning, S. (2000) *The Springboard: How Storytelling Ignites Action in Knowledge-Era Organizations*, Boston, MA: Butterworth-Heinemann.

De Padua, D.B. (1976) 'Rice post-production handling and processing: its significance to agricultural development', paper presented at the *International Workshop on Accelerating Agricultural Development*, SEARCA, Laguna, Philippines, 26–30 April.

Fairhead, J. and Leach, M. (1996a) *Misreading the African Landscape: Society and Ecology in a Forest-Savanna Mosaic*, Cambridge: Cambridge University Press.

Fairhead, J. and Leach, M. (1996b) 'Rethinking the forest-savanna mosaic: colonial science and its relics in West Africa', in M. Leach and R. Mearns (eds), *The Lie of the Land*, London: International African Institute.

Fairhead, J. and Leach, M. (2003) *Science, Society and Power: Environmental Knowledge and Policy in West Africa and the Caribbean*, Cambridge: Cambridge University Press.

Frankel, F.R. (1971) *India's Green Revolution: Economic Gains and Political Costs*, Princeton, NJ: Princeton University Press.

Gonzalez, A.H. (2013) *Pathways to Sustainability in Community-Led Total Sanitation. Experiences from Madhya Pradesh and Himachal Pradesh*, D. Phil thesis, Universitat Politechnica de Valencia.

GOI (2012) *Census of India 2011*, New Delhi: Government of India.

Greeley, M. (1987) *Post-harvest Losses, Technology and Development*, Boulder, CO: Westview Press.

Harriss, J. (1977) 'Bias in perception of agrarian change in India', in B.H. Farmer (ed.), *Green Revolution?* London: Macmillan.

Hellden, U. (1991) 'Desertification: time for an assessment?' *Ambio* 20(8): 372–83.

Hueso, A. and Bell, B. (2013) 'An untold story of policy failure: the Total Sanitation Campaign in India', *Water Policy* 15(6): 1001–17 <http://dx.doi.org/10.2166/wp.2013.032>.

Ibbott, R. (2014) *Ujamaa: The Hidden Story of Tanzania's Socialist Villages*, London: Crossroads Books.

Iraq Inquiry (2016) *The Report of the Iraq Inquiry*, London: UK Government, <www.iraqinquiry.org.uk/the-report> [accessed 26 February 2017].

Jolly, R. (2015) Letter to *The Independent* (London) and *The Guardian* (London) newspapers, 6 July.

Keeley, J. and Scoones, I. (2003) *Understanding Environmental Policy Processes in Africa: Cases from Ethiopia, Mali and Zimbabwe*, London: Earthscan.

Leach, G. and Mearns, R. (1988) *Beyond the Woodfuel Crisis: People, Land and Trees in Africa*, London: Earthscan.

Leach, M. and Mearns, R. (eds) (1996) *The Lie of the Land: Challenging Received Wisdom on the African Environment*, Oxford: International African Institute in association with James Currey; Portsmouth, NH: Heinemann.

Lehrer, J. (2008) *Proust was a Neuroscientist*, Boston, MA: Houghton Mifflin.

Levy, T.E. (2002) *Vitamin C, Infectious Diseases and Toxins: Curing the Incurable*, Philadelphia, PA: XLibris Foundation.

Lewis, D. (2013) 'Reconnecting development policy, people and history', in T. Wallace and F. Porter with M. Ralph-Bowman (eds), *Aid, NGOs and the Realities of Women's Lives: A Perfect Storm*, pp. 115–26, Rugby, UK: Practical Action Publishing.

Lipton, B.H. (2008) *The Biology of Belief: Unleashing the Power of Consciousness, Matter and Miracles*, London: Hay House.

MOIP (1972) *Report of the Irrigation Commission 1972*, New Delhi: Ministry of Irrigation and Power.

NARC/ADB (1991) *Nepal Agricultural Research Study*, Kathmandu: National Agricultural Research Council and the Asian Development Bank.

Sanchez, P., Shepherd, D., Soule, M., Place, F., Buresh, A., Mokwune, A., Kwesiga, F., Nidiritu, C., and Woomer, P. (1997) 'Soil fertility replenishment in Africa: an investment in natural resource capital', in R. Buresh, P. Sanchez, and F. Calhoun (eds), *Replenishing Soil Fertility in Africa*, SSSA Special Publication Number 51, Madison, WI: Soil Science Society of America, American Society of Agronomy.

Schulz, K. (2010) *Being Wrong: Adventures in the Margin of Error*, London: Portobello Books.

Scott, J.C. (1998) *Seeing Like a State: How Certain Schemes to Improve the Human Condition Have Failed*, New Haven, CT: Yale University Press.

Smaling, E., Nandwa, S. and Janssen, B. (1997) 'Soil fertility in Africa is at stake', in R. Buresh, P. Sanchez, and F. Calhoun (eds), *Replenishing Soil Fertility in Africa*, SSSA Special Publication Number 51, Madison, WI: Soil Science Society of America, American Society of Agronomy.

SRI-Rice (2015a) *SRI methodologies*, Cornell University, <http://sri.ciifad.cornell.edu/aboutsri/methods/index.html> [accessed 26 February 2017].

SRI-Rice (2015b) *SRI concepts and methods applied to other crops*, Cornell University, <http://sri.ciifad.cornell.edu/aboutsri/othercrops/index.html> [accessed 26 February 2017].

Starkey, P. (1988) *Animal-drawn Wheeled Toolcarriers: Perfected yet Rejected*, Braunschweig/Wiesbaden: Friedrich Vieweg & Sohn.

Swift, J. (1997) 'Desertification: narratives, winners and losers', in M. Leach and R. Mearns (eds), *Lie of the Land*, pp. 73–90, Oxford: International African Institute in association with James Currey; Portsmouth, NH: Heinemann.

Tiffen, M., Mortimore, M. and Gichuki, N. (1993) *More People, Less Erosion: Environmental Recovery in Kenya*, Chichester, UK: John Wiley and Sons.

UNEP (1984) *General Assessment of Progress in the Implementation of the Plan of Action to Combat Desertification 1978–1984: Report of the Executive Director*, Governing Council, Twelfth Session, UNEP/GC.12/9, Nairobi: UN Environment Programme.

Uphoff, N. and Coombs, J. (2001) *Some Things Can't Be True But Are: Rice, Rickets and What Else?* Ithaca, NY: Cornell International Institute for Food, Agriculture and Development, Cornell University.

Waller, J. (2002) *Fabulous Science: Fact and Fiction in the History of Scientific Discovery*, Oxford: Oxford University Press.

WCED (1987) *Our Common Future: Report of the World Commission on Environment and Development*, Oxford: Oxford University Press.

Wharton, C.R. (1969) 'The Green Revolution: cornucopia or Pandora's Box?' *Foreign Affairs* 47: 464–76.

World Bank (1988) *Rural Development: The World Bank Experience 1965–1986*, Washington, DC: World Bank.

WSP (2007) *Community-Led Total Sanitation in Rural Areas: An Approach that Works*, New Delhi: Water and Sanitation Program, World Bank.

CHAPTER 2
Biases and blind spots

Abstract

That people want to know realities cannot be assumed: strategic ignorance, not wanting to know, is common. Biases of perception can result from direct personal experience, as in development tourism. Blind spots and neglected topics are themselves a neglected topic. Some that are now less neglected are gender relations, harmful traditional practices, unpaid care, masculinities and men, sexuality, child sex abuse, and corruption. Others that have been backwaters of research include cookstove air pollution, neglected tropical diseases, entomophagy, and effects of climate change on ocean ecology. Water, sanitation, and hygiene provides revealing cases of biases, blind spots, and neglected areas, including diarrhoea reductionism and the links between faecally transmitted infections and undernutrition. Analysis of these examples and other evidence sheds light on the aetiology and morphology of biases, blind spots, and neglected areas. Causal explanations include professional specialization, tunnel vision, and incentives; difficulties of measurement, institutional silos, and inertia; and professional and personal preferences. Past and present biases, blind spots, and neglected topics in different disciplines and professions share characteristics which are pointers to future priorities for research and action. The biggest blind spot of all is ourselves.

Keywords: strategic ignorance, biases, blind spots, neglected topics, WASH, undernutrition, professional and personal preferences, research, incentives, priorities

> What the eye does not see, the heart does not grieve over. (Old English Proverb)

> Development professionals can be susceptible to a host of cognitive biases, can be influenced by their social tendencies and social environments, and can use deeply ingrained mindsets when making choices. (World Bank, 2015)

> ...there are known knowns...known unknowns...also unknown unknowns...(Donald Rumsfeld, 2002, on Saddam Hussein's weapons of mass destruction)

Overview and purpose

Error and myth are often associated with biases and blind spots. By biases, I mean professional preferences for and tendencies towards behaviours, choices, locations, people, priorities, topics, qualities, and methods

http://dx.doi.org/10.3362/9781780449449.002

which give an unbalanced, distorted and/or incomplete view of realities. By blind spots I mean domains, locations, topics, factors, aspects, dimensions, approaches and/or methods which are systemically not recognized or neglected.

This chapter is an invitation for the reader to join in exploring some of these biases and blind spots. I have found this fascinating. They are everywhere in everyday as well as professional life. Their ubiquity and inherent interest make it strange that as a topic they have themselves been something of a blind spot.

A welcome exception has been the 2015 World Development Report, *Mind, Society and Behaviour* (World Bank, 2015), and the sources it cites. The choice of subject was a breakthrough, and the report is a revealing compilation and synthesis of insights from research. It has sections on 'biases in assessing information' and 'biases in assessing value', and a whole chapter on 'The biases of development professionals'. It summarizes much research on behaviour, psychology, and perceptions, in particular relating to irrationality in decision-making. However, there is little overlap with the subject matter of this chapter, such as the biases of outsiders' brief rural visits; biases of preferences for areas for study and action; and blind spots and neglected topics left largely unrecognized and unilluminated by normal professionalism. In a spirit of critical reflection let me invite readers to search for, find, and correct blind spots, biases, errors, and omissions in this chapter and in the rest of the book. For they are surely there.

Strategic ignorance

In much development discourse, and in most of this chapter, development actors are assumed to want to know. This assumption reflects ignorance of the psychology and sociology of ignorance. For blind spots and ignorance are often chosen. Strategic ignorance (McGoey, 2012) refers to deliberately not knowing or knowing but not wishing to be known to know. A probable example of the latter was the newspaper phone hacking scandals in the UK in the first half of the 2010s where much turned on whether or not editors and others knew about the illegal activities of their journalists. Strategic ignorance can take many forms and be manifest in many contexts.

One arena is meetings. An issue can be kept off the agenda. Someone with unwelcome information can be kept quiet by the chair. Any other business can be rushed. Someone whose views are not wanted can be excluded from the meeting (for an example see Eyben, 2012: 12). Or a meeting itself can be postponed, even indefinitely. Another tactic is not to respond to a point and change the subject. Under the heading 'Diplomatic science', Walter Huppert (2013: 271) recollects that when, from 1998 to 2004, he was a member of the board of the International Water Management Institute (IWMI) he argued at a number of board meetings that corruption was so significant in the sector that it should be researched by IWMI. The director-general appointed during this period was 'a very engaged and highly competent professional' but:

> Each time I raised the subject there was a kind of awkward silence by the DG and amongst other board members followed by a quick change of subject. Nevertheless , I was too shy to insist on an in depth discussion of the topic...In 2008, the annual report of Transparency International and of the Water Integrity Network dealt with corruption in the water sector. At that time the...DG had left his job at IWMI. When I read this report, I discovered to my great surprise that it was nobody else but this DG himself who had written the chapter on corruption, pointing to new and promising ways on how to deal with that topic and arguing that they deserve increased attention. No longer being the DG of IWMI allowed him to raise his voice on matters like these. (Huppert, 2013: 271)

Another tactic is shelving a report, keeping it confidential, editing it, postponing its completion and release,[1] limiting its circulation, or at the individual level postponing reading it or leaving it unread. I have done the latter. When responsible for coordinating evaluation for the Kenya Special Rural Development Programme in 1969–71, I believed gravity reticulation water projects were a very good thing. Harland Padfield, an experienced sociologist, wrote a think-piece with cautions and criticisms. I feared that these would threaten the substantive programme. I remember that after glancing at his paper I did not want to read it, let alone pass it on to others, and again and again postponed studying it properly or arranging for it to be discussed.

Designing tests that will fail is a tactic in agriculture – testing an unwelcome innovation with key elements missing or badly implemented thereby ensuring failure. It can be hard to tell whether this is unconscious or contrived wilful incompetence. The first trial of SRI (System of Rice Intensification) by West African Rice Development Association (WARDA) scientists did not find benefits from the system. This was predictable as they had omitted the key element of aeration of the roots of the rice plant during its first nine weeks. When government researchers in Rhodesia (as it then was) tested the Savory system of rotational grazing, they did it in a manner that its originator said guaranteed failure (Alan Savory, pers. comm.). These are contested areas, and it is fair to recognize that scientists tied to rigid research designs are at a disadvantage compared with farmers or pastoralists whose management can be flexible and adaptive; and that this disadvantage may rise exponentially the more complex and interlocking the system being developed or tested.

For the powerful, strategic ignorance can be a survival strategy. Without it many politicians and officials would find life difficult. The achievement of targets presents many examples. The rural sanitation sector in many countries has claimed that communities are open defecation-free when they are not. Officials know that statistics are misleading (see Chapter 1) but to question them openly could expose them to political and even career risk. A conversation I had with an Indian Administrative Service officer sticks in my mind. I asked her if she knew how targets were falsely reported to her as achieved. She replied, 'I don't want to know'. She knew her staff were lying and they probably knew that she knew. But all kept quiet. So it is that strategic ignorance is aided and abetted by two siblings: tacit connivance and strategic silence.

Biased experience: development tourism revisited

A widespread phenomenon of biases of experience and perception in which to varying degrees strategic ignorance, shortage of time, convenience, accessibility, and stage management combine, is rural development tourism, the brief rural visit by the urban-based person. Pleasurable collaboration and dialogue with co-researchers in Sri Lanka and Tamil Nadu in 1973–74[2] and later brainstorming with colleagues in IDS led to the identification of the biases of 'rural poverty unseen' (Chambers, 1983: 10–27). Here they are in summary with updates in italics:

Spatial bias includes tendencies for outsiders to visit places and meet people accessible from urban centres when those who are worse off are often further away. Tarmac bias is one dimension. Visiting the centres of villages when the poor people are around the peripheries is another. *Airport bias can be added. This is the tendency for places visited and even research locations to be within convenient distance of an airport. However, people who are worse off are not always peripherally located: beggars and labourers seeking work can be found in core locations. In famines or other distress people move to roadsides and to central places.*

Project bias is the tendency for outsiders to want to visit and to be taken to projects where there has been an external input, to the neglect of other usually more typical areas. The same projects, visited and described repeatedly, build up a project myth. *Project bias remains. An example is the specially privileged, much visited and atypical Millennium Development Villages in Africa.*

Person bias is the tendency to meet leaders, men, the wealthy, and elites to the neglect of those who are excluded and left behind, including women, those who are poorer, of low status, minorities, those who are stigmatized, physically weak, powerless, and/or inarticulate. *Who is not met or heard remains a critical question, and besides those listed above also often includes children, the disabled, the sick, the elderly, and widows, especially where several of these characteristics coincide in the same person or persons.*

Seasonal bias is the tendency to visit during the dry season, when harvests are in, travel is easier and more reliable, and people better off, better fed, and less sick. *Seasonal bias has been to some extent mitigated in many environments by extension of tarmac roads but remains serious, pervasive, and still under-recognized and inadequately offset.*

Diplomatic bias is the reluctance to broach sensitive subjects, or to ask to meet people who are marginalized. *It has become much more acceptable and expected for poor people and women to be met.*

Professional bias is the tendency to look for, to inquire about, and notice whatever are the concerns of one's discipline or profession. *Recognition of the multidimensionality of poverty has reduced the biases of professional specialization.*

Security is an addition to the original 1983 listing. Substantial areas are out of bounds to visitors, especially in fragile states, but those areas are where people are most likely to be suffering and most in need of assistance.

Urban slum bias can also be added. The rural biases also apply in urban contexts. We can talk now of development tourism without the rural prefix. Some slums, like Kibera in Nairobi, have been much visited, including by celebrities. Pressures of time, convenience, and accessibility may combine to make urban visits more common, together with the justification that quite often an increasing proportion of poor people are urban dwellers.

The biases of development tourism will continue to evolve. To know better, each generation will need to recognize and correct them.

Past blind spots: a selection reviewed

Since the early 1980s significant past blind spots have been studied and illuminated, accompanied by changes in language, mindsets, values, and policies. Some of these can be clustered under gender, cultural, social, and space. Others remain as backwaters of research.

Gender, cultural, social, and space

Gender biases. These have been pervasive in overlooking discrimination against women and girls. Gender biases against females persist and even intensify in some contexts and dimensions. But there has been much progress. Four decades ago there were few national statistics about women. Now they are quite extensive. Gender has been the subject of many books, conferences, and movements. Still, there remains a long road before universal gender equality is reached. What remains neglected or a blind spot and not on the agenda for research or for action varies by country, culture, religion, and local context. That said, certain neglected issues can be noted, all of them now receiving more attention.

Harmful traditional practices. As outlined by the Gender and Development Network (2015), harmful traditional practices (HTPs) are being confronted more and more. Recently they have been grouped together and given this collective name. The main ones have been identified as:

- female genital mutilation/cutting (FGM/C)
- early (often child) marriage
- dowry
- son preference and selective abortion
- honour killings
- bride price.

HTPs are all contested: they entail conflicts between traditional social norms in many local societies and the norms of outsiders and community members who have other perspectives. Difficult moral and ethical questions are raised about whose values and norms count. As neglected areas these practices have different characteristics. Dowry, bride price, and usually early marriage, are publicly acknowledged and not concealed, whereas selective abortion and honour killings are kept out of sight. Bottom lines are, however, that all are power-related, tend to be supported or enforced by men and, sometimes, as with FGM/C, older women, and all lead to or reflect discrimination against females.

Unpaid care. Unpaid work can affect men as well as women in their gendered roles, but unpaid care is assumed to be and overwhelmingly is a woman's role. Rosalind Eyben (2012: 7) has defined care 'as meeting the material and/ or developmental, emotional and spiritual needs of other people through direct personal interaction'. It has, she argues, been persistently neglected and repeatedly in many ways kept off the agenda. The executive summary of the World Development Report on gender equality (World Bank, 2012), for instance, excludes care from its list of major 'sticky issues' (Eyben, 2012: 12). It is so widespread, with so many social and economic implications, so convenient for men, and so unseen, that many do not want to recognize it, and so practise the strategic ignorance of keeping it out of sight and off the agenda.

Masculinities and men. These were at first not high on the list of feminist and gender concerns but came to be recognized as important for progress towards equitable gender relations (see Cornwall and White, 2000, for an early contribution on this). Gender equity has now been replaced in the discourse by the stronger phrase gender equality. This cuts both ways. Men can be losers and left behind, for instance in HIV testing in Africa (Shand et al., 2014) and teenage boys in Bangladesh who experience the downside of positive discrimination towards females (Dee Jupp, pers. comm.). Men and boys have a key part to play in overcoming persistent and pervasive patriarchy, male privilege, and multiple discriminations against females.[3]

Sexuality. This has been described as 'a central aspect of being human throughout life and encompasses sex, gender identities and roles, sexual orientation, eroticism, pleasure, intimacy and reproduction' (Jolly et al., 2006). Sexuality has been slow to be recognized, only emerging as a substantial development concern at the turn of the century (Jolly, 2000). LGBT (lesbian, gay, bisexual, transgender) and intersex people, and sex workers, have been regarded predominantly as a problem rather than people with rights. Sexuality has been seen negatively, not as a source of well-being. Those who are not heterosexual have been widely and often still are victimized for their sexual orientation, denied access to resources or employment, and subjected to violence and even criminal prosecution. Sexual orientation is thus closely linked with poverty. Sexual rights are more and more recognized. Research, advocacy, and action have gone forward together, and a once blind spot is now less and less of a neglected area.

Child sex abuse. In the early 1980s child sex abuse was barely recognized. Freud had interpreted women's accounts of it as fantasies manifesting repressed sexual desires for the abuser. The first prominent whistle-blower in the UK was Marietta Higgs in Cleveland. She removed from their parents 121 children whom she had found to have been abused and put them in care. For this she was virulently attacked, demonized in the press, dismissed, and her career ruined; 96 of the children were sent home but 75 per cent of her diagnoses were later confirmed (Gerard, 1997). It is now recognized that child sex abuse has been widespread worldwide and especially perpetrated by men protected by patriarchy within the sacred secrecy of the family home. For long it was kept hidden, with rear guard cover-ups by alliances and networks of threatened parents, and in hierarchical institutions like the Catholic and other churches, monasteries, and nunneries, through secrecy, solidarity, and denial. But the Catholic Church has done a huge turn around and in open democratic societies the exposure and investigations of child sex abuse continue.[4]

At this stage we can note that factors responsible for the neglect of these areas include patriarchal and intergenerational power and solidarity, culturally embedded customs, taboos, shame, and lack of visibility associated with norms of social and spatial privacy especially of family and home.

Backwaters of research

Lack of research has shielded other blind spots to varying degrees, leaving them as backwaters. Five disparate areas provide evidence of diverse reasons why they can remain relatively neglected.

Corruption. This is both a blind spot and a major and in some countries ubiquitous problem with very damaging effects. It is notoriously difficult to research. Early pioneering work by Robert Wade (1982) showed how systemic and systematic corruption was in the early 1980s in the irrigation sector in

India. Research can be threatening for the researcher: Wade was reported to have had to leave India. He had described, for instance,

> [a] circuit of transactions in which the bureaucracy acquires control of funds, partly from farmers in the form of variable levies, and partly from the state's public work budget, then passes a portion to politicians and especially Ministers, who in turn use the funds for distributing short-term material inducements in exchange for electoral support. (Wade, 1982: 319, cited in Huppert, 2013: 268)

He revealed that irrigation system managers deliberately created uncertainty about water supplies so that they would be paid to assure them; and the disintegrating cement structures for all to see off the main roads in India in the early 1980s were testimony to the prevalence of malpractices in construction. Another indicator in some countries is bumpy rides from potholes in newly constructed roads. Far more damaging are likely to be the many invisible effects of corruption in funds fiddled and creamed off to be hidden in foreign accounts. While this is universally acknowledged, and a commonplace of gossip, institutions and individuals find themselves constrained to employ strategic ignorance, even actively taking precautions not to know.

Corruption can with less difficulty be discussed retrospectively or in casual encounters. In his article 'Viewpoint – rent-seeking in agricultural water management: an intentionally neglected core dimension', Walter Huppert (2013) reflects on his observations from past decades and on the major adverse effects of corruption in irrigation system management. Casual encounters with strangers one will never meet again can be revealing. I learned much from a conversation on the subject waiting for a train on an Indian railway station: my informant regaled me with the percentage breakdowns of the take by officials and politicians at all levels from top to bottom. However, corruption often remains a known unknown, a blind spot, an elephant in the room, too difficult and dangerous to research.

Entomophagy. Eating edible insects (Glover and Sexton, 2015) is an area of enormous potential benefit to humankind that is still struggling to come out of the woodwork (if I may be forgiven). Edible insects are defined by human behaviour, what people are known to eat: besides insects this includes arachnids (spiders)[5] and myriapods (centipedes). Over 1,400 species of insects in this inclusive non-biological sense have been recorded as eaten by humans, with crickets, grasshoppers, ants, caterpillars like the Mopani worm in southern Africa, and eggs, larvae, and pupae among the most common; even scorpions are on the list. Entomophagy is a win–win: insects are highly nutritious and a good source of proteins, fats, and essential minerals, and rearing them en masse would likely be much more environmentally friendly than cattle for meat. Insects are reportedly five times more efficient than cattle in converting food into edible tissue and with their high reproductive rates their food conversion efficiency may be even higher.

Bias against entomophagy illustrates the combined effects of habit, socially conditioned (or possibly instinctive) revulsion, lack of market supply because of lack of demand, falling outside the mainstream of nutritional and agricultural research, and being seen as a food of the poor.

Neglected tropical diseases. NTDs are a prominent example of how blind spots can be recognized and acted on – named, identified as a category, documented, and funds obtained for research, prevention, and cure – all of these raising the prestige and rewards for working in them. Malaria, tuberculosis, and HIV/AIDS have received overwhelming attention and share of international funding for prevention and cure, but NTDs affect some 1–2 billion people or more. WHO has recognized 17 NTDs. In order of decreasing prevalence,[6] some of the most widespread are:

- soil-transmitted helminths (worms), *Ascaris* (roundworms), *Trichuris* (whipworms), and hookworms, affecting perhaps 1.5 billion people
- schistosomiasis: over 200 million
- dengue: 100–200 million cases a year
- lymphatic filariasis: 120 million
- zoonotic trematodes in food: 40 million
- onchocerciasis (river blindness): 37 million
- trachoma: 21 million (one of several estimates).

Others like leprosy, African sleeping sickness, Guinea worm disease, and polio have been greatly reduced or almost eliminated. New candidates like Ebola and Zika appear but are far from neglected. NTDs are also significant as a category defined not by strictly scientific or medical criteria based on biological characteristics. They are caused by a variety of pathogens such as viruses, bacteria, protozoa, and helminths, clubbed together for their shared characteristics of scale of human relevance and previous relative neglect.

NTDs show what can be done when funding agencies (the Gates Foundation, the Carter Foundation, and others), governments, and the medical and scientific establishment commit resources to a new priority. A significant indicator in the case of NTDs was the launch of a peer-reviewed international journal, *PLOS Neglected Tropical Diseases* with volume 1 in 2007. Indeed, the very labelling of a topic as neglected can draw attention and enhance its profile, prestige, and research funding.

Cookstove air pollution. Three billion people are said to rely on indoor cooking from solid fuels, with 4.3 million deaths resulting annually, more than from either malaria or tuberculosis, and contributing to heart disease, chronic obstructive pulmonary disorder, low birthweight children, and other harmful impacts. But cookstove air pollution has received relatively little attention, perhaps because it is confined largely to women's space (where the kitchen is separate from other rooms), largely out of sight, chronic not episodic, not a distinct disease, and mainly affecting women and children (GACC, 2015).

Climate change and ocean ecology. Neglect of the effects of climate change on ocean ecology further illustrates how several factors can combine to deter recognition and research despite importance.[7] The oceans absorb 93–94 per cent of the warming from greenhouse gases compared with only 6–7 per cent by land and atmosphere. However, the sea's influence on climate and global warming has been under-studied as have marine biological changes associated with climate change; 28,586 significant terrestrial and atmospheric climate-related biological changes with time-series data were identified by the Intergovernmental Panel on Climate Change in its Fourth Assessment Report (IPCC, 2007), but only 85 for marine and freshwater systems (Richardson and Poloczanska, 2008). More generally, the relative neglect of marine ecology is reflected in only 11 per cent of published papers in the fields of ecology, conservation biology, and biodiversity research having dealt with marine systems.

The neglect of the effects of global warming on marine ecology until the 2010s can be attributed to the interlocking combination of many factors. Among these are:

- Measurability and location: difficulty of observation and the significance of small differences, the general limitation of satellite observation to the water surface, the concentration of studies in coastal waters, and sheer physical scale: 70 per cent of the Earth's surface is ocean with an average depth of 4 kilometres.
- Complexity of currents, and factors like cooling from melting ice, albedo, winds, plankton, fishing and over fishing, coastal pollution, among others.
- Temporal scale: change is secular, over a long time scale, requiring longitudinal studies.
- Citizen science with higher public interest in terrestrial aspects with direct impact and related public observation (e.g. of bird distribution, time of budding) has no strong equivalent at sea.
- The oceans are international requiring international cooperation, which is less necessary terrestrially, given the nation state structure.
- Funding: high cost and requiring secure and sustained long-term research funding.
- Scientific articles on oceans and warming have received fewer citations than their terrestrial equivalents. Scientists devoting their careers to oceans and warming may then be or have been at a disadvantage compared with their terrestrial and atmospheric counterparts when promotions boards review their publication records.

Two other examples of relatively neglected areas are canal irrigation at night (Chambers, 1988: 133–57) and what happens in the root zones of crops. These draw attention to linked and recurring factors that contribute to these and many other nutritional, scientific, and medical neglected areas in research, namely, difficulties and inconvenience of observation and measurement.

Out of the closet: blind spots of WASH

Water, sanitation, and hygiene (WASH) is a source of examples of past and present (though diminishing) blind spots and biases. In order to shed further light on the morphology of blind spots, let us examine it in more detail than the cases above.

Faeces (aka shit): horrible, out of sight, out of mind. Open defecation remains widespread, practised by about a billion people (WHO, 2017). It has been a classic blind spot. Shit is dirty and smelly and evokes disgust. In most cultures it is embarrassing[8] and shameful, especially for women, to be seen defecating. It is a taboo subject. People 'turn a blind eye'. It is kept out of sight and out of mind. To overcome this, in community-led total sanitation (Kar with Chambers, 2008) people in communities are facilitated to recognize that open defecation means that 'we are eating one another's shit'. The local crude word is always used to avoid glossing over the nasty reality.[9]

Professionally, in parallel, shame and disgust have been coming out of the closet. Nick Haslam (2012: 10) reported that shame and disgust had received exponentially increasing attention in psychology research and publications, as shown in Table 2.1. Disgust is a central theme in Valerie Curtis' book (2013), *Don't Look, Don't Touch, Don't Eat: The Science behind Revulsion*. For all but coprophiliacs, shit is revolting. Community responses to this revulsion have been to concentrate defecation in areas only visited for that purpose, or somewhere distant, or in the privacy of a latrine or toilet.

Table 2.1 Numbers of psychology articles with shame and disgust in their titles

	1960s	1970s	1980s	1990s	2000s
Shame	16	49	234	665	924
Disgust	1	None	16	60	366

Source: Haslam (2012: 10), based on 'a major database of psychology publications'

Infant poo. Andres Hueso has called infant poo the blind spot of blind spots (pers. comm.). Explanations can be sought in terms of biases: cleaning children's faeces is overwhelmingly women's work and women often lack time and resources to deal with it hygienically; it is less smelly and disgusting than adults'; it is widely regarded as harmless, although it carries a heavier pathogen load than that of adults. So in rural areas where there is open defecation, it is common practice to leave infant poo in the open near dwellings or to throw it on rubbish heaps together with rags or other material used for wiping bottoms. For many it would be too expensive or time consuming to do anything else.

Incontinence. The International Continence Society estimates that urinary and/or faecal incontinence affects one in four women over the age of 35, and one in 10 adult men. It increases with age. Particularly liable to incontinence are men, women, and children with physical disabilities and/or learning difficulties, and women and adolescent girls who have recently given birth or who have fistula. It can cause embarrassment, fear of leakage and smell, ostracism, isolation, and teasing. Long overlooked by WASH professionals, it is only in 2016 coming to be recognized as a widespread physical and social problem. It is also more difficult to manage and mitigate, and so more serious as an affliction, in developing countries (Giles-Hansen, 2015).[10]

Faecal sludge management. Dealing with the contents of toilets not connected to sewers was another neglected topic until two to three years ago when it rose sharply on the agenda of international WASH conferences, particularly for urban contexts. Latrines and toilets fill up. Their contents can be removed or covered over. When they are removed there are questions of safe disposal: sometimes the contents are dumped in rivers or water bodies, or in the open. When pits are covered over, another pit has to be dug.

Faecally transmitted infections. The term FTI (Chambers and Von Medeazza, 2013, 2014) is inclusive of all infections that are faecally transmitted. This is to avoid two common exclusions. The first is 'faecal-oral' which excludes parasite pathways through the skin as with hookworm and schistosomiasis (see for example Mara et al., 2011). The second is 'waterborne' which excludes infections such as hookworm, trachoma (WHO, 2013), and tapeworms, which are not waterborne. When I first became interested in FTIs and could not find a comprehensive list and compiled my own, I was astonished to discover how many there were, including:

- *diarrhoeas,* including cholera, shigellosis, rotavirus, cryptosporidiosis, and campylobacter
- *environmental enteric dysfunction* (EED)
- *intestinal parasites,* including giardia, amoebiasis, *Ascaris* (roundworm), hookworm (which feeds on blood and causes anaemia), *Trichuris* (whipworm), and tapeworms (with perhaps 2 billion people infected by worms)
- *other pathogens,* including hepatitis A, B, and E, typhoid fever (bacteria, salmonella), liver fluke, poliomyelitis and other enteroviruses, schistosomiasis (200 million people affected), trachoma (up to 80 million affected), neurocysticercosis (causing about one-third of cases of epilepsy worldwide), and other zoonoses transmitted through intermediate hosts.

Epidemiologists and other professionals have to specialize and have incentives to narrow their vision and work in order to conduct 'rigorous' research and secure the publications in peer-reviewed journals essential for promotion and a successful career. The more difficult an infection is to study, the closer the focus has to be. The incentive system, professional norms, and inherent difficulties of measurement and attribution may explain why I did not find any study of the combined effects of FTIs when several are present in the same child or adult.

Diarrhoea: from measurability to reductionism. Diarrhoeas have been studied far more than other FTIs. Nothing should detract from their seriousness.[11] However, their relative significance needs to be qualified. Their dramatic clinical manifestations, their visibility, the ease with which they can be recorded, and the fact that they can kill, have led to their receiving attention to the relative neglect of the other FTIs, many of which are to varying degrees subclinical and asymptomatic but continuously debilitating. The rigour of much medical research demands measurement and statistics, to which diarrhoeas lend themselves, whereas subclinical FTIs are less visible, and take more time and cost to measure. Diarrhoea as morbidity reported through recall is easy to obtain though unreliable. Measurability has repeatedly attracted attention to the diarrhoeas for which the ratio of research time to peer-reviewed article (and chances of recognition and promotion) is likely to be lower than for most other FTIs.

In consequence, the focus on diarrhoeas is out of all proportion. The 2008 *Lancet* Maternal and Child Undernutrition Series was modelled entirely through diarrhoea. In journals, article after article covers diarrhoea. This then becomes incestuous: review articles are again and again tied to the diarrhoeas to the neglect of other FTIs, because there are comparable numerical data (e.g. Curtis et al., 2000; Curtis and Caincross, 2003; Waddington et al., 2009). A synthetic review of impact evaluations of the effectiveness of WASH interventions was based on reducing childhood diarrhoea (Waddington et al., 2009). The highly valued and rigorous *Cochrane Systematic Review* article, 'Interventions to improve water quality and supply, sanitation and hygiene practice, and their effects on the nutritional status of children' (Dangour et al., 2013), assessed impact in terms of diarrhoeal morbidity, as inevitably did a review of the reviews, 'The cost of a knowledge silo: a systematic re-review of water, sanitation and hygiene interventions' (Loevinsohn et al., 2014). The latter lists 13 earlier systematic reviews, which are all of the *diarrhoeal* impacts of WASH. To cap it all, a WASH Evidence Gap Map shows diarrhoea morbidity as overwhelmingly the most studied outcome, while other FTIs do not feature at all (International Initiative for Impact Evaluation, 2015). Because they are measurable and measured, a convenient and universal indicator, the diarrhoeas have lent themselves also to institution building. The International Centre for Diarrhoeal Disease Research, Bangladesh (ICDDR,B) is world-renowned. There is no International Centre for FTI Research.[12]

Environmental enteric dysfunction: out of sight, out of mind. The most nutritionally significant FTI is almost certainly EED (earlier known as tropical sprue, then tropical enteropathy, then environmental enteropathy).[13] It is also known popularly as 'leaky gut'. It is an asymptomatic pathological condition of chronic exposure to faecal pathogens. EED continuously consumes nutritional energy (see Crane et al., 2014; IAEA, 2015). Though recognized at least as early as 1960 as 'tropical sprue', it came into prominence following Jean Humphrey's seminal article, 'Child undernutrition, tropical enteropathy, toilets and handwashing', published in *The Lancet* in 2009. In EED, infections damage the wall of the small intestine: villi are atrophied and blunted and their area reduced so that they can absorb fewer nutrients. Resulting gut hyperpermeability evokes an energy and protein-consuming immune response to fight the infections in the blood. Studies of Gambian infants living in dirty conditions had found them to enter 'a near-continuous state of growth-suppressing immune response: dietary nutrients [are] repartitioned away...in favour of glucose oxidation and synthesis of acute-phase proteins and other immune mediators' (Humphrey, 2009: 1034). Subsequent studies (e.g. Lin et al., 2013; Prendergast et al., 2014; Ngure et al., 2014) have confirmed the association of undernutrition with faecal contamination and unhygienic conditions. It is also suggestive that battery hens who live in their own filth are fed antibiotics which are known in the business as 'growth permitters' (Humphrey, 2009). EED is now recognized as a continuous subclinical condition which inhibits growth.

Diarrhoeas and EED compared. Jean Humphrey has described the diarrhoeas as only the visible tip of a much larger subclinical iceberg (pers. comm., November 2011), a view that has been cumulatively confirmed by research. Why then is there such a bias towards the diarrhoeas compared with EED? An answer can be found in their contrasting characteristics, as shown in Table 2.2.

Table 2.2 Contrasting characteristics of diarrhoeas and EED

Diarrhoeas	*EED*
Episodic	Continuous
Dramatic	Asymptomatic
Visible	Invisible
Painful, distressing	Not felt
Readily and cheaply measurable directly or by recall	Laborious and very expensive to measure, with ethical issues*
Deaths countable and attributable	Deaths cannot be attributed
Amenable to randomized controlled trials	Randomized control trials out of the question
Statistics available, quotable, widely quoted, memorable	No statistics
Easy to grasp and explain	Requires detailed explanation

*The priority of developing a cheap, reliable, and non-invasive way of measuring EED has been increasingly if belatedly recognized. A C-Sucrose breath test while not wholly reliable has been used in Australia. I do not understand why it has not been widely adopted elsewhere. Perhaps it is another blind spot. In the meantime a search has intensified for biomarkers in faeces, with stable isotopes seen as a promising possibility (IAEA, 2015).

Water bias. In earlier decades I was several times told that whatever the budget, about nine times as much was spent on rural water as on rural sanitation. This will vary a lot and may be less and less true, but compared with rural sanitation rural water has a lot going for it. Water and water supplies, compared with sanitation, are:

- cleaner and odourless
- more popular with people, politicians, officials, and donors
- easier and nicer to inspect
- more photogenic
- more demanding of engineering skills and services
- easier to spend budgets on fast and well
- implementable in a more controlled and top-down manner
- easier to measure and monitor.

For decades there has been a large annual World Water Week conference in Stockholm, to which sanitation has crept in as a poor relation. Sanitation, with only about one-tenth of the main programme, compensates for this in part with fringe meetings before and during the conference.[14]

Rural sanitation has then been neglected compared with water. Exceptions have been local and national campaigns. The Millennium Development Goal (MDG) for clean water was far surpassed, while the goal for sanitation was missed by a big margin (UNICEF and WHO, 2015).[15]

FTIs and undernutrition: a classic blind spot. The blind spot of the link between FTIs and undernutrition[16] shows how a net of interlocking motivations and biases can conceal a powerful relationship.

From their review 'Environmental enteropathy: critical implications of a poorly understood condition', Poonam and Petri (2012) conclude that 'the clinical impact of environmental enteropathy is just starting to be recognized. The failure of nutritional interventions and oral vaccines in the developing world may be attributed to environmental enteropathy, as the intestinal absorptive and immunological functions are significantly deranged.' EED may be the most significant FTI, but when all the FTIs are taken together, the diversity, extent, and probable debilitating impact of non-diarrhoeal FTIs on nutritional status is even more striking. Combinations of EED with worms, giardia, and other continuous infections can be expected to have interactive as well as cumulative effects on a child, damping down and reducing activity, play, and learning, as well as affecting more measurable indicators of growth. In sum, the non-diarrhoeal FTIs are then likely to have much greater adverse effects on children's nutritional status, and so on morbidity and mortality, than was earlier recognized.

Professional nutritionists, those who research into nutrition, and those who passionately wish to intervene to prevent and mitigate the multiple deprivations of undernutrition, focus on feeding, and are frustrated that their programmes do not reduce stunting more. Nothing that follows should undermine their efforts. But we now know that at least half of child undernutrition can be attributed to open defecation and environmental conditions. Dean Spears (2013) compared 140 national demographic health surveys. After controlling for other obvious variables, he found that over half (54 per cent) of undernutrition was accounted for by open defecation, rising to almost two-thirds (65 per cent) when population density was factored in. In mountainous areas in Vietnam, five-year-old children have been found to be 3.7 cm taller in communities where everyone practises improved sanitation than in communities where open defecation and unimproved sanitation prevail (WSP, 2014). Prendergast and Kelly (2012: 756), in their article 'Enteropathies in the developing world: neglected effects on global health', state that EED is:

> ubiquitous among people living in unhygienic conditions and is likely to mediate stunting and anaemia and to underlie poor oral vaccine efficacy and human immunodeficiency, while interacting effects of infection and enteropathy drive a vicious circle that can propagate severe acute malnutrition which underlies half of under five year old deaths.

The 'Asian enigma' that Asians with higher average per capita incomes are shorter than Africans with lower incomes stands largely or entirely explained by FTIs, with EED likely to be the most significant.

In spite of this overwhelming accumulation of evidence, the dominant discourse of nutrition and undernutrition has been and remains related to food intake and assuring that enough food of good quality is reliably and continuously available to infants, children, and adults. The mindset has been fixed and focused on direct delivery. Major international efforts focus on improving and assuring food security for poor, marginalized, and isolated people. Journal articles and books concerned with hunger and nutrition repeatedly focus on quantity and quality of food, feeding programmes, and micronutrients, and in recent years, issues of governance, rights, and justice, often to the total or near-total neglect of sanitation, hygiene, and FTIs, or only a passing reference (e.g. Paul et al., 2011). This has a long history: WASH has no mention in V.K.R.V. Rao's authoritative book, *Food, Nutrition and Poverty in India* (Rao, 1982). Since then a whole succession of books and publications have overlooked the FTIs and WASH, including the importance of privacy and convenience for women: not one of the 25 chapters in *Empowering Women through Better Healthcare and Nutrition in Developing Countries* (Sharma and Atero, 2012) is on sanitation. Nutrition professionals have spread their span of relevance to include governance, food justice, food security, and agriculture. This is shown by a series of *IDS Bulletins*: 'Lifting the curse: overcoming persistent undernutrition in India' (IDS, 2009); 'Standing on the threshold: food justice in India' (IDS, 2012), and 'Seeing the unseen: breaking the logjam of undernutrition in Pakistan' (IDS, 2013). But these bulletins have no article on WASH or FTIs. It is mentioned in passing and not followed up. That half to two-thirds of child undernutrition can be attributed to FTIs is nowhere acknowledged. The blind spot is resilient.[17]

Recurring dimensions of blind spots

We can now draw on the evidence of biases and blind spots – related to gender, cultural, social, and space; research backwaters; and WASH and nutrition – to identify significant and recurring clusters of explanation. The first three are mainly from FTIs and undernutrition but with wider relevance.

Personal and psychological preferences

Personal and psychological preferences can focus attention away from blind spots. An example is preference for the oral to the anal – preferring infant food to infant poo, the clean, odourless, and pleasant to the dirty, smelly, and disgusting. Valerie Curtis (2013) has examined the human emotion of disgust and described the science behind revulsion. Most adults would rather feed a child and wipe its face than dispose of its poo and wipe its bottom. Interestingly there has been a shift in psychology from the preoccupation of Freud and the early psychoanalysts with the anal to the current focus, almost tunnel vision if the metaphor can be excused, on the oral. Thus Nick Haslam in his delightful and insightful *Psychology in the Bathroom* (2012: 6–8) observes that there are numerous psychological journals dedicated to the study of eating and drinking, and eating disorders such as anorexia nervosa and bulimia nervosa, but no psychological scientific journals devoted to the elimination of food and its disorders. Yet those with gastrointestinal and urinary problems (such as irritable bowel syndrome – one person in 10, or incontinence which is even more common) far outnumber those with eating disorders. There is what Rozin (2007) has called a 'hole hole', a lack of study of human orifices, one may add especially the anus, kept out of sight and out of mind. Similar personal biases, whether recognized and admitted or not, may be expected, for instance preferring water to sanitation.

Shame, taboos, privacy, and power

Power, secrecy, shame, and privacy preserve blind spots. Patriarchal power is implicated in the family. Patriarchy has played a part in delaying the recognition and study of, in rising order of difficulty, sexual relations, domestic violence, and intra-family child sex abuse. Other topics regarded as shameful, dirty, or to be hidden have been kept off the agenda – open defecation to an extent, and more so menstruation. With harmful traditional practices, women as well as men can be guardians and gatekeepers. Topics can be taboo, sensitive, and risky for discussion: FGM/C, early marriage, dowry, son preference and selective abortion, the tyrannizing of daughters-in-law, honour killings, and bride price. So, too, it is with sexuality where LGBT orientations are or have been regarded as deviant, sinful, or non-existent or their practices or relationships illegal.[18]

Threatening to expose the powerful

Those who are getting away with behaving badly or illegally will want to protect their activities as blind spots. This applies across corruption, criminality, and tax evasion, and socially to exploitation, slavery, and human rights abuses in their many forms including child sex abuse. Corruption, once a taboo topic regarded as too politically sensitive for discussion, is now more in the open.[19]

Institutional and professional marginality and silos

For long in many governments, nutrition was an insignificant orphan, shuffled from department to department. For its part sanitation tended to be urban-biased, dominated by engineers, and a junior sibling to water. In each department, battles had to be fought for recognition and funding. Nutrition and rural sanitation were also difficult areas in which to achieve notable measured success. Struggling for status and resources the focus was on resources and survival, not luxuries like exploring FTI–undernutrition links.

Professional specialization, inertia, incentives, and tunnel vision

Specialization breeds incestuous specialization. Nutritionists who have been professionally trained in nutrition then go on to work on nutrition. Similarly, the sanitation sector has been populated quite largely by those trained in engineering. College and university teachers who do the training have their notes and lectures and under pressure have little incentive to change them. Indeed, conservative academic colleagues might oppose including WASH in nutrition courses, or nutrition in those concerned with WASH.

There are incentives too for specialization. Epidemiologists and other research professionals narrow their focus in order to be able to publish in peer-reviewed journals. They study the studiable, seeking to minimize the time and effort to produce the publications needed for a successful career. 'I should be able to get a couple of articles out of this' is the sort of remark one can hear. This has concentrated attention on the diarrhoeas to the neglect of other FTIs and NTDs. More generally, gaps between disciplines and what is easy to study probably still harbour neglected areas – both as known unknowns and as the fully blind spots of unknown unknowns.

Reliable research results

Reliable research results are then a powerful criterion: what can be studied with assured outcomes receives priority. Professional norms and incentives and funding sustain ignorance by directing attention to topics which can be relied on to deliver results. MA and PhD thesis supervisors act responsibly in steering students towards research with the potential to generate outcomes adequate to earn their degrees, and that in reasonable time. It also helps the academic careers of supervisors to have a record of having overseen successful

PhDs: I recollect being a referee for a promotion to professor where the person concerned had an unimpressive publication record but a dazzling record of over 15 good PhDs that he had supervised (exceptionally, he was promoted).

At the level of individual or small group research in field conditions, responsibility and incentives consequently bias research towards low-risk topics which promise results in a short period. This privileges the regular, predictable, controllable, measurable, and short term and rules out or discourages empirical fieldwork on, say, inter-annual seasonal variations, the more so where experimental method and statistics are required. Neglect of rain-fed agriculture can result: at one time nine out of 10 theses in agriculture in India were on irrigated agriculture, where water supply can be regulated and crops assured (Anil Gupta, Indian Institute of Management, pers. comm., *c.* 1970s or 1980s). Or again, research on marine mammals is vulnerable to unpredictable behaviour: a PhD on whales took seven-and-a-half years, with a delay of two years when the whales failed to appear. For reasons also of amenability to experimental method, accessibility, and low cost, a sensible supervisor and student will prefer, say, innumerable small invertebrates on sandy beaches where tides create predictable diurnal change and numbers lend themselves to statistics.

Counter incentives

There are, though, counter incentives in the wide citation, recognition, and influence that can come from identifying a blind spot or neglected area which others then follow up on and funders support. Three seminal examples from the research cited earlier should inspire others. In chronological order they are:

- Anthony Richardson and Elvira Poloczanska's 2008 Policy Forum note, 'Ocean science, under-researched and under threat', published in *Science*
- Jean Humphrey's September 2009 research note in the *Lancet*, 'Child undernutrition, tropical enteropathy, and toilets and handwashing'
- Dean Spears's (2013) analysis of the secondary data of 140 demographic health surveys to find that open defecation accounted for 54 per cent of stunting, and 65 per cent when population density was factored in.

The first two of these were brief, just two pages and three pages respectively. All three articles were based on the analysis of secondary data. All three challenged conventional wisdom and practice. All three led to the funding of a new generation of research. All three made their authors international figures. Their examples should embolden others to uncover and open up other blind spots and neglected areas. Besides which, doing so should be enthralling and fun.

Biases and blind spots: past and present

Biases and blind spots are not static. Nor are they free of context. Some areas, like gender, have registered major shifts, even transformations, in some places and contexts. Others, like the biases of development tourism, will always be there except when they are deliberately offset. Other phenomena, like strategic ignorance, are part of the human condition and will never disappear. In order to look forward, seeking to know better, let us examine aspects of change in the past three to four decades, and try to tease out dimensions which influence decisions for research and action. For me, a baseline that comes readily to hand is from *Putting the Last First* (Chambers, 1983: 173). The 'first' were the powerful, elites, professionals, the wealthy, and so on, and the 'last' those who were powerless, low status, less educated, poorer, and so on. The first and last had contrasting values, preferences, contexts, interests, and priorities, as in Table 2.3.

The purpose of the listing was to draw attention to the neglect of the last and the need to offset it. Since then many changes have taken place: there has been a massive demographic shift from rural to urban, though rural poverty, ill-being, and deprivation remain widespread and significant; insecurity, fragile states, and refugee crises have become more prominent. However, poverty has, with the MDGs and more so the Sustainable Development Goals and 'leave no one behind', long since moved up the agenda, with innumerable initiatives and experience with anti-poverty programmes; many rural areas have become less remote and cut off, through extension of all-weather roads, penetration of the market, and the spread of mobile phones, radio, television, and internet; gender and other biases have been partially offset; and overall services and many dimensions of well-being have improved. Most of the dimensions in the table still apply, but the balance and mix of biases and blind spots relevant for knowing better, and for research and action, have moved on.

Drawing on this listing, and on the evidence and examples in this chapter, we can note some of the more significant professional and personal biases and preferences to review when making choices for research and action now (Table 2.4).

This is not at all to imply that the 'bias against' column is better. There are many other considerations: cost, cost-effectiveness, scale and intensity of impact, human resource use, and so on. But scores in the 'bias against' column should indicate scope for offsetting biases and finding and opening up neglected topics or blind spots.

Biases and blind spots: the future

What are the blind spots and neglected topics now? How does one set about identifying them? And what should we do now to know better in the future?

There can be no simple or polarized answers, but one starting point is to look for topics with some features of the right-hand column in Table 2.4, drawing also on Chapter 1. These may be variously confronting conventional wisdom and beliefs, interstitial between disciplines, socially delicate and sensitive, politically risqué, transgressing social norms, exploring taboos, kept

Table 2.3 Professional values and preferences as perceived in 1983

First	Last
A. For technology research and projects	
Urban	Rural
Industrial	Agricultural
High cost	Low cost
Capital-using	Labour-using
Mechanical	Animal or human
Complex*	Simple
Large	Small
Modern	Traditional
Exotic	Indigenous
Marketed	Subsistence
Quantified	Unquantified
Geometrical	Irregular
Visible and seen	Invisible or unseen
Tidy	Untidy
Predictable	Unpredictable
Hard	Soft
Clean	Dirty
Odourless	Smelly
B. For contacts and clients	
High status	Low status
Rich	Poor
Influential	Powerless
Educated	Illiterate
Male	Female
Adult	Child
Light-skinned	Dark-skinned
C. For place and time	
Urban	Rural
Indoors	Outdoors
Office, laboratory	Field
Accessible	Remote
Day	Night
Dry season	Wet season

*Complex as 'first' and simple as 'last' was a creature of its time, before complexity theory was prominent. As the words are now understood they misfit these categories.

Table 2.4 Professional and personal biases and preferences to review and offset when making choices for research and action

Bias towards	Bias against
Interests of powerful, rich, elite	Interests of powerless, poor, low status
Supporting power	Threatening power
Disciplinary mainstream	Disciplinary backwaters, gaps between disciplines
Measurable, statistical analysis	Hard to measure, qualitative analysis
Readily researchable	Difficult to research
Accessible context	Inaccessible
Prominent, visible	Hard to see, out of sight
Non-contextual, widely applicable	Context-specific, limited application
Predictable	Unpredictable
Controllable, low-risk outputs	Uncontrollable, high-risk outputs
Outputs readily publishable	Output publication problematic
Politically correct	Politically incorrect
Culturally acceptable	Taboo, confronting social norms
Matters of pride	Matters of shame
Publicly acceptable	Private, sensitive
Marketed, paid, quantified	Subsistence, unpaid, unquantified
Convenient, comfortable	Inconvenient, uncomfortable
Safe, secure	Dangerous, conflictual
Clean, odourless	Dirty, smelly

secret by the person, the family, an organization or society, occurring at night or requiring work at night, inconvenient, unpleasant and/or uncomfortable, dangerous, politically incorrect, disapproved of by mainstream colleagues, difficult to measure, not amenable to statistical validation, or currently rubbished or ridiculed by the establishment. There is also a troubling boundary which may keep blind spots out of research because proposals would not pass an ethics audit.

With these and other pointers, let me challenge readers to reflect and think of remaining or new neglected areas and blind spots. For research and action I have a short list. Readers will have many more.[20]

- *Child abuse within the family*. This is reported to be found in all cultures but is widely denied and covered up. Yet quite apart from its immediate awfulness for children, it often leaves a socially disastrous legacy for society when they grow up as disturbed adults.
- *Corruption and illegality* at many levels and in many contexts, including tax evasion, and conditions where gangs and mafias are in league with police and both will be hostile to the investigator.

- *Understanding young males and their tendencies to violence.* In some places, positive discrimination for females appears to have left young males, their frustrations and alienation, their doing badly in school and dropping out, relatively overlooked. More generally, young males are a worldwide problem and opportunity.
- *Identifying neglected areas and blind spots important for those who are 'last'* – those who are powerless, who live in poverty, those who are physically weak, vulnerable, isolated, less able, aged, marginalized, stigmatized, discriminated against.
- *Finding out how the 62 top global mega-rich (whose wealth equals that of the poorer half of humankind) can find fulfilment by devoting their resources to reducing inequalities and enhancing well-being.*

To identify topics, and once identified to get them developed and resourced, there are many practical questions. Open-ended brainstorming workshops to determine priorities for funding and action may be less common than they should be. In any case they tend to be bounded by commitments already made or funded or by the professional competencies and interests of those taking part, or both. One way forward is to bring bearers of different areas of knowledge together to interact, learn from each other, and provoke reflection. This has been done by the Santa Fe Institute, for instance in convening economists and physicists to talk to one another (Waldrop, 1994: 135–43). Since the 1980s it has been increasingly widespread in agriculture, with scientists and farmers sharing their different knowledge and skills. And combinations and multi-disciplinary insights often occur most readily in the same person. Which brings us to the biggest blind spot of all.

The blind spot of ourselves

For me and for readers of this book, there are questions about our own mindsets, biases, and preferences. How we see and construe the world is framed by our cultures, upbringing, education, professional training, and life experiences. Economists, anthropologists, engineers, medics, geographers, sociologists, statisticians, educationalists, linguists, agriculturalists, ecologists, biological and other scientists, political scientists, accountants, psychologists, journalists, politicians, officials, academics, NGO workers, consultants... whoever we are, with whatever single or multiple disciplinary and experiential backgrounds, each of us, uniquely, has our own cognitive lenses and mental frames for seeing and interpreting the world, with our own motivations, distractions and drivers of commitment and passion.

I began this chapter with the World Bank's World Development Report (WDR) 2015. More than any other publication I know, except the Human Development Reports of UNDP, the WDRs can claim to have an annual impact on development thinking and action. WDR 2000, *Attacking Poverty* (World Bank, 2000), for instance, was of seminal and enduring value. With WDR

2015, *Mind, Society and Behaviour*, there was a perhaps once-and-for-all opportunity for the Bank to lead development thinking in a radically reflexive direction (see also Chapter 6).

To its credit, the chapter titled 'The biases of development professionals'
(World Bank, 2015: 180–91) identifies four sources of bias in decision-making:
confirmation bias – selecting and privileging information that confirms
beliefs; shortcuts – the use of shortcuts when faced with complexity; sunk
cost bias – continuing a poor project because of investments already made;
and effects of context on judgement and decision-making. The authors also
conducted a survey of the perceptions of World Bank staff. And they ended
the report with a section on learning and adapting. But they did not rise to
the challenge to reflect critically on their own mindsets. They could have set
a wonderful example and asked, 'Why should all development professionals,
like ourselves, reflect critically on our own mindsets and behaviour?' For we
will always have our own biases and blind spots, and realism should always
benefit from holding up a mirror to ourselves and how our knowledge is
formed and framed.

Agenda for reflection and action

- *Strategic ignorance.* Is strategic ignorance a factor? What has it left, or
  might it leave, in darkness? If so does it matter? What should be done
  about it?
- *Biases in what is seen and shown.* Are biases of development tourism
  implicated? How can they be offset?
- *Blind spots.* Are biases and personal and professional preferences hiding
  or protecting significant blind spots?
    - interests, values, and topics of the 'first', not those of the 'last'
    - threats to power
    - difficulties of measurement
    - inconvenience and discomfort
    - disapproval of colleagues
    - political correctness
    - professional and institutional silos
    - specialization
    - risks – of delays, unreliable results, failing to publish
    - others in Table 2.4.
- *New blind spots and neglected areas.* What do these questions point to?
  Are there new needs and (brilliant) opportunities? Who can you inspire
  and enthuse as allies or champions to explore and shed light on them?
- *Implications.* What are the implications:
    - for policy and practice;
    - for research and research funding?
  and
- *Have those who are last been consulted?* How? What are their priorities?

Notes

1. In an earlier draft I wrote, 'In the UK the completion of the Chilcot inquiry into the events leading up to the illegal invasion of Iraq was postponed for year after year allegedly for consultations to give those implicated fair opportunity to comment on drafts. The brazen transparency of this scandalous cover-up left me as a British citizen almost speechless with rage, feeding an unwelcome cynicism and destroying the vestigial remains of my former naïve trust in the basic honesty of the British establishment.' But the report was published just before going to press. I have to, if not eat my words, at least qualify this. In the event it was more balanced, judicious, and damning than I had expected and much less of a cover-up than I had feared.

2. Let me acknowledge my debt to Madduma Bandara, Nanjamma Chinnappa, Hiran Dias, Barbara Harriss-White, John Harriss and Wicks Wickremanayake for experiences in the field, and Benny Farmer for master-minding and managing the project.

3. Policy and practical aspects of the roles of men and boys in the struggle for gender equality have received much attention recently; for instance in EMERGE (2015).

4. The BBC television celebrity, the late Jimmy Savile, was exposed with allegations of repeated, habitual child sex abuse in hospitals and studios on a scale which beggars belief, indicating consistent strategic ignorance on a very wide scale.

5. I can testify from Cambodia that deep fried spider is a good crunchy snack, though I flinched at the eyes.

6. These estimates are from various sources and should be treated as order of magnitude approximations. However, that the NTDs affect 1–2 billion or more people is beyond dispute. Estimates are complicated by differences such as degrees of infection, as with trachoma, and one-off incidence, as with dengue.

7. For the detail that follows I am indebted to David Schoeman.

8. I was appalled to arrive at boarding school and find the toilets had no doors and faced each other. This we surmised was to discourage us from masturbating.

9. For an international glossary of words for shit with over 200 entries see CLTS Knowledge Hub (2009), and choose your favourite one. For rather personal reasons mine is *ngik* (Samburu).

10. Giles-Hansen (2015) is the main source for this paragraph. I am grateful to Sue Cavill for drawing my attention to this blind spot and source.

11. Statistics for the incidence of diarrhoeal deaths tend to be far too high and out of date, repeated, remembered, and like many beliefs slow to be corrected and updated (see Chapter 1).

12. It must be pointed out, however, that the ICDDR,B conducts much ground-breaking research beyond the diarrhoeas, and now includes EED.

13. As understanding and needs evolve, renaming can make sense. Tropical was a misnomer since EED was not limited to the tropics (it is widespread in North India, for instance). Enteropathy was descriptively clearer than sprue. I have adopted environmental enteric dysfunction because this is

increasingly used in the technical literature (e.g. Crane et al., 2014; IAEA, 2015), which perhaps adopts it to be more inclusive for a condition the details and boundaries of which are still far from established.

14. The official pre-conference programme for the 2016 World Water Week achieved a new high water mark for bias: on two of the five conference days not a single session was listed on a sanitation and hygiene topic. However, in the actual programme there were quite a number of sessions on WASH that had not been listed earlier.

15. The MDG targets were to halve by 2015, from a 1990 baseline, the proportion of people without safe water and without improved sanitation. The water target was met in 2010, while in 2015 the sanitation target had been missed by almost 700 million people, only 68 per cent of the global population having an improved facility against the target of 77 per cent (UNICEF and WHO, 2015).

16. Stunting – short height for age – is the preferred indicator for undernutrition. I use the term undernutrition rather than malnutrition because the latter can refer to overeating and bad diets for children and adults who have the means to eat enough healthily, often leading to obesity. In undernutrition I include deficiencies of micro-nutrients such as inadequate iron or zinc.

17. At the time of writing, early 2016, the blind spot is increasingly being recognized (see e.g. Chase and Ngure, 2016). By the time this is published and read, it may be largely history in research communities. But it will take some time for the implications to be recognized in curricula, teaching, training, and practice.

18. In a discussion with transgender people in India in 2016, an African was asked the legal and social position of transgender people in his country. He said he did not know that there were any such people. In his country homosexual practices were illegal and carried heavy penalties. One can speculate that people there who are transgender dare not come out and so are generally not known to exist.

19. However, in 2016 for practical reasons, wanting to have an influence, I was advised not to use the word *corruption* in a policy note for a government, and reluctantly substituted *malpractices*. I came to realize, however, that the latter had the advantage of being not only less stigmatizing and more acceptable than the former, but also more inclusive, being applicable to a wider range of damaging practices.

20. In an earlier listing I included 'Pre-pubertal sexual activities'. At a Participatory Rural Appraisal workshop near Harare a Zambian researcher who had been doing participatory research with pre-pubertal children described their extensive sexual activities. Parents at the workshop were horrified and wondered if their children were doing the same. 'How common is this? How much does it matter?' But I judge this area to be much less important than the other four.

References

Chambers, R. (1983) *Rural Development: Putting the Last First,* Harlow, UK: Longman.

Chambers, R. (1988) *Managing Canal Irrigation: Practical Analysis from South Asia*, New Delhi: Oxford and IBH; Cambridge: Cambridge University Press.

Chambers, R. and Von Medeazza, G. (2013) 'Sanitation and stunting in India: undernutrition's blind spot', *Economic and Political Weekly* June 22: 15–8.

Chambers, R. and Von Medeazza, G. (2014) *Reframing Undernutrition: Faecally-transmitted Infections and the 5 As*, IDS Working Paper 450, Brighton, UK: Institute of Development Studies.

Chase, C. and Ngure, F.M. (2016) *Multisectoral Approaches to Improving Nutrition: Water, Sanitation, and Hygiene*, Washington, DC: Water and Sanitation Program, World Bank.

CLTS Knowledge Hub (2009) *International glossary of shit*, Institute of Development Studies, <http://www.communityledtotalsanitation.org/resource/international-glossary-shit> [accessed 27 February 2017].

Cornwall, A. and White, S. (eds) (2000) 'Men, masculinities and development: politics, policies and practice', *IDS Bulletin* 31: 2 <http://dx.doi.org/10.1111/j.1759-5436.2000.mp31002001.x>.

Crane, R.J., Jones, K. and Berkley, J. (2014) 'Environmental enteric dysfunction: an overview', *CMAM Forum Technical Brief*, August 2014.

Curtis, V. (2013) *Don't Look, Don't Touch, Don't Eat: The Science behind Revulsion*, Chicago: University of Chicago Press.

Curtis, V., Cairncross, S. and Yonli, R. (2000) 'Review: domestic hygiene and diarrhoea – pinpointing the problem', *Tropical Medicine and International Health* 5(1): 22–32.

Dangour, A.D., Watson, L., Cumming, O., Boisson, S., Che, Y., Veeleman, Y., Cavill, S., Allen, E. and Uauy, R. (2013) 'Interventions to improve water quality and supply, sanitation and hygiene practices, and their effects on the nutritional status of children', *Cochrane Database Systematic Review* 8 <http://dx.doi.org/10.1002/14651858.CD009382.pub2>.

Engendering Men: Evidence on Routes to Change for Gender Equality (EMERGE) (2015) *New document library*, <http://xyonline.net/content/emerge-engendering-men-evidence-routes-change-gender-equality-new-document-library> [accessed 5 April 2017].

Eyben, R. (2012) *The Hegemony Cracked: The Power Guide to Getting Care onto the Development Agenda*, IDS Working Paper No. 411, Brighton: IDS.

GACC (2015) *Public health fact sheet*, Global Alliance for Clean Cookstoves, <http://cleancookstoves.org/resources/350.html> [accessed 27 February 2017].

Gender and Development Network (2015) *Harmful Traditional Practices: Your Questions, Our Answers* [pdf], London: Gender and Development Network <http://gadnetwork.org/gadn-resources/2015/1/13/harmful-traditional-practices-your-questions-our-answers?rq=harmful%20traditional%20> [accessed 27 January 2017].

Gerard, N. (1997) 'Into the arms of the abusers', *The Observer Review*, 25 May 1997.

Giles-Hansen, C. (2015) *Hygiene Needs of Incontinence Sufferers: how can water, sanitation and hygiene actions better address the needs of vulnerable people suffering from urinal and/or faecal incontinence in low and middle income countries*, desk-based review, WaterAid and SHARE.

Glover, D. and Sexton, A. (2015) 'Edible insects and the future of food: a foresight scenario exercise on entomophagy and global food security', *Policy Anticipation, Response and Evaluation Evidence Report 149*, Brighton, UK: IDS.

Haslam, N. (2012) *Psychology in the Bathroom*, Basingstoke, UK: Palgrave Macmillan.

Humphrey, J. (2009) 'Child undernutrition, tropical enteropathy, toilets, and handwashing', *Lancet* 374: 1032–5 <http://dx.doi.org/10.1016/S0140-6736(09)60950-8>.

Huppert, W. (2013) 'Viewpoint – rent-seeking in agricultural water management: an intentionally neglected core dimension', *Water Alternatives* 6(2): 265–75.

IAEA (2015) *Report: Technical Meeting on Environmental Enteric Dysfunction, the Microbiome and Undernutrition*, Vienna: Division of Human Health, International Atomic Energy Agency.

IDS (2009) *Lifting the Curse: Overcoming Persistent Undernutrition in India*, Bulletin 40(4), Brighton, UK: IDS.

IDS (2012) *Standing on the Threshold: Food Justice in India*, Bulletin 43, Brighton, UK: IDS.

IDS (2013) *Seeing the Unseen: Breaking the Logjam of Undernutrition in Pakistan*, Bulletin 44(3), Brighton, UK: IDS.

International Initiative for Impact Evaluation (2015) *Water, sanitation and hygiene evidence gap map*, <http://gapmaps.3ieimpact.org/evidence-maps/water-sanitation-and-hygiene-evidence-gap-map> [accessed 27 February 2017].

IPCC (2007) *Fourth Assessment Report*, Geneva: Intergovernmental Panel on Climate Change.

Jolly, S. (2000) *What Use is Queer Theory to Development?* Brighton: BRIDGE, IDS.

Jolly, S., Cornwall, A. and Standing, H. (2006) *Sexuality and Development*, IDS Policy Briefing issue 29, Brighton, UK: IDS.

Kar, K. and Chambers, R. (2008) *Handbook on Community-Led Total Sanitation*, Brighton: IDS; London: Plan.

Lin, A., Arnold, B.F., Afreen, S., Goto, R., Huda, T., Haque, R., Raqib, R., Unicomb, L., Ahmed, T., Colford, J.M. Jr, and Luby, S. (2013) 'Household environmental conditions are associated with enteropathy and impaired growth in rural Bangladesh', *American Society of Tropical Medicine and Hygiene* 89(1): 130–7<http://dx.doi.org/10.4269%2Fajtmh.12-0629>.

Loevinsohn, M., Mehta, L., Cuming, K., Nicol, A., Cumming, O. and Ensink, J. (2014) 'The cost of a knowledge silo: a systematic re-review of water, sanitation and hygiene interventions', *Health Policy and Planning* 2014: 1–15 <http://dx.doi.org/10.1093%2Fheapol%2Fczu039>.

Mara, D., Lane, J., Scott, B. and Trouba, D. (2011) 'Sanitation and health', *PLoS Medicine* 7(11): e1000363 <http://dx.doi.org/10.1371/journal.pmed.1000363>.

McGoey, L. (2012) 'Strategic unknowns: towards a sociology of ignorance', *Economy and Society* 41(1): 1–16 <http://dx.doi.org/10.1080/03085147.2011.637330>.

Ngure, F.M., Reid, B.M., Humphrey, J.H., Mbuya, M.N., Pelto, G. and Stolzfus, R.J. (2014) 'Water, sanitation and hygiene (WASH), environmental enteropathy, nutrition, and early childhood development: making the links', *Annals of the New York Academy of Sciences* 1308: 118–28 <http://dx.doi.og/10.1111/nyas.12330>.

Paul, V.K., Sachdev, H.S., Mavalankar, D., Ramachandran, P., Sankar, M.J., Bhandari, N., Srinivas, V., Sundaraman, T., Govil, D., Osrin, D. and

Kirkwood, B. (2011) 'Reproductive health, and child health and nutrition in India: meeting the challenge', *The Lancet* 377(9762): 332–49 <http://dx.doi.org/10.1016/S0140-6736(10)61492-4>.

Poonam, S.K. and Petri, W.A. (2012) 'Environmental enteropathy: critical implications of a poorly understood condition', *Trends in Molecular Medicine* 18(6): 328–36 <http://dx.doi.org/10.1016/j.molmed.2012.04.007>.

Prendergast, A. and Kelly, P. (2012) 'Enteropathies in the developing world: neglected effects on global health', *American Journal of Tropical Medicine and Hygiene* 86(5): 756–63 <http://dx.doi.org/10.4269%2Fajtmh.2012.11-0743>.

Prendergast, A., Rukobo, S., Chasekwa, B., Mutasa, K., Ntozini, R., Nduduzi, N., Mbuya, N., Jones, A., Moulton, A., Stolzfus, R. and Humphrey, J. (2014) 'Stunting is characterized by chronic inflammation in Zimbabwean infants', *PLoS ONE* 9(2): e86928 <http://dx.doi.org/10.1371/journal.pone.0086928>.

Rao, V.K.R.V. (1982) *Food, Nutrition and Poverty in India*, New Delhi: Vikas Publishing House.

Richardson, A. and Poloczanska, E. (2008) 'Ocean science, under-resourced and under threat', *Science* 320(1294–5): 41 <http://dx.doi.org/10.1126/science.1156129>.

Rozin, P. (2007) 'Exploring the landscape of modern academic psychology: finding and filling the holes', *American Psychologist* 62: 754–66 <http://dx.doi.org/10.1037/0003-066X.62.8.754>.

Shand, T., Thomson-de Boor, H., Van den Berg, W., Peacock, D. and Pascoe, L. (2014) 'The HIV blind spot: men and HIV testing, treatment and care in sub-Saharan Africa', *IDS Bulletin* 45(1): 53–60 <http://dx.doi.org/10.1111/1759-5436.12068>.

Sharma, S. and Atero, A. (eds) (2012) *Empowering Women through Better Healthcare and Nutrition in Developing Countries*, New Delhi: Regency Publications.

Spears, D. (2013) *How Much International Variation in Child Height Can Sanitation Explain?* Policy Research Working Paper 6351, Washington, DC: World Bank.

UNICEF and WHO (2015) *Progress on Sanitation and Drinking Water 2015 Update and MDG Assessment* [pdf], New York: UNICEF; Geneva: WHO <www.wssinfo.org/fileadmin/user_upload/resources/JMP-Update-report-2015_English.pdf> [accessed 6 September 2016].

Waddington, H., Snilsvelt, B., White, H. and Fewtrell, L. (2009) *Water, Sanitation and Hygiene Interventions to Combat Childhood Diarrhoea in Developing Countries*, Synthetic Review 001, Delhi: International Initiative for Impact Evaluation.

Wade, R. (1982) 'The system of administrative and political corruption: canal irrigation in South India', *Journal of Development Studies* 18(3): 287–328.

Waldrop, M. (1994) *Complexity: The Emerging Science at the Edge of Order and Chaos*, New York: Penguin Books.

World Bank (2000) *Attacking Poverty, World Development Report (2000/2001)*, New York: Oxford University Press.

World Bank (2012) *Gender Equality and Development, World Development Report 2012*, Washington, DC: World Bank.

World Bank (2015) *Mind, Society and Behaviour, World Development Report 2015*, Washington, DC: World Bank.

World Health Organization (WHO) (2013) *Investing in Mental Health: Evidence for Action*, Geneva: WHO.

World Health Organization (WHO) (2017) *Overview*, Sanitation <http://www.worldbank.org/en/topic/sanitation/overview> [accessed 5 April 2017].

WSP (2014) *Investing in the Next Generation: Children Grow Taller, and Smarter, in Rural Villages of Lao PDR Where All the Community Use Improved Sanitation* [pdf], Washington, DC: Water and Sanitation Program, World Bank <https://www.wsp.org/sites/wsp.org/files/publications/WSP-LaoPDR-Stunting-Research-Brief.pdf> [accessed 27 January 2017].

CHAPTER 3
Lenses and lock-ins

Abstract

Epistemic relativism recognizes knowledges as plural artefacts. They form and are formed by the lenses through which we see the world. Many knowledges in development are relative and contextual. Knowledges can be framed and understood in terms of contrasting multi-dimensional paradigms, one of things and procedures, and the other of people and processes. Views of poverty illustrate how economics and anthropology differ in approaches, methods, mindsets and vocabularies. An example from China shows how different methods can lead to sharply different conclusions about who are the poor households. In the early 21st century, knowing about development realities has been increasingly constrained and distorted through the spread of mechanistic approaches: the methodologies of randomized control trials and systematic reviews, promoted in the name of rigour in research; and a sequence of procedures such as logframes, results-based management, payment by results and competitive bidding required in the name of accountability, impartiality, and effectiveness for projects and procedures. The power and patronage of funding have promoted and required these methodologies and procedures. Though seen as 'best practices' they limit and distort learning and have high hidden transaction and opportunity costs in finance, staff time, motivation, and morale. To know better in development needs alternatives.

Keywords: lenses, knowledges, paradigms, reductionism, measurability, mechanistic methodologies, procedures, hidden costs

> Surely one of the most visible lessons taught by the twentieth century has been the existence, not so much of a number of different realities, but of a number of different lenses with which to see the same reality. (Michael Arlen)

> Not everything that can be counted counts, and not everything that counts can be counted. (Albert Einstein, on the wall of his study in Princeton)

> …those development programs that are the most precisely and easily measured are the least transformational, and those programs that are most transformational are the least measurable. (Andrew Naitsios, former Administrator of USAID)

> The great advantage of being in a rut is that when in a rut one knows exactly where one is. (Arnold Bennett)

http://dx.doi.org/10.3362/9781780449449.003

Basic framing

Knowledges as plural artefacts

Knowledge is not singular. There are many knowledges.[1] The plurality of knowledges is self-evident when we consider local technical knowledge and that of outsiders (Howes and Chambers, 1979; Brokensha et al., 1980; Chambers, 1983). Local knowledges are incorrigibly plural and permanently provisional and changing. In assessing whether rigorous scientific knowledge is singular and established for all time, one can distinguish three categories: where Newtonian physical materialism and Euclidian and mathematical logic apply, and where knowledge does indeed seem to be singular and universal, or largely so; physical areas where we can theorize but do not know;[2] and social domains where knowledge is contextual and transient. Past and recent history shows how frequently received scientific 'truth' is qualified, amended, and even overturned. Every year the *New Scientist* presents surprises, examples which question what was earlier accepted in a field of scientific inquiry. And this is continuously the case in many domains of the plurality of development knowledges.

Methodological paradigms

To frame and inform this chapter, let us start with a basic view of contrasting methodological paradigms.[3] A things–people binary can provide an illuminating entry point. It points up contrasts between disciplinary and professional orientations and favoured methodologies and methods. The things paradigm is more associated with and useful in engineering, accountancy, and economics, while the people paradigm fits and is found more in anthropology and sociology. The contrasts between the two columns in Table 3.1 indicate differences which are evident in much practice. At the same time, there are many cross-overs and cross-applications. There are dangers of caricature. I am presenting this only as a heuristic device, not a defining description: a great many economists embrace mixed methods, and many anthropologists value and generate statistics.

Limited by lenses

Epistemic relativism: views of poverty

It is almost self-evident that we are conditioned by our education, specialization, skills, professionalism, and positionality[4] to prefer and practise one approach or methodology or another. Personal, psychological, and professional factors contribute to the biases noted in Chapter 2. A statistician among statisticians, or a social anthropologist among social anthropologists, or those who have been educated and socialized into the traditions, values, and methods of any single discipline or profession, will tend to prefer and

Table 3.1 Two methodological paradigms

Point of departure and reference	Things	People
Antecedent keywords	Top-down Blueprint Planning Preset Closed	Bottom-up Process Participation Evolving Open
Outcomes, findings	Universal Non-contextual Quantitative	Particularistic Contextual Qualitative
Typical methods and methodologies	Questionnaires RCTs Logframes Payment by results	RRA PRA Systems analysis Participatory methodologies
Valuing	Measurement Precision Statistical rigour Replicability	Judgement Insight Inclusive rigour (see Chapter 4) Relevance
Typical approaches, methods	Reductionist Standardized Sequences preset Questionnaires	Inclusive Varied Sequences evolve Observation
Interaction with local people	Questioning Extractive	Facilitating Empowering
Local people seen as	Informants	Collaborators
Outputs	Statistics Correlations	Qualitative insights Case studies
Classical concept of poverty	Income poverty 'Objective' Non-contextual	Multi-dimensional 'Subjective' Contextual

Source: adapted and updated from Chambers (1997: 37)

employ mainly or only those approaches and methods which are dominant and accepted in their specialization, and may not question how these frame and categorize what they learn and influence how they see the world. Personality plays a part too. Some prefer the security of what is certain and known, while others tolerate and enjoy ambiguity and pluralism. And, as we have explored in Chapter 2, the biases of control, convenience, researchability, measurability, and professional values and incentives, whether consciously or unconsciously, can apply. What sort of people we are, our social environment, and our professional norms and incentives, influence how we learn and what we learn, and the knowledge or knowledges that we generate, embrace, and consider valid. To varying degrees we are then locked in to particular views.

Lock-in may seem an overly strong term.[5] Yet, disciplinary training and university and other education, however beneficial[6] they are, can be seen as a form of indoctrination which moulds mindsets and embeds words, concepts, and ways of construing the world. Let us compare economics and anthropology. Many economists and anthropologists are polymath pluralists. Nevertheless, the orientation of many economists corresponds with the things paradigm in Table 3.1 and that of many anthropologists with the people paradigm. This can be illustrated by the views of poverty which they have held historically.

Economists: quantitative, reductionist, and non-contextual

Development thinking and views of poverty have been dominated by economists. A venerable history goes back to the pioneering research of Booth and Rowntree in England in the late 19th century. Booth invented the term *poverty line* (Spicker, 2007: 42), and Rowntree's study in York set the pattern of questionnaires, household budgets, and measurement of poverty primarily in terms of income,[7] which spread worldwide. The questionnaire survey and the concept of income-poverty had much going for them: income does matter to poor people; time-series data show progress or otherwise; being independent of context, international comparisons can be made; and poverty line statistics fulfil the needs of the state to simplify and count poverty in order to make it legible, enabling it to grasp a key element in a large and complex reality (Scott, 1998).[8] Thinking in terms of income poverty was reinforced by the dominance of economists and economic thinking in the World Bank, ministries of finance and planning, and in aid. There can be few countries in the world that do not now have a poverty line.

The resulting concept of poverty has then been a statistical artefact from reported survey-generated numbers for income or more usually consumption as a proxy for income. A mental and policy lock-in can then have an incestuous circularity of policies, prescriptions, and per capita income measures of progress.

As late as the World Development Report 1990, poverty was taken as this income-poverty. As a concept it was classically reductionist, excluding what could not readily and comparably be expressed in numbers. As Spicker (2007: 7) put it, 'In some cases, the methods used to identify poverty drive the debate to such an extent that they change the way the subject is understood'. What has been counted becomes what counts and becomes how we see the world of those others, people living in poverty. 'Our' knowledge is then an artefact of dominant methodology. Or, in the words of irreverent doggerel:

> Economists have come to feel
> What can't be counted isn't real
> The truth is always an amount
> Count numbers, only numbers count

Until the mid-1990s, the term income-poverty, to distinguish it from other aspects of poverty, was rarely if ever used, gaining currency only in the debates which preceded the World Social Summit of 1995.

Anthropological particularism: qualitative, inclusive, and contextual

For a long time, economics followed a largely independent trajectory from other social sciences, which were even sometimes described as 'non-economic social sciences'. For social anthropologists defining and measuring poverty were not priorities. Their main concern was with observing and interpreting social relations and behaviour, and their main approach participant observation.[9] When they used the word *poverty* it was with an idiosyncratic, locally, and culturally specific meaning, influenced by the interaction of context and their own conceptual framework. For Margaret Haswell, working with an agricultural society in West Africa, 'Fundamentally, the nature of poverty can be defined as that point at which there occurs an imbalance between man and land of such an order that men can no longer rely upon the natural fertility of the land for their survival' (1975: 71). Richard Waller (1999), in his essay *Pastoral Poverty in Historical Perspective*, started with pastoralists' own discourse on poverty and description of who is poor. Other writers, like Polly Hill in her study of Rural Kano in northern Nigeria (1977), did not find it necessary to define poverty but rather implicitly combined local meanings with common ideas about deprivation. In these traditions, poverty has been understood as a varying and often indeterminate blend of non-numeric emic and etic concepts.[10]

Disciplinary convergence

Reductionist mindsets and tendencies remain strong among economists, but there have been convergences and a broadening of concepts. Economists themselves have been among the strongest critics of income-poverty reductionism and advocates of multi-disciplinarity and methodological pluralism. The Nobel Prize winner Gunnar Myrdal noted 46 years ago that

> In presenting their concepts, models and theories, economists are regularly prepared to make the most generous reservations and qualifications – indeed to emphasize that in the last instance development is a human problem...Having thus made their bow to what they have become accustomed to call the non-economic factors, they thereafter commonly proceed as if those factors did not exist. (Myrdal, 1970: 28–9)

And such back-sliding persists. But some economists – Amartya Sen, Richard Jolly, and Ravi Kanbur come to mind – have been leaders in widening concepts, marrying quantitative and qualitative and non-contextual and contextual, and introducing new measures of poverty and well-being. The Human Development Report launched in 1990 introduced the Human Development Index which, besides per capita income, included measures of education and life expectancy. And targets have become more ambitious: the first of the Millennium Development Goals set in 2000 was to halve between 1990 and 2015 the proportion of people whose income was less than a dollar a day.

The first of the Sustainable Development Goals adopted in September 2015 is explicitly more inclusive: 'to end poverty *in all its forms* everywhere' (my emphasis).

Findings as artefacts of methodology

Economists, anthropologists, and other professionals, even psychologists, do not often look in a mirror and reflect on how their methods structure and distort their findings. The need for critical awareness of how findings can be an artefact of methodology can be illustrated by two examples.

Open defecation in rural India. Findings on sensitive subjects are vulnerable to underestimation in questionnaire surveys (see for example Chambers, 1983: 56; 1997: 93–7). A matter of concern in rural India is the proportion of the rural population who, although they have toilets, still practise open defecation. Two National Sample Surveys asking this of members of households together reported 1.7 per cent and 4.4 per cent. Surveys which asked balanced questions about individuals, for example, 'Does [NAME] defecate in the open or use a latrine?' found 39 per cent (Barnard et al., 2013) and 44 per cent (Coffey et al., 2014a) while qualitative interviews with 100 respondents found 56 per cent (Coffey et al., 2014b). It seems that all questionnaire findings on such topics should be themselves critically questioned.[11]

Caizhen Lu and who are the poor? Caizhen Lu in her ground-breaking and iconoclastic study *Poverty and Development in China: Alternative Approaches to Poverty Assessment* (2012: 182–210) presented the findings of four approaches to identifying the poor households among the same 473 households in four Chinese villages. The approaches were:

- the official poverty list (OPL) drawn up by village officials and leaders for submission upwards;
- the national poverty line (NPL);
- a participatory wealth ranking (PWR) by community members themselves;
- a multi-dimensional poverty index (MDI).

She compared the proportions of the total households identified as poor. These ranged from less than 1 per cent with the NPL, to 18 per cent with a local price-based poverty line, 34 per cent with the MDI, 40 per cent with the OPL, and 60 per cent with local people's own PWR. Households identified by only one method were: NPL, one; PWR, 34; MDI, 47; and OPL, 63. The PWR and the MDI stood out for sharing some of the same criteria; for instance, having sick and disabled people, female-headed households, elderly households, low education, and minority ethnic Miao households.

Lu discusses the policy implications of the disparities between the outcomes of the different methods and the striking low overlaps between the findings of the four approaches. Astonishingly, only four of the 473 households were identified as poor by all four approaches. Disturbing questions follow for other contexts about how and by whom those who are poor are identified for programmes of support, and who is included and who is left out. The least one can conclude is that the methodologies and implementation of all household and individual targeted programmes merit critical and reflexive appraisal and ground-truthing in the field.

Relativism and realism: the Rashomon effect

Rashomon is four accounts of an incident between Japanese samurai. Depicted in the film of that name, each account is plausible. At the end you know that something happened, but you do not know which version to believe, or whether the reality was something different yet again. One speculates that the versions were self-serving mixes of falsehood and malleable memory, embedded and believed through repetition, a phenomenon noted in Chapter 1. The Rashomon effect with Caizhen Lu's study is less impenetrable because we can interrogate the four approaches. The challenge is frontal. After this study there is less excuse than ever for uncritical methodological monoculture.

So we enter a world of relativism of knowledge and knowledges with both theoretical and practical implications. There are many choices of how to find out, how to learn, how to investigate, how to conduct research, how to set about impact evaluation, and so on. If the outcomes can depend to anything like such a degree on methodology and process, we have to ask what determines or drives these, and how much does that limit, extend, or distort the knowledges, conclusions, and concepts of realities that are derived and the policies and practices that follow. If we are locked into using the lens of any one methodology, we are locked into the biases, structure, and categories of just one particular view. Rigour in this relativism can, however, be sought through mixed methods and triangulation, and the wisdom of knowing which combination of methodologies and procedures best fits need and context. In practice, however, we are again and again trapped and locked in personally, professionally, and institutionally to ways of learning and acting which are mechanistic, costly, reductionist, and dysfunctional.

Locked in by mechanistic methodologies

Mechanistic methodologies for research and for project procedures have become widespread, being privileged or required by funders, whether these are governments, foundations, donors, or lenders.

Locked in to research methodologies

In the early 21st century there has been a steady shift of major research resources to sponsoring and supporting methodologies with strict protocols and rules to be followed in sequence. In research these are: *randomized control trials* (RCTs), studies which compare before and after in randomized samples that receive a treatment with untreated comparable randomized samples as controls – these have become very widespread; and *systematic reviews* (SRs) of evidence from sources which pass stringent criteria of rigour which limit them largely to RCTs.

To considering these I bring the perspective of a spectator alarmed by reductionism and the huge resources devoted to RCTs and SRs. I do not aspire to technical or statistical competence in assessing them. I appreciate the commitment, energy, hard work, and professional competence of those who take part in them. The question I ask is how cost-effective are they for useful learning compared with alternatives.

Randomized control trials

Randomized control trials have been touted as the 'gold standard' of methods. For technical critiques see authoritative papers by Angus Deaton (2009) and Paul Shaffer (2011). Extravagant claims have been made for them:[12] 'we have a new, powerful tool: randomized control trials (RCTs), which give researchers, working with a local partner, a chance to implement large-scale experiments designed to test their theories' (Banerjee and Duflo, 2011: 14).

Esther Duflo and Abhijit Banerjee and the Poverty Action Laboratory (J-PAL) at MIT have been driving forces backed by generous funding. As seems common with mechanistic methodologies, the spread of RCTs was explosive,[13] and they could claim that: 'By 2010 J-PAL researchers had completed or were engaged in over 240 experiments in forty countries around the world, and very large numbers of organizations, researchers, and policy-makers have embraced the idea of randomized trials' (Banerjee and Duflo, 2011: 14–5).

The financial and human resource costs of RCTs on such a scale must have been prodigious. One case where they have affected policies and practice that has been repeatedly cited is PROGRESA, a programme for conditional cash transfers which has been adopted and adapted in many countries. (For the positive case for PROGRESA see Banerjee and Duflo, 2011: 78–81, and for a serious methodological critique Faulkner, 2013.) In many other cases and notably in rural sanitation, findings of RCTs have often been inconsequential and unconvincing, an exception in rural sanitation (as of mid-2016) being community-led total sanitation (CLTS) and stunting in Mali (Alzua et al., 2015). Alternative ways of learning have been sidelined, underfunded, and underdeveloped. The opportunity costs of research crying out to be done, and not done because of resources pre-empted by RCTs, is beyond computation.

Even critics of RCTs recognize that, though costly, they can be appropriate when treatments can be standardized; receiving environments and controls are uniform, predictable, and separable; there are plausible causal links between treatments and measurable indicators of outputs, outcomes, and/or impacts; controls can be protected from contamination; and ethical issues can be dealt with. This can be made to apply in some medical research: a pill, or an immunization, is a standard intervention; the receiving environment, the human body, is highly predictable and homeostatically controlled within tight limits. Effects with large samples and placebo controls may be plausibly attributed to the intervention. However, when the RCT involves people, some of whom have and some of whom do not have the intervention treatment, there can be troubling ethical issues.

These conditions do not obtain with interventions in communities or other situations which are complex, multi-dimensional, uncontrollable, unpredictable, and idiosyncratically variable. Nevertheless, RCTs have repeatedly been applied in such contexts. With communities, there are also difficulties in standardizing interventions. Weaknesses in these conditions include:

Contamination. The treatment in intervention communities can affect the controls, again more likely the longer the interval. With CLTS in Himachal Pradesh, a general campaign brought the treatment to the controls and forced abandonment of a study. The follow-up on the baseline in an Indonesian study (Sijbesma et al., 2011) found that control communities, frustrated that they were excluded, pressurized local government and NGOs to give them more attention and similar interventions, with some success.

Causality. Causality is a black box. Correlations or lack of correlations raise but do not answer questions of causality. As Deaton has pointed out (2009: 448), 'as with all experiments the mechanisms are unclear'. And yet again and again for practical and policy purposes what we need from studies and evaluations is not just what works or does not but why it works or why it does not.

Before–after incomparability. This faces three problems, which become worse the longer the interval between baseline and final study. The first is that households and respondents do not remain constant. After an interval of years households and their members have often changed. Some migrate, temporarily or permanently, households split up, people die, children are born, individuals or households move in and settle, and so on. After a 10-year interval, these problems can be very taxing and time-consuming to tackle, and diminish the power of the conclusions. And the rapid rate of social and other change makes comparisons increasingly difficult (see Sijbesma et al., 2011, for a full discussion).

Weak in external validity. What is found is contextual and not necessarily generalizable (EES, 2007). While these weaknesses are well recognized, other drawbacks seem to have been largely or totally overlooked. These concern choice of topics; data and findings; costs and opportunity costs; and irreversibility and risks.

Choice of topics. The choice of topic may be biased to the standard, and, as noted, evaluations and studies that are most amenable to RCTs have simple interventions, a standard receiving environment, and measurable outcomes, as with immunizations, bed nets and malaria, menstrual hygiene pads, and textbooks. A disturbing question is whether the drive for accountability biases choices of development interventions towards such standardized 'things' which are relatively amenable to 'rigorous' evaluation through RCTs, and away from others which are harder to measure but more transformative (see the Naitsios quotation at the head of the chapter).

Data and findings. These can be subject to three limitations:

1. *The frequency of no significant findings.* No significant findings may be significant but tend to be regarded as failures. They are under-reported in scientific journals. With RCTs they may also result from deficiencies in design and implementation and changes in external conditions. Many conditions are liable to produce low or negligible impacts. Three stand out as particularly significant. First, when the methodology and implementation are flawed or not standardized, as with some WASH and undernutrition studies. Second, when effects are likely to be smaller in the short term than the long term but the interval between treatment and measurement is short: when the Poverty Action Laboratory at MIT conducted an RCT on microfinance in 104 neighbourhoods in Hyderabad the difference after 15–20 months was minimal – 7 per cent for treatment against 5 per cent for controls. This gave rise to vigorous argument and disputes (Banerjee and Duflo, 2011: 170–2). The third condition is when there is complex multi-causality, a treatment inherently variable in quality (such as CLTS triggering and follow-up), receiving environments inherently variable, as with rural communities, and the causality of the measured outcome is complex. These three conditions have tended to occur with RCTs intended to identify health, and in particular nutritional, impacts of WASH (which also tend to be very costly). A single exception to this is the RCT in Mali (Alzua et al., 2015) where conditions and implementation were well standardized and controls apparently little contaminated. Such conditions would be difficult to find and create again.
2. *Systemic distortion and spurious correlations.* Questionnaires are well known for the biased responses they can evoke through the interview situation. Then there is the 'bugger-off effect' of giving answers that will dispatch bothersome investigators quickly (Thomas Clasen, pers. comm., 2013). But more serious and almost totally overlooked in

the RCT literature is the likelihood of systematically biased responses evoked by the uniformities of the interview situation, with prudent, socially acceptable, or otherwise biased, incomplete, or evasive responses. Correlations found may then be spurious, based not on reality but on uniformities in social relations, motivations, and distortions in interviews. There is ample evidence of systematic misreporting on sensitive subjects in surveys (Tourangeau et al., 2000: 287). It is probably rare for a survey to be designed with the skill of the SQUAT survey in North India, in which there was no indication until half way through an interview that there was an interest in sanitation. And the findings of that survey were very significant (see Coffey et al., 2014a, b). A separate point is that subsequent behaviour can be affected through repeated interviews (Zwane et al., 2011).

3. *Missing major factors.* A study in India shows how the major findings with practical and policy implications can come not from the RCT but from a much cheaper and less demanding approach. The intervention was complex, to deepen democracy in rural India. At considerable expense an RCT study found no significant impact. However, a longitudinal qualitative study over four years in 10 per cent of the 200 RCT communities (100 intervention and 100 control) found that the most significant variable was the commitment and quality of the facilitators of the intervention. This did not feature in the RCT: 'many positive impacts, however subtle or unexpected, were only observed in those panchayats [village-level government entities] that had good facilitators' (Ananthpur et al., 2014: 20). This finding came from participant observation, was not dependent on the RCT, and could have emerged without it at a fraction of the cost.

Costs and opportunity costs. First, most RCTs are very costly, especially when health-related. Twice when I have asked researchers the budget costs of their health-related RCTs, one in Nepal and one in Malawi, they would not tell me, possibly because they were embarrassed that they were so high. Well-informed sources estimate that costs of RCTs can range from $0.5 m for a very simple study to over $10 m for a health-related study, much depending on scale, duration, the policy and norms of the sponsoring organization (a major variable), and what sorts of measurements, for instance laboratory tests, are required.

Second, RCTs are human resource intensive. An RCT typically requires quite a large team of field researchers to administer questionnaires. RCTs are also costly for communities and respondents. Their time is not costed in.

Third, opportunity costs are high. Because they are engaged on an RCT, researchers are denied the opportunity to learn other approaches and methods, or what they would have revealed. Questionnaires are extractive. Empowering alternatives from which local people gain and learn are forgone. The opportunity costs of win–win alternatives forgone are high (see Chapter 5). But they are not recognized.

Fourth, other learning opportunities are smothered or ignored. Much useful learning comes from outliers and exceptions. RCTs tend to average things out. There is little learning from whatever is not statistically significant. But many of the best practical insights come from positive and negative deviants (Gladwell, 2009; Rose, 2016).

Delaying learning and action. Policy and practice in a world of accelerating change need quick insights. Delays have ever higher costs. The perceived need for rigorous research on environmental effects on stunting led to a major, complicated, managerially demanding study in Zimbabwe which from conception to conclusion will have taken at least six years.[14] Its findings may have major implications. But in the meantime the blind spot of enteric environmental disorder (EED), which is a large part of what it is studying, will have affected the growth and life prospects of perhaps hundreds of millions of children. It would be tragic if this study were to delay action.

Irreversibility and risk. Irreversibility (see Chambers, 2005: 20–5) and risk are under-recognized weaknesses compounded by and compounding others. Once funded and committed to an RCT there is no going back. It is a juggernaut on rails with a fixed sequence, sucking in and pre-empting human resources and tying them down to required activities at each stage. The options are yes or no: to continue or to cancel. Risks are amplified by contamination and confounding by exogenous variables. Changes in government policy cannot be controlled: an RCT on local governance in Karnataka was confounded when government funding to all local government entities was increased sevenfold (Ananthpur et al., 2014). Multiple problems of before–after comparability are, in the view of Christine Sijbesma and her colleagues (2011), becoming more challenging and making the classical study increasingly problematic. Irreversibility and inflexibility in the context of rapid and unpredictable change amplify other shortcomings.

Trade-offs. As if these shortcomings were not enough, there are difficult trade-offs. As noted, the shorter the interval between baseline and follow-up study to identify effects, the smaller those effects are likely to be and the less convincing the findings. On the other hand, the longer the interval, the more demanding the comparison in terms of the comparability of conditions and the greater the dangers of contamination making it harder to draw conclusions. And it may be neither feasible nor ethical to prevent control communities from seeking contaminating treatments (Sijbesma et al., 2011).

Privileging RCTs, neglecting other evidence. A final weakness derives from valuing RCTs over other sources. These may be qualitative data or widely recognized phenomena. An example in the World Development Report 2015, *Mind, Society and Behaviour,* is the treatment of evidence on CLTS. There is overwhelming evidence from many countries that hardware subsidy programmes for rural household latrines seriously inhibit the self-help of CLTS. Abolishing or avoiding such subsidies has been key to probably well over 30 million rural people now (2016) having benefited from CLTS. For the authors of the WDR, though, this may have fallen in their category of 'some promising anecdotal evidence'. They privileged evidence from two RCTs which were of questionable value and then misread them to draw the dangerously misleading and totally false conclusion that '...where CLTS was combined with subsidies for toilet construction, its impact on toilet availability within households was much higher' (World Bank, 2015: 17).[15]

This litany of fallibilities, risks, and costs of RCTs is rarely if ever recognized in its fullness. Ideology, long-term funding, institutional inertia, professional training and capabilities, the political economy of funding for RCTs, and overlooking the counterfactual of opportunity costs, have combined to give them for a time the unstoppable momentum of a supertanker. Chapters 4 and 5 present evidence and argument that there are cheaper, quicker and more timely, more ethical, more inclusive, more empowering, and more rigorous, often win–win ways for knowing better (for the relevant definition of rigour see the Glossary of meanings and Chapter 4).

Systematic reviews

Proponents of RCTs will make an argument for them from the standpoint of the rigour of systematic reviews. SRs are usually as defined in the Cochrane Collaboration, which has strict protocols for which studies are rigorous enough for inclusion. Studies which qualify are then analysed and their conclusions summarized. Though widely accepted and practised, SRs are open to criticism.

First, triage on the grounds of lack of rigour eliminates learning from a mass of observation and evidence, much of it credible. As Rehfuss and Bartram (2013) have pointed out, 'limiting systematic reviews to...RCTs may dismiss as noise much of what others consider to be the signal'. However, SRs do start inclusively. They then screen using successive criteria. One (Benova et al., 2014) narrowed down 4,162 unique papers to 14; another (Loevinsohn et al., 2014) screened 20,299 papers down to 214 for a second stage in which only five were considered candidates for in-depth review. When the 2009 SR of WASH interventions to combat childhood diarrhoea in developing countries (Waddington et al., 2014) conducted word searches of data bases, Google generated so many that they limited consideration to the first thousand. Triage narrowed selection down to 65 impact evaluations judged rigorous enough for quantitative analysis. A later SR (Dangour et al., 2013) of impacts of WASH interventions on child nutrition narrowed down to 14 studies of which five were RCTs and nine less rigorous non-randomized studies with comparison groups. In these studies, thus, the vast majority of the relevant evidence – noise or signals depending on one's view – was relegated to darkness. The protocol favours RCTs though in practice non-randomized studies with comparison groups are included. However, Wolf-Peter Schmidt (2014) has found even case-control studies which come up with plausible results to have been excluded.

Second, SRs appear vulnerable to biased reductionism. The five RCTs in the Dangour et al. SR were all water-related (one was the provision of soap) perhaps reflecting the water over sanitation preference noted in Chapter 2. None was on sanitation, rather limiting, to say the least, the policy relevance of the findings.

Third, a repeated lament in SRs is the poor quality of the studies reviewed. Dangour et al. (2013) reported that none of their 14 studies was at low risk of bias, several had multiple potential risks, and none of them masked the WASH intervention from participants. Some of the analysis in the SR was limited to the five cluster-randomized control trials but these had durations of only nine to twelve months.

Fourth, the combined limitations of RCTs and RCT siblings outlined earlier may skew SRs towards finding small results. In the Dangour study, in which the durations were short, the impact found was slight, and the conclusions drawn guarded: that there was 'suggestive evidence from these 5 of a small benefit of WASH interventions on measures of growth in childhood' (Dangour et al., 2013, 26). This did not prevent a splash in *The Guardian* (London) blowing this up into a major discovery; publicity, however desirable, which may have had more to do with communications professionals than with the scale of the findings. This and other SRs may only substantiate rather weakly what is already known from much other 'less rigorous evidence' that has been systematically excluded. And yet much of that other, less 'rigorous' evidence, points to very strong causal links between sanitation and stunting, for instance the work of Dean Spears (2012, 2013) (see Chapter 2). For policy purposes, such SRs and the RCTs on which they draw are not needed. Their limited findings may indeed do harm by delaying policy action.

Fifth, as trenchantly pointed out in their systematic review of SRs, 'The cost of a knowledge silo: a systematic re-review of water, sanitation and hygiene interventions', Loevinsohn and his colleagues (2014) show that SRs are, like the RCTs on which they are based, weak on causal pathways, which are often more varied and with more impacts than the studies recognize or reveal. They reviewed a selection of 27 of the 65 cases in the SR *Water, Sanitation and Hygiene Interventions to Combat Childhood Diarrhoea in Developing Countries* (Waddington et al., 2009). Doing this with both a health lens and a development lens, they brought to light a more nuanced and complex reality with more actions, pathways, and impacts, than in the original SR.[16]

Finally, the reductionisms of RCTs and SRs are mutually reinforcing. They are locked in an incestuous embrace. In the case of water, sanitation, and hygiene, they are glued together (if I may be forgiven) by diarrhoea. Diarrhoea reductionism (see Chapter 2) is almost universal. Because diarrhoeas can be measured, they are basic in WASH studies which need statistics. So comparisons in SRs are based on diarrhoea statistics, accepted almost as automatically as, say, we accept the base 10 in our mathematics. This can shed some light on the blind spots of causal links between WASH interventions and undernutrition but its tunnel vision leaves, as we have seen, the multiple causalities of other faecally transmitted infections – intestinal parasites, EED, and the many others – in the dark to which they are accustomed. As in this example, by privileging RCTs over other approaches, the strengths and defects in RCTs are not just reproduced but may be amplified in SRs, with the added authority of appearing to be doubly rigorous because of the rigid standards of each.

To know better, one way forward is more of the same with improvements. The many credible and well-researched critiques of RCTs and to a lesser extent SRs may provoke some better practice, especially mixing in qualitative methods with preliminary and parallel studies to shed light on causality and unanticipated outcomes. However, as I have argued, the costs and opportunity costs of both are enormous. One can only agree with Paul Shaffer (2011) that the choice of approach should be driven by the research question and not the alleged superiority of the methodology; and costs, opportunity costs, and cost-effectiveness should be added to the criteria for choice of methodology.

Cost-effective alternatives to RCTs and SRs

There are many ways of knowing better. Drawing on examples from the WASH field in Chapter 2, three alternatives stand out for their cost-effectiveness.

Comparative analysis of secondary data. This has been extraordinarily cost-effective in the three seminal contributions cited in Chapter 2 (e.g. page 45), with their extensive implications for research, policy, and practice. Dean Spears not only analysed over 140 demographic health surveys (finding that open defecation combined with population density explained 65 per cent of child undernutrition; Spears, 2014) but also in another study (Spears, 2014b) compared Indian census data from 2001 and 2011 to create a colour map of changes in the density of rural open defecation for all the over 643 rural districts in India, finding that in almost all North India it had increased in those 10 years. These studies were at a tiny fraction of the cost of an average RCT and have probably been more influential than all the WASH-related RCTs together.

Literature reviews. These are almost always useful. They enable others to gain an overview. Good ones synthesize and summarize. In the WASH field, a succession of UNICEF literature reviews has provided invaluable summaries of what is believed to be known for many aspects of WASH, ranging from effects on diarrhoeas of handwashing with soap to the safe disposal of children's faeces. A review of 115 grey literature sources from 11 websites, *Testing CLTS Approaches for Scalability* (Venkataraman, 2012), has been much more directly valuable for practice than many RCTs.

Cross-sectional studies. Cross-sectional studies often with large samples can, when credible, come up with findings of interest and potential relevance for policy and practice. In western Kenya a large-scale study of schools including household questionnaires found that the only WASH factor associated with school absence was the cleanliness of the toilets (Dreibelbis et al., 2012). In Bangladesh, a more in-depth study in 16 schools found that key factors in well-managed school sanitation were quality construction and community or government financial support, and that the supporting conditions were school management committee involvement, a sanitation champion, and clear teacher responsibility for maintenance (Chatterley et al., 2014). Both have contextual limitations but both generated useful insights.

Numerous other cost-effective alternatives in development practice can be found through eclectic methodological pluralism (Chapter 4) and participatory methodologies (Chapter 5).

Locked in by mechanistic procedures

Procedural demands by governments, government agencies, lender and donor agencies, foundations, and other funders have tightened over the past three decades. For Dutch aid, which is typical, it has been noted that 'The past 15 years have seen [a] shift from a trust-based system to a largely protocol-driven approach' (van Es and Guijt, 2015: 110). Widespread shifts away from trust have been in the name of efficiency, effectiveness, value for money, and accountability. Who can be against these? There have been some good effects. Earlier, project and programme design, monitoring, and evaluation were often too loose and projects poorly monitored. When I worked for the Ford Foundation in India in the early 1980s we expected that project funding would often need to be rolled over because of failure to implement in a timely fashion. And across the sector there were NGOs that believed it was enough to mean well and want to do good. All that has gone and good riddance.

Logframes and beyond

But the pendulum has taken an extreme swing. We are now (in 2016) in another world. Accountability is on all funders' lips. Bilateral donors justify upwards accountability as being responsible to their taxpayers. The upside of this includes more reflection on goals, more timely implementation, and better monitoring. But these are the tip of an iceberg with a massive downside out of sight. Procedural demands on recipients have been multiplying, tightening, and becoming more time-consuming, constraining and demoralising. This began when the logframe was introduced in the 1990s. To some at the time, its linear logic was such a misfit to complex and unpredictable realities that it would die a natural death. But consultants were trained in it, and trained other consultants who then trained and advised aspiring grantees when they found the logframe difficult to complete. The more donors demanded log-frames, the more the consultants were in demand, and the more sustainable their livelihoods became and remain.

In the name of efficiency, effectiveness, and accountability upwards, a succession of systems and labels followed: delivering value for money (who could be against that?), results-based management (RBM) (of course, common sense), theories of change (think through how you think good change will follow), all with *evidence-based* as a mantra, and most recently Payment by Results (PbR) (recipients bear the risks, donors pay on delivery, and upwards accountability is assured). With the only partial exception of theories of change, these are all interpreted to require some mix of preset measurable results such as outputs, milestones, targets, outcomes, and impacts (depending on what these words are taken to mean). None of these is wholly damaging in its direct effects. They have shaken complacency and made applicants think and question what they propose to do. To work out a theory of change can be useful. Evidence can be a valuable source of learning and lead to a change of direction (if that is permitted). But the cumulative impact of this successive tightening of procedures has been disastrous. And the frogs in the gradually heating pot have not recognized, or if recognized, not effectively resisted, the long-term trend.

Starting with the logframe, there are many arguments for and against. Since its popularization in the 1990s there have been many critical and insightful reviews (e.g. Gasper, 2000, 2008). Whatever positive aspects can be adduced, it diminishes flexibility and has often been found stressful by implementers. It can be against the interests of people living in poverty. The head of an NGO in a remote part of Nepal had a logframe but no contact with the distant donor in Kathmandu. As he became familiar with local conditions, he saw it would be better not to follow the logframe but to work with bonded labourers. The discrepancy between what he was to report on and what he passionately felt he had to do became so disturbing that he needed support and counselling. Fortunately a visiting anthropologist was able to provide these and act as a go-between in negotiating changes in the logframe. The revised project was so outstanding that it was chosen to be visited by the donor minister when she came to Nepal. In another case in Bangladesh, ActionAid felt they could not start work on Reflect (see pp 124–6) at least until a mid-term review of their logframe. Donors will plead that they are flexible if approached, but those at the sharp end are usually reluctant to do this, fearing transaction costs and harm to their reputation and prospects of future funding.

The negative aspects of the logframe have been overshadowed by its successors. Mostly, these have been additions not alternatives to the logframe. In *Time to Listen* (Anderson et al., 2012), the authors report on and summarize findings from open-ended listening to over 6,000 people in the aid chain in 21 countries. These were people who had received international assistance, observed the effects of aid efforts, or been involved in providing aid. There is a whole chapter on 'proceduralization', defined as: 'the codification of approaches that are meant to accomplish positive outcomes into mechanical checklists and templates that not only fail to achieve their intent but actually lead to even worse outcomes' (Anderson et al., 2012: 67).

It is, then, not just that the negative aspects of the new procedures have grown. It is the damning finding that their net effects are negative. Four factors were found: complying with procedures was increasingly time-consuming; pressures to spend fuelled corruption (the widespread complaint was that too much aid comes too fast); relationships were distorted through focusing on resource transfers and undermining local contributions and ownership; and waste was encouraged. Just one example of many was:

> when the need to spend down funds by the end of a reporting period prompts unnecessary and repetitive conferences or workshops in expensive hotels, rather than ensuring that these funds are used throughout an activity to engage local people effectively. Procedures should allow for underspending and reward it. (Anderson et al., 2012: 141)

Proceduralization has had bad effects within donor organizations. It has saddled staff with ever more laborious and time-consuming internal procedures. In the UK's Department for International Development (DFID) a grant has to have a business case. A business case for £50,000 is not much different in its demands on staff time from one for £50 m. In many agencies, in the name of cost-effectiveness, the number of staff has been pared down at the same time as the procedures have become more onerous. Viscosity and delays result. Some of the more dedicated staff have left in frustration. The ratio of donor staff time to funds to be disbursed has dropped continuously so the size of grants has had to grow.[17] Grants and loans have to be in larger chunks, while at the same time many more demands are made on the time of applicants in completing proposals.

The nadir of dysfunctional proceduralization has been payment by results, originating in the World Bank in 2008 (Eyben et al., 2015: 27) and later promoted by DFID which proudly proclaimed itself to be leading the world in developing results-based aid, and now PbR. It makes sense, in the reported words of the International Development Secretary (in an undated press release), for DFID 'to take a tougher, more business-like approach by requiring results up front before payment is made. Better sharing of risk in this way will drive value for money as partners become more incentivised to deliver'.

This is perverse. It is centralizing power at the top and top-down in the aid chain. It is not sharing risk but passing all the risk to the recipient. Recipients need substantial working capital to tide over the period until (if they are successful) they are paid. This discriminates against smaller NGOs and other small organizations and favours large contractors or already well-resourced governments.[18] And there are pressures against participation, inherently unpredictable as that is, and best not tied to a timetable.

So forced to achieve targets for payment by results, organizations can face stark choices: abandon participation, go bankrupt, plead for clemency, relax standards of verification, gloss your reports, or lie, or some combination of these. One small organization was driven almost to bankruptcy through a PbR contract which the donor terminated for failure to deliver: reportedly, the senior management had to forgo remuneration for six months.[19] Box 3.1 describes the unseen, unreported, field reality communicated to me with the proviso that neither the organization nor the country should be revealed. We dare not speak truth to power.

The UK's International Development Secretary was reported to have claimed to be pursuing 'a relentless drive for value for money ... We're making sure that every pound is spent as efficiently and effectively as possible' (*The Independent* (newspaper), 22 July 2015).Box 3.1 describes how this played out and was experienced in the field. Far from delivering value for money, the tightening of controls in the name of accountability perversely diminished the cost-effectiveness of British aid. This is not what those of us had in mind who campaigned for 0.7 per cent of GDP to be committed to the aid budget. Well-meaning blindness, accountants who confuse accountability with accountancy and a creeping audit culture have done damage, largely unseen, at the cost of the British taxpayer, and more importantly, through acts of commission and omission, to poor, vulnerable, and marginalized people. I expressed my anger in a blog (Chambers, 2014),[20] and sent the International Secretary a copy of *Time to Listen* (Anderson et al., 2012) recommending that she buy 2,000 copies to give to all DFID staff.

Let me be clear. I am not at all arguing for a smaller aid budget, but for more staff in DFID and more flexible, less demanding, and more empowering procedures, with transparency, trust, and face-to-face relationships (see Chapter 6). These, I argue, would be more cost-effective than current mechanistic procedures.

Competitive bidding

The tightening of accountability and controls has spawned competitive bidding. The laudable aim is to eliminate the favouritism of 'old boy networks' and to have a 'level playing field'. But this is the visible tip of an iceberg of hidden costs. There is a huge downside. Competitive bidding fosters rivalry between organizations which should be openly sharing and collaborating with each other. If bids are for large blocks of money, these are most readily submitted by large organizations, typically commercial consultancies. Nor has this eliminated the old boys. At the higher levels, there are revolving doors between donor agencies and large commercial consultancy organizations. The old boy network has become a big boy network.

For small organizations, the alternative is to form or join consortia, typically of NGOs. For them, though, to bid has high transaction costs of negotiation, agreement, fitting the proposal to their own missions and priorities as well as adapting to those of others, iterating over details, agreeing relative

---

Box 3.1 Payment by results experience from an INGO working in an African country, 14 November 2014

'It would be great if the feedback can be anonymous from our team here:

PbR framework approach is very complex and I'm not sure we were prepared for the intensity of it when we were successful.

Our existing skills were never assessed here in ... to understand our gaps and capacities in managing this type of framework.

The level of risk to achieving results becomes too high and after a year and a half designing, redesigning, and planning for the program, the funding has been hibernated for a number of months.

I can't tell you how many hours, days, and weeks it took to develop the proposals and the high level of information required.

To have this money removed will now potentially threaten our work with communities who we heavily engaged with and government officials.

We have had to shelter our local partners from the risk of PbR and have provided them with grants – they cannot absorb this risk.

The reality of PbR in the field is that you need dedicated staff just to "feed the machine" of paperwork, tables, huge templates, and requirements for the donor which reduces our efficiencies.

Our coordination team was continually focused on donor requirements, rather than program quality on the ground.

Reporting is extremely complex and cumbersome – taking highly skilled, not programmatic staff.

Apparently PbR is meant to increase effectiveness and efficiency of aid – instead I think perhaps it is reducing efficiencies.

Achieving outcomes in WASH can sometimes be unpredictable and the evidence base is weak ... areas such as hygiene promotion, CLTS, or capacity building are extremely difficult – how can you quantify the quality of this approach and "assessing" its quality and effectiveness is highly subjective.

For example ... we have a 17-page document trying to unpick how to measure and verify each "payment result".

There is little if no room for flexibility to changing conditions or accepting and highlighting failures/learning.

You either succeed based on the plan or you go home! We removed all but one innovation in our project and stuck with tried and tested approaches where possible.'

---

budget shares, and so on. Small NGOs are discriminated against – they add to the transaction costs for the larger NGOs and make agreement more difficult and more time-consuming. So there are mutually reinforcing biases towards larger organizations.

Whose convenience counts? Whose transaction costs? Would-be bidders have their transaction costs raised by the insensitive use of power by funders to fit their own convenience, with deadlines they unilaterally decide. Donor staff have been known to clear their desks before *their* summer holidays, getting a call for bids out at a time and with deadlines which force would-be bidders to spend *their* summer holidays negotiating on their mobile phones. Then there can be a tight deadline because in the funding agency 'money has to be got out of the door' before the end of the financial year. The idea that saving money is a virtue appears rather Victorian. A failure to disburse funds has become an embarrassing, even culpable, delinquency. Or internal donor procedures delay putting out a call for bids which then has very tight deadlines, forcing bidders to drop everything else. In one case, bids were invited, at least four organizations devoted much time and effort in preparing them, only to be told out of the blue and without apology that it had been decided not to go ahead.

Opening up bidding for smaller amounts to provide opportunities for smaller civil society organizations has a different pathology. Jacqui Stevenson, in a well-researched blog,[21] analysed the transaction costs of unsuccessful bids for funding from the UN Trust Fund for Women for research on violence against women. The fact that 2,212 applications were submitted is a testimony if one was ever needed to the unmet need for funding for such work. After a second round, 17 were funded and 2,195 rejected. Each initial proposal was estimated to have taken five to ten days of unpaid (almost entirely women's) time to prepare and submit. On a normal 250-day working year this averages out at over 65 unfunded person years taken from work with and for women for failed bids. Any hidden benefits to failed bidders through the thinking and preparation will have been many times outweighed by the costs of dashed hopes and demoralization, the diversion of staff time from programme activities, and the negative effects on women's organizations and the women with whom they work. In any subsequent evaluation of the research, the extraordinary scale and spread of these hidden transaction costs, so distant and unseen by those administering the fund, should be set against whatever benefits were found. But these costs defy easy measurement. And such an evaluation is as unlikely as it would be unsettling. The blinkers of distance, isolation, and power, or feeling the system allows no alternatives, should not excuse any repetition of such behaviour. Let me hope that this section will provoke such outrage that whoever can will convene and fund a group of informed, committed, and creative people to discover or to brainstorm, test, and spread better procedures.[22]

Shared characteristics

Methodological and procedural lock-ins have four characteristics in common.

First, all require *fixed methods in fixed sequences*. These constrain innovation, adaptable responses to the unforeseen, and ability to seize emerging opportunities. There are 'best practices'. All have linear, sequential tramlines. There are standard practices and sequences for RCTs, SRs, logframes and PbR alike. With RCTs and SRs credibility depends on conformity. PbR is claimed by its advocates to encourage innovation, but in the African example in Box 3.1 prudent risk-minimization reduced it. And the preset targets of logframes and more so of PbR are difficult or believed to be impossible to alter. Even when a procedure might seem to offer scope for flexibility, it can be interpreted and treated as rigid. Take theory of change for instance. Theories of change held by active agents in a change process will evolve with changing circumstances and perceptions: but formal theories of change have been described as 'logframes in disguise', and rarely modified in the course of a project or process.[23]

Second, these approaches are *driven and demanded by large funders*. This is the power of money, more potent when there are individuals and organizations that need funding for survival.[24] RCTs have been promoted with large grants from agencies like the Bill & Melinda Gates Foundation and DFID. The high financial costs of RCTs and SRs may even make them attractive to donor staff under pressure to spend their budgets by the end of each funding period.

Third, there are *systemic failures of feedback to funders*. 'All power deceives'. All individuals and organizations that control rewards and sanctions are liable to be told what they are believed to want to hear, with discordant feedback, or feedback that might harm the reporting person or organization, withheld. Speaking truth to power carries risks, in the case of grantees, fears of losing future grants.[25] I have sat through a whole day's workshop on methodologies. Most of us had strong reservations about RCTs, and would have raised our concerns had there not been present a programme officer of the funding organization which we believed favoured them, and from which we had received or hoped for grants. It was only in the last minutes of the day that someone (I am ashamed to admit not me) dared to raise the subject, by which time there was no time to discuss it. And this was despite the programme officer having said at the start of the day that he welcomed critical feedback, and making himself inconspicuous by staying silent the whole day. Few if any funders realize the extent of the systemic learning disability of power from which they suffer.

Fourth, and perhaps most important of all, all these methods and procedures have *high hidden costs,* out of sight of the powerful funders. These take two main forms: opportunity costs in finance and human resources; and costs in frustration, demotivation, and relationships.

Opportunity costs in finance and human resources

Opportunity costs in finance and human resources and their long-term commitment can be very high. These are the counterfactuals of what the funds and people might otherwise have been dedicated to, the costs of missed benefits from activities not undertaken. Counterfactuals are integral to RCTs in their controls, but not counterfactuals to RCTs themselves. RCTs and SRs engage many professionals. RCTs can require the commitment of many field staff over substantial periods. When they are tied down to questionnaire surveys they are concerned less with surprises and insights and more with ticking boxes. Alternative pathways and methods – training to be facilitators, or generating participatory statistics, or using qualitative approaches and methods or other, more flexible learning approaches (see Chapter 5) – are options that are usually closed to them. This limits the boundaries of their personal and professional development. As for disabling procedures, as we have seen, their transaction costs can be enormous but beneath funders' radars. Where donors have had different reporting requirements, work has been multiplied. Competitive bidding, as we have also seen, can make huge unremunerated demands on time. The monitoring and reporting requirements of the upward accountability procedures of logframes, RBM, PbR, and their siblings, make heavy demands on staff time collecting and analysing data, filling in templates, and the like. And furthest out of sight are the costs and opportunity costs to people in communities – in providing information, responding to surveys, and most of all, and least recognized of all, not being facilitated and empowered to take action themselves. Funders are too far away to see, or perhaps even imagine, such benefits forgone.

Costs in frustration, demotivation, and relationships

These costs are also high but hidden. This is not surprising. They are not readily measurable. Nor do they force themselves on the consciousness of funders.

Deep and widespread frustration is documented in *Time to Listen* (Anderson et al., 2012). The time spent preparing reports, trying to understand what is needed, agonizing over what to include and what not to include and how to express things, consulting colleagues and writing and rewriting in the light of their comments, can be immensely frustrating as many can attest, particularly when it is at the cost of things not done that would have made a real difference.

Demotivation follows frustration. Fixed project requirements demotivate good people who need flexibility and hurt the poor people they wish to serve. Some of the high hidden costs of competitive bidding are in demotivation, yet demotivation costs are not part of our development lexicon. The disappointment of a failed bid in which one has invested time, money, and effort can be deeply demoralizing. A valued colleague, an international leader in her field, told me that she could not face more of the painful and repetitive struggle with laborious procedures to gain funding for her team: she had had enough and was taking early retirement, an uncountable loss to those in her sector and many suffering discrimination who could have benefited had she continued.

Relationships are affected in many ways. For instance, laborious procedures put distance between donors and those they fund and who would like to meet face-to-face; targets, milestones, and other requirements encourage a supervisory and auditing culture and relationships; competitive bidding sets organizations against one another, encouraging secrecy; vertical communication is inhibited and distorted; and participatory and democratic relationships are undermined.

We are long overdue for a sustained effort to incorporate hidden costs such as these in evaluations. The fact that they are difficult to quantify is no reason for overlooking them. To know better in evaluations, we need to know everything, not just what can be quantified. Judgemental estimates can take us some way. There is here another blind spot to be explored.

Trends, irreversibility, and alternatives

Two trends outlined in this chapter are in tension. On the one hand, plural knowledges, epistemic relativism, methodological pluralism, and inclusiveness are gaining acceptance intellectually; and on the other, lock-ins to required mechanistic methods and approaches increasingly prevail procedurally. Standardization and reductionism dominate the world in which many development professionals have to live and work. Power-related procedures have tightened their grip. Seen as cost-effective and convenient for powerful funders, they constrain and disable those funded.

Confronting the power of money, words and warnings have had little leverage. In 2007 the European Evaluation Society issued a dire warning and authoritatively argued the case about the limitations of RCTs and how erroneous it was to promote them as the best or only rigorous and scientific way to improve impact evaluation and assessment (EES, 2007). But money called the tune: funding to the Poverty Action Laboratory in MIT was decisive and in the following years hundreds of RCTs in developing countries received donor support.

Such trends fuelled by funds, together with irreversibility, sunk costs, long shelf life, and dissonance reduction, have combined to compound the problem. Mechanistic lock-ins, whether funded methodologies or mandatory procedures, not only endure but can be additive and tighten and spread, reinforced and reproduced through teaching and training, and favoured by discourse and fashion. It is easier to introduce or add to a controlling procedure or standard methodology than to abolish or simplify it, the more so when it purports to serve rigour or upwards accountability. Some RCTs require commitments of several years, prolonged where there is a struggle to clean the data and see whether findings can be less inconsequential. Sunk costs and other commitments make it less embarrassing to continue than to terminate a flawed project.

Prevention or prophylaxis against new lock-ins requires vigilance and prompt, honest, and critical feedback. This means monitoring funders and the conditions they propose or promulgate. Those within funding agencies and those they fund can be key actors and allies if they are willing. When a procedure or requirement is introduced, one strategy is for would-be recipients to refuse to comply. But this is risky and may mean not being funded.[26] Collective action through representative NGO or research organizations is another line of action. But even their criticisms, in prudent self-interest and the interests of their members, have tended to be muted. Blogs, reports, presentations in meetings, expressions of frustration, meeting funders – there are many other channels of communication. But the risks of speaking truth to power remain and can be unexpected.[27]

Just how complex, variable, and subtly nuanced the realities of procedures and power are is manifest in a landmark contribution to understanding of the aid chain and its relationships. *The Politics of Evidence and Results in International Development: Playing the Game to Change the Rules?* (Eyben et al., 2015) gives insights into the origins and damaging effects of mechanistic procedures (not a term the authors use). The book originates in what Rosalind Eyben called 'The Big Push Back' against the trend of increasing top-down requirements, which she soon transformed into 'The Big Push Forward' with a more positive orientation. The book is an invaluable resource for all who seek to understand the realities, nuances, and possibilities of the aid chain as it was in 2015. In parallel with *Time to Listen* (Anderson et al., 2012), it should be studied and reflected on by all who hold funding power. The ground-truths revealed by these two books are disturbing, laying bare as they do some of the perverse and unintended negative effects of funder power and requirements.

Over the past two decades there has, then, been an insidious creep to lock the dynamics of the development sector into ever more mechanistic, rigid, formulaic, and dysfunctional procedures, imperiously required by funders. The most sinister aspect is what this has done to our vocabularies, mindsets, and memories (see Chapter 6). It takes an effort for those who were active in the mid-1990s to remember what relationships and procedures were like then. Of course, there was much to improve. But there was a freedom for flexibility and adaptation and for relationships with more open communication and trust. Both formal (the tip of the iceberg) and hidden (the rest of it) transaction costs were far, far lower. The iceberg has grown and grown. The freezing, to pursue the metaphor, has been gradual but consistent and sustained. Even critical academic analyses like *Negotiating Knowledge* (Hayman et al., 2016) can fail to recognize and confront adequately what has happened. Those entering development agencies now are brainwashed and acculturated into another world: they cannot know what has been lost, nor appreciate how badly and unnecessarily constrained development actors have become in the ever-tightening straitjackets they are forced to wear as they negotiate the unpredictable obstacle courses of development.

I conclude, then, that to know better in development demands a radical rethink and alternatives to current trends. Ways have to be found to abolish or at least mitigate disabling and demoralizing procedures. But once introduced and embedded they are infuriatingly resilient,[28] and not just irreversible but with tendencies to intensify and spread. The evidence in this chapter shows that they are not in the interests of people living in poverty. But those who groan and grumble in private fear to speak the truth to the power of purse strings in public. It needs vision and courage to transform lock-ins by doing, seeing, and saying things differently. Solutions have to be positive and persuasive with critical feedback informed and inspired by realism, new vision, and better alternatives.

This sets the scene for the second half of this book in which I explore a paradigm of complexity and participation as a basis for alternative approaches. These, I shall argue, promise better value for resources, above all for those who are last in our unequal world.

Agenda for reflection and action

Personal orientation

- In which methodological paradigm do you find yourself and are you most comfortable? Does it matter?
- What has formed and framed your view of poverty? What adjectives and other words do you use to describe it? How do you think it fits with the views of poor people themselves?

Institutional action outside funding agencies

- Can you slow, stop, or reverse the spread of procedural lock-ins?
- Can you reduce their costs and the damage they do?
- Can you detect early signs of new lock-ins and help others prevent them?
- Can you refuse to comply or negotiate wriggle room?
- Can you help funders to appreciate realities?
- Can you support those in funding agencies who see the need for change?

Additional for funders

- Do power and distance distort your learning? What can you do about it?
- Can you make your internal procedures and external requirements less onerous?
- With any new procedure can you ensure unhurried, small-scale pilot testing?
- Can you find ways to make grants or loans adequate but no larger than they need to be?
- Can you allow unspent funds to be carried over into the next financial year?
- Can you resist pressures for inappropriate RCTs and find alternatives?
- Can you fund research on the hidden transaction costs of project procedures and bidding for grants?

Notes

1. Those who programmed my laptop were out of touch and out of date, for the plural – knowledges – shows with a wavy red line to indicate a misspelling, both in the text and in this note. The singular knowledge

of programmers may only perceive and permit one knowledge – theirs. (Since writing this I must eat my words: my laptop has taught itself or been taught and removed the red line.)

2. It is striking how limited our understanding of the universe is, and how plural and provisional theories of its nature are, with little understood imponderables like dark matter, dark energy, gravity, quantum processes, and what if any limits there are to the universe in time and space, reminding me of Einstein's remark, 'Two things are infinite: the universe and human stupidity, and I'm not sure about the universe'.

3. The concept of paradigm, and these two paradigms, are elaborated in Chapter 4.

4. Positionality is another word the programmers do not like. Its use is, after all, relatively recent and I have only just begun to dare to use it. Here I use it to refer to a person's social situation, context, and relationships.

5. Tempting though it is, I will not explore the analogy of *lock-in* as the term for hiding those who wish to continue drinking in a bar after closing time.

6. At an RRA (Rapid Rural Appraisal) Conference at IDS in 1979, Rosalind Eyben recounted her preference for secondary school pupils to university graduates as field research assistants, saying something like 'By the time they leave university, the damage has been done'.

7. These bald summaries omit the qualifications and subtleties of the work of Booth and Rowntree. For a summary and some criticisms see Holman (1978: 2–13).

8. In *Seeing Like a State*, James Scott (1998) does not mention poverty lines. Knowing the extent and location of poverty was not a priority in the cases he presents, but his arguments and analysis apply as well to poverty, once it became important for the state to know about it.

9. While participant observation has been their overarching approach, social anthropologists have employed a wide range of methods. See for example Pelto and Pelto (1978).

10. See also *The Anthropological Lens* (Peacock, 1986).

11. For this illustration of extraordinary differences in survey findings, I am grateful to Payal Hathi of the Rice Institute and a note she prepared for the Ministry of Drinking Water and Sanitation.

12. One extravagant claim for RCTs is: 'Britain has given the world Shakespeare, Newtonian physics, the theory of evolution, parliamentary democracy – and the randomized trial', quoted by Deaton (2009: 438). Never mind the jingoism, the irony is that with RCTs the mechanistic paradigm of Newtonian physics is part of the problem.

13. Why mechanistic methodologies spread so fast would repay research.

14. I am not passing any judgement. The topic – behaviour and effects of clean and dirty environments on infant and child growth and health, and testing measures – is of immense importance. It is just unfortunate that the quasi-medical methodology has such high costs, including opportunity costs of professionals' time and delays in learning. Perhaps there could have been less 'rigorous', cheaper, and faster alternatives with participatory and iterative learning (for which see Chapters 4 and 5).

15. For an open letter from the CLTS Knowledge Hub and the World Bank team's response, see CLTS Knowledge Hub (2015) visit http://www.communityledtotalsanitation.org/blog/open-letter-response-world-development-report-2015.
16. The curious reader is referred to the original of Loevinsohn et al. (2014) for detail of the painstaking and credible methodology applied to this systematic review of systematic reviews.
17. I am not alone in having twice learned that my budget for a project was too small. In one case it was funded after we had increased it to more than we wanted or felt was needed. However, we adapted, I hope responsibly and cost-effectively.
18. The Indian Government in 2016 agreed a PbR contract with the World Bank for $1.5 bn for rural sanitation, with independent verification. The Indian Government is thus a very large, well-funded contractor and does not seriously need the money, but may welcome the conditionality. I recollect a possibly apocryphal anecdote from the 1980s. In the presence of other Indian officials, a World Bank representative was negotiating and arguing with his Indian opposite number. In a tea break the Indian said to him: 'You are weakening, for goodness sake – don't!' Credible conditionality can empower down the aid chain.
19. The story is not simple. As so often, multiple causes contributed to the liquidity crisis of the organization. But it seems without question that PbR was a major one. And both donor and recipient displayed ignorance and irresponsibility in a *folie à deux* by agreeing astronomically unrealistic targets.
20. A 2016 blog by Duncan Green elaborates on negative aspects as well as presenting some positive angles.
21. The original research was conducted by Luisa Orza. For more detail of the calculations see the original blog in Stevenson (2015).
22. In about 2010 when Dutch INGOs were facing brutally intensified requirements for funding, a group agreed to meet and brainstorm alternatives. But to my knowledge, nothing happened.
23. In late 2015 when I asked some 150 professional evaluators in the biennial conclave of the Community of Evaluators South Asia how many of them had changed a theory of change in the course of a project, only about five raised their hands. In the USA at a similar meeting of the American Evaluation Association in 2016 the proportion was much higher.
24. 'I spoke with the heads of INGOs that you would instantly recognize, as they have become household names. I came away acutely aware that while we criticize commercial business for giving primacy to ensuring stakeholder value over customers, these huge non-profits have simply substituted donors for shareholders and seem to forget that their primary clients are the poor they are intended to serve', Pamela Hartigan, personal communication, January 2013.
25. When Melissa Leach took over as Director of IDS she stimulated and encouraged us to reimagine ourselves. On a door in the men's toilet someone put up a sheet proclaiming 'I am IDS' conscience. Help me to reimagine myself'. Underneath someone had written: 'LET'S SPEAK TRUTH TO

POWER'. Someone else had written under that: ' YES, IF SOMEONE WILL FUND US'.
26. I was involved in a team bidding for funding from DFID for a research project. This was in the 1990s when DFID could still make fairly small grants. Having submitted our proposal, DFID demanded a logframe. We refused. There was a tense silence for a few weeks and then we heard we had been successful. But this was not a competitive bid. And we were in a strong position because two months earlier the minister had said in a speech that the research had already started.
27. DFID called a meeting of NGOs and research organizations to elaborate the procedures for applying for a large pot of money for work on sanitation. More than three projects were unlikely to be supported. This required either very large organizations or consortia. The CLTS Knowledge Hub which I represented was small and would have to join a consortium. Those in the meeting had been frustrated by delays on the DFID side. No one spoke up about this, so towards the end I did, urging DFID to move faster. I do not think anyone in DFID took this badly. But we were not included in any of the consortia of organizations with whom we had good working relations. Later I was told that my remarks had been taken to indicate that we were not interested in bidding.
28. In the late 1990s ActionAid (now ActionAid International) had a damagingly heavy reporting system. Two attempts to reform it – one by redesign and one by asking heads of departments their absolute minimum data needs – ended up as bad as the original. The radical chief executive sent six people away to be cut off for a week and come back with ruthless recommendations. These gave birth to ALPS (Accountability, Learning and Planning System) which has evolved to survive today, and influenced several other INGOs.

References

Alzua, M.L., Pickering, A., Djebarri, H., Lopez, C., Cardenas, J.C., Lopera, M.A. Osbert, N., and Coulibaly, M. (2015) *Final Report: Impact Evaluation of Community-Led Total Sanitation in Rural Mali*, Working Paper, Argentina: Universidad Nacional de La Plata.

Ananthpur, K., Malik, K. and Rao, V. (2014) *The Anatomy of Failure: An Ethnography of a Randomized Trial to Deepen Democracy in Rural India*, Washington, DC: Poverty and Inequality Team, Development Research Group, World Bank.

Anderson, M.B., Brown, D. and Jean, I. (2012) *Time to Listen: Hearing People on the Receiving End of International Aid*, Cambridge, MA: CDA Collaborative Learning Projects.

Banerjee, A. and Duflo, E. (2011) *Poor Economics: Rethinking Poverty and the Ways to End it*, Noida, India: Random House.

Barnard, S., Routray, P., Majorin, F., Peletz, R., Boisson, S., Sinha, A. and Clasen, T. (2013) 'Impact of Indian Total Sanitation Campaign on latrine coverage and use: a cross-sectional study in Orissa three years following programme implementation', *PloS ONE* 8(8): e71438 <http://dx.doi.org/10.1371/journal.pone.0071438>.

Benova, L., Cumming, O. and Campbell, O. (2014) 'Systematic review and meta-analysis: association between water and sanitation environment and maternal mortality', *Tropical Medicine and International Health* 19(4): 368–87 <http://dx.doi.org/10.1111/tmi.12275>.

Brokensha, D.W., Warren, D.M. and Werner, O. (eds) (1980) *Indigenous Systems of Knowledge and Development*, Lanham, MD: University Press of America.

Chambers, R. (1983) *Rural Development: Putting the Last First*, Harlow: Longman.

Chambers, R. (1997) *Whose Reality Counts? Putting the First Last*, Rugby, UK: Practical Action Publishing.

Chambers, R. (2005) *Ideas for Development*, London and Sterling VA: Earthscan.

Chambers, R. (2014) 'Perverse payment by results: frogs in a pot and strait-jackets for obstacle courses' [blog], IDS (posted 3 September 2014) <https://participationpower.wordpress.com/2014/09/03/perverse-payment-by-results-frogs-in-a-pot-and-straitjackets-for-obstacle-courses/?utm_content=buffer3133a&utm_medium=social&utm_source=facebook.com&utm_campaign=buffer> [accessed 16 December 2016].

Chatterley, C., Javernick-Will, A., Linden, K., Alam, K., Bottinelli, L. and Venkatesh, M. (2014) 'A qualitative comparative analysis of well-managed school sanitation in Bangladesh', *BMC Public Health* 14(6) <http://dx.doi.org/10.1186/1471-2458-14-6>.

CLTS Knowledge Hub (2015) *An open letter in response to the World Development Report 2015*, Institute of Development Studies, <http://www.communityledtotalsanitation.org/blog/open-letter-response-world-development-report-2015> [accessed 27 February 2017].

Coffey, D., Gupta, A., Hathi, P., Khurana, N., Spears, D., Srivasta, N. and Vyas, S. (2014a) 'Revealed preference for open defecation', *Economic and Political Weekly* 49(38): 43.

Coffey, D., Gupta, A., Hathi, P., Khurana, N., Spears, D., Srivasta, N. and Vyas, S. (2014b) *Culture and the Health Transition: Understanding Sanitation Behaviour in Rural North India*, Working paper, RICE Institute.

Dangour, A.D., Watson, L., Cumming, O., Boisson, S., Che, Y., Veeleman, Y., Cavill, S., Allen, E. and Uauy, R. (2013) 'Interventions to improve water quality and supply, sanitation and hygiene practices, and their effects on the nutritional status of children (Review)', *Cochrane Database Systematic Reviews* 8: CD009382 <http://dx.doi.org/10.1002/14651858.CD009382.pub2>.

Deaton, A. (2009) *Instruments of Development Randomization in the Tropics and the Search for the Elusive Keys to Economic Development*, Working Paper 14690, New York: National Bureau of Economic Research.

Dreibelbis, R., Greene, L.E., Freeman, M.C., Saboori, S., Chase, R.P. and Rheingans, R. (2012) 'Water, sanitation, and primary school attendance: a multi-level assessment of determinants of household-reported absence in Kenya', *International Journal of Educational Development* 33(5): 457–65 <http://dx.doi.org/10.1016/j.ijedudev.2012.07.002>.

Duflo, E and Banerjee, A (2011) Poor Economics: a radical rethinking of the way to fight global poverty. Random House, London.

EES (2007) *EES Statement: the importance of a methodologically diverse approach to impact evaluation – specifically with respect to development aid and development interventions*, Nijkerk, The Netherlands: European Evaluation Society.

Eyben, R., Guijt, I., Roche, C. and Shutt, C. (eds) (2015) *The Politics of Evidence and Results in International Development: Playing the Game to Change the Rules*, Rugby, UK: Practical Action Publishing <http://dx.doi. org/10.3362/9781780448855>.

Faulkner, W. (2013) *Negotiated Validity: Three Perspectives on IFPRI-PROGRESA's Sampling*, London: The Evaluator.

Gasper, D. (2000) 'Evaluating the "logical framework approach": towards learning-oriented development evaluation', *Public Adminis-tration and Development* 20(1): 17–28 http://onlinelibrary.wiley.com/ doi/10.1002/1099-162X(200002)20:1%3C17::AID-PAD89%3E3.0.CO; 2-5/full.

Gasper, D. (2008) 'The logical framework: a list of useful documents', *Monitoring and Evaluation News*, 1 January.

Gladwell, M. (2009) *Outliers: The Story of Success*, London: Penguin Books.

Green, D. (2016) 'Payment by results in aid: hype or hope?' [blog], *The Guardian* <www.theguardian.com/global-development-professionals-network/2016/ apr/12/payment-by-results-aid-evidence-for-against?CMP=ema-1702&CMP> (posted 12 April 2016) [accessed 16 December 2016].

Haswell, M. (1975) *The Nature of Poverty: A Case History of the First Quarter-Century after World War II*, Basingstoke: Macmillan.

Hayman, R., King, S., Kontinen, T. and Narayanaswamy, L. (eds) (2016) *Negotiating Knowledge: Evidence and Experience in Development NGOs*, Rugby, UK: Practical Action Publishing.

Hill, P. (1977) *Population, Prosperity and Poverty: Rural Kano 1900 and 1970*, Cambridge: Cambridge University Press.

Holman, R. (1978) *Poverty: Explanations for Social Deprivation*, Oxford: Martin Robertson.

Howes, M. and Chambers, R. (1979) 'Indigenous technical knowledge: analy-sis, implications and issues', *IDS Bulletin* 10(2): 5–11.

Loevinsohn, M., Mehta, L., Cuming, K., Nicol, A., Cumming, O. and Ensink, J. (2014) 'The cost of a knowledge silo: a systematic re-review of water, sani-tation and hygiene interventions', *Health Policy and Planning* 2014: 1–15 <http://dx.doi.org/10.1093%2Fheapol%2Fczu039>.

Lu, C. (2012) *Poverty and Development in China: Alternative Approaches to Poverty Assessment*, Abingdon, UK: Routledge.

Myrdal, G. (1970) *The Challenge of World Poverty: A World Anti-Poverty Programme in Outline*, Harmondsworth, UK: Penguin Books.

Peacock, J.L. (1986) *The Anthropological Lens: Harsh Light, Soft Focus*, Cambridge: Cambridge University Press.

Pelto, P.J. and Pelto, G.H. (1978) *Anthropoloigcal Research: the Structure of Inquiry*, 2nd edition, Cambridge: Cambridge University Press.

Rehfuss, E. and Bartram, J. (2013) 'Beyond direct impact: evidence synthesis towards a better understanding of effectiveness of environmental health interventions', *International Journal of Hygiene and Environmental Health* 217(2–3): 155–9 <http://dx.doi.org/10.1016/j.ijheh.2013.07.011>.

Rose, T. (2016) *The End of Average: How to Succeed in a World that Values Sameness*, London: Allen Lane, Penguin Random House.

Schmidt, W. (2014) 'The elusive effect of water and sanitation on the global burden of disease', *Tropical Medicine and International Health* 19(5): 522–7 <http://dx.doi.org/10.1111/tmi.12286>.

Scott, J. (1998) *Seeing Like a State: How Certain Schemes to Improve the Human Condition Have Failed*, New Haven, CT: Yale University Press.

Shaffer, P. (2011) 'Against excessive rhetoric in impact assessment: overstating the case for randomised controlled experiments', *Journal of Development Studies* 47(11): 1619–35.

Sijbesma, C., Sikoki, B., Suriastini, W. and Ponsonby, M. (2011) 'Methodological lessons and findings from an impact evaluation of a WASH project in Indonesia', refereed paper 1096, *35th WEDC International Conference*, Loughborough, UK.

Spears, D. (2012) *How Much International Variation in Child Height Can Sanitation Explain?* Working Paper, New Delhi: Rice Institute.

Spears, D. (2013) *How Much International Variation in Child Height Can Sanitation Explain?* Policy Research Working Paper 6351, Washington, DC: World Bank.

Spears D, (2014a) *Increasing average exposure to Open Defecation in India 2001-2011*, http://riceinstitute.org/wordpress/wp-content/uploads/downloads/2014/06/Spears-2014-increasing-OD-density.pdf [accessed 28 August 2014].

Spears D, (2014b) *The nutritional value of toilets: sanitation and international variation in height*, 2014 version, first circulated 2012 http://riceinstitute.org/wordpress/wp-content/uploads/downloads/2013/07/Spears-height-and-sanitation-6-2013.pdf [accessed 28 August 2014].

Spicker, P. (2007) *The Idea of Poverty,* Bristol: Policy Press.

Stevenson, J. (2015) 'All the things we could do, if we had a little money: the costs of funding women's rights work' [blog], *Huffington Post* <www.huffingtonpost.co.uk/jacquistevenson/womens-rights-funding_b_7449872.html> (posted 5 June 2015) [accessed 16 December 2016].

Tourangeau, R., Rips, L.J. and Rasinski, K. (2000) *The Psychology of Survey Response*, Cambridge, UK: Cambridge University Press.

Van Es, M. and Guijt, I. (2015) 'Theory of change as best practice or next trick to perform? Hivos' journey with strategic reflection', in R. Eyben, I. Guijt, C. Roche, and C. Shutt (eds), *The Politics of Evidence and Results in International Development*, pp. 95–114, Rugby, UK: Practical Action Publishing.

Venkataraman, V. (2012) *Testing CLTS Approaches for Scalability: Systematic Literature Review*, Washington, DC: Plan International USA; Chapel Hill, NC: The Water Institute, University of North Carolina.

Waddington, H., Snilsvelt, B., White, H. and Fewtrell, L. (2009) *Water, Sanitation and Hygiene Interventions to Combat Childhood Diarrhoea in Developing Countries*, Synthetic Review 001, Delhi: International Initiative for Impact Evaluation.

Waller, R. (1999) 'Pastoral poverty in historical perspective', in D.M. Anderson and V. Broch-Due (eds), *The Poor Are Not Us: Poverty and Pastoralism in East Africa*, Oxford: James Currey.

World Bank (2015) *Mind, Society and Behaviour,* World Development Report 2015, Washington, DC: World Bank.

Zwane, A.P., Zinman, J., Van Dusen, E., Pariente, W., Null, C., Miguel, E., Kremer, M., Karlan, D.S., Hornbeck, R., Ginéb, X., Duflo, E., Devoto, F., Crepon, B., and Banerjee, A. (2011) *The Risk of Asking: Being Surveyed Can Affect Later Behavior* 108(5): 1821–6 <http://dx.doi.org/10.1073/pnas.1000776108>.

CHAPTER 4
Rigour for complexity

Abstract

Rigour is set in the context of coexisting paradigms: Newtonian for physical things; and complexity for people and social processes. Newtonian rigour is reductionist. For complexity with emergence, non-linearity and unpredictability, rigour can be sought through critical inclusiveness. Canons for an inclusive rigour for complexity are: eclectic methodological pluralism and mixed methods; seeking diversity and balance; improvisation and innovation; adaptive iteration; triangulation; inclusive participation and plural perspectives; optimal ignorance and appropriate imprecision; and interactive and experiential ground-truthing. Pervasively these are underpinned by rigour from participation, reflexivity, and responsible relevance. Inclusive rigour is inherent in well-facilitated participatory methods and approaches, visualizations, group-visual synergy, the democracy of the ground, and participatory statistics. The Participatory Impact Assessment and Learning Approach in Vietnam, Ghana, and Myanmar is an example of eclectic methodological pluralism and creative adaptability. The sugar industry in Kenya and rural sanitation in India illustrate how complex, wicked, messy conditions require multiple action and learning strategies. Transparent reflexivity, personal behaviour and attitudes, and good facilitation are fundamental. Fully inclusive rigour for complexity often demands radical personal, institutional, and professional reorientation.

Keywords: Newtonian, complexity, paradigms, canons, plural, inclusive, reflexivity, rigour

> I can calculate the movements of heavenly bodies, but not the madness of men. (Isaac Newton on the South Sea Bubble, quoted in Ramalingam, 2013: 165)
>
> World is crazier and more of it than we think, Incorrigibly plural. (*Snow*, by Louis MacNeice)
>
> Rigour: the quality of being extremely thorough and careful. (Oxford English Dictionary)

Exploring: an invitation

This chapter is an exploration. I may have missed something but until recently rigour for complexity seems to have been a blind spot. Exploring is fun but also risky. There can be the thrill of Aha!s and the unexpected but also holes

http://dx.doi.org/10.3362/9781780449449.004

to fall into. What follow are neither normal ideas of rigour nor an exposition on complexity. This is rather an attempt to find signposts and compasses to guide travel and provisionally map a terrain. I invite readers to join me and challenge them to reflect for themselves and map and share better ways of navigating and knowing.

The paradigmatic context

Paradigms: from Kuhn to complexity

The word paradigm was popularized by Thomas Kuhn in his classic *The Structure of Scientific Revolutions* (1962). For him a paradigm was a strong network of commitments – conceptual, theoretical, instrumental, and methodological – in physical sciences such as astronomy, physics, and chemistry. In his analysis of paradigm changes, he reviewed many examples besides the better known ones associated with Galileo, Copernicus, Newton, Lavoisier, and Einstein. In his historiography of science, Kuhn showed how revolutionary transformations had taken place, meeting at first resistance, especially among older scientists, and then increasingly with a 'gestalt switch', a transformation of vision, a conversion experience that could not be forced. The new paradigm then became 'normal science', implanted and sustained through textbooks, and generating research which sought to solve puzzles within the paradigm until an accumulation of anomalies precipitated a further shift to another paradigm. Kuhn's focus was on the physical sciences. He was little concerned with biology or with the social sciences apart from noting that they were different.

To include the social sciences, and for all sciences to include behavioural, relational, and psychological dimensions, I propose a more inclusive meaning for paradigm as: 'a coherent and mutually supporting pattern of concepts and ontological assumptions; values and principles; methods, procedures and processes; roles and behaviours; relationships; and mindsets, orientations and predispositions' (see Figure 4.1).

A contrast can then be drawn between Newtonian and Complexity paradigms.[1] The Newtonian paradigm is fitting for physical things that are controllable, measurable, predictable, and with a linear logic towards equilibrium; the Complexity paradigm is fitting for people and processes that are uncontrollable, harder to measure, unpredictable, and with non-linear logic towards emergence. Roles and behaviours, relationships, mindsets, orientations, and predispositions contrast between the two paradigms. As we saw in Chapter 3, top-down, standardized, mechanistic procedures have increasingly dominated in many agencies and governments and in development policy and practice, reflecting a shift of balance from Complexity to Newtonian.

Binary contrasts like this polarize, exaggerate differences, and even caricature. They can be simplistic. Norman Uphoff (1992) has made a

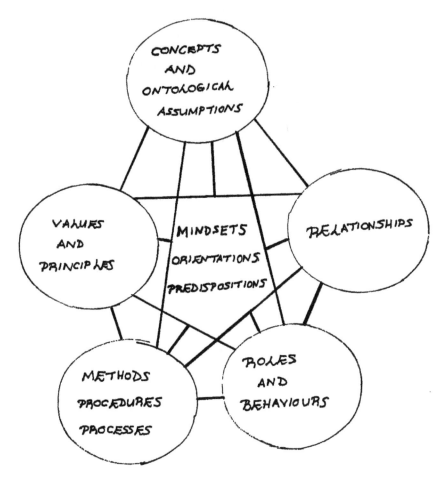

Figure 4.1 Basic elements in a paradigm

convincing case for approaches which are not either-or but inclusively both-and. A balanced view can be that it is neither either-or nor both-and, but the right combination and mix of these according to context and need. That said, and for all their limitations and with all the qualifications which are in order, binaries often have heuristic and practical value. They can help identify syndromes of elements and relationships. The two postulated paradigms are outlined in Figures 4.2 and 4.3, and Table 4.1.

Analysis and illustration of the many characteristics, linkages, contrasts, and tensions postulated by the table and the figures could make a book in themselves. Each double-headed arrow is an assertion and a set of hypotheses. How valid and useful they are for analytical and practical purposes is a matter

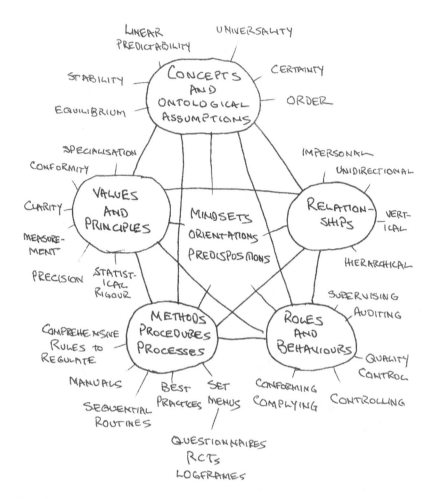

Figure 4.2 Elements in a paradigm of Newtonian practice

for judgement, verification, refutation, and/or modification. If they provoke reflection and improvement, they will have served a purpose.

Inclusive rigour for complexity

Meanings and forms of 'rigour'

Each paradigm has its appropriate definition and form of rigour. The dominant meaning of rigour is 'lack of bias' (Befani et al., 2014: 2). Those authors observe authorities exhibiting a hierarchy of degrees of rigour from

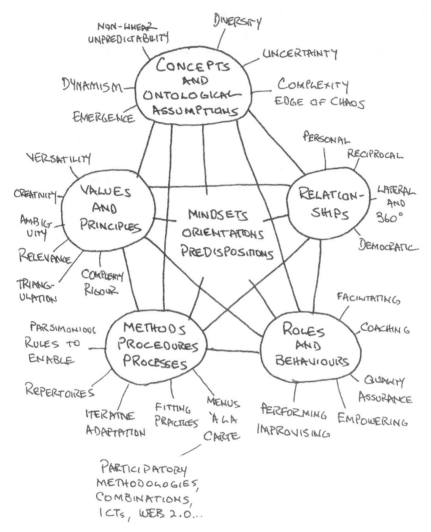

Figure 4.3 Elements in a paradigm of adaptive pluralism

randomized control trials (RCTs), through quasi-experiments, mixed methods, and qualitative methods. In this interpretation, the highest degrees of rigour are achieved through reductionism – simplifying and standardizing in order to generate statistics which can be analysed according to well-accepted rules of best practice which can be found in manuals. This reductionist rigour is applied in controlled or controllable scientific and medical research and can be appropriate for some phenomena and conditions which are or can be standardized and controlled, and are relatively stable, uniform, and predictable.

Table 4.1 Characteristics of Newtonian and Complexity paradigms

Paradigm	Newtonian	Complexity
Ontological origins and assumptions	Things, the physical world Newtonian science Order Laws of nature Linearity, predictability	People, the social world Complexity science Edge of chaos Emergence Non-linearity, unpredictability
Pervasive concepts	Universality Uniformity, stability, equilibrium Controllability, predictability	Local specificity Diversity, dynamism, emergence Uncontrollability, unpredictability
Methods, procedures, processes	Standardized Sequential routines Fixed menu Manuals Best practices	Pluralist Iterative adaptation À la carte and combinations Source books Fitting practices
Embodying and expressing	Comprehensive rules to regulate Conventions, conformity	Parsimonious rules to enable Originality, inventiveness
Roles and behaviours	Supervising Auditing Controlling Conforming, complying	Facilitating Coaching Empowering Performing, improvising
Favoured and prevailing approaches and methods include	Questionnaires RCTs Logframes	Interactive analysis Participatory methodologies Participatory M and E
Relationships	Vertical Hierarchical Impersonal Unidirectional	Lateral and 360 degree Democratic Personal Reciprocal
Goals, design, and indicators	Planned, preset, fixed	Negotiated, evolving, emergent

This form of rigour is problematic in conditions of complexity where there is multiple causality combined with being diverse, difficult to control or uncontrollable, emergent, non-linear, and unpredictable. The question then is, what is rigorous when, in various combinations, treatments are not or cannot be standardized, receiving environments are diverse, controls liable to contamination, measurements difficult, unreliable or impossible, causality multiple and intertwined, and/or problems messy, wicked, and not amenable to obvious or straightforward solutions. In short, what is rigour for knowing and acting in complexity?

Rigour for knowing in conditions of complexity needs a different definition. One option would be to use a word other than rigour. This might be taken to imply that rigour could not be achieved for conditions of complexity or only by applying Newtonian reductionist simplifications. Van Hemelrijck and Guijt (2016), drawing on and referring to their practice in the pioneering Participatory Impact Assessment and Learning Approach (PIALA, see later) evaluation broaden the definition of rigour to:

> the quality of thought put into the methodological design and conduct of every step in the evaluation – including sampling, triangulation of methods, facilitation of processes, data collation, cross-validation, and causal analysis – to ensure both consistency and responsiveness to the purposes and constraints of the evaluation...

They also discuss the trade-offs between rigour, inclusiveness, and feasibility. Or, in the Root and Tuber Improvement and Marketing Programme (RTIMP) evaluation report (Van Hemelrijck and Kyei-Mensah, 2015):

> Rigour is understood in terms of methodological consistency and reliability of methods and the rigorous facilitation of participatory processes. Acknowledging that an evaluation is never power-neutral and entirely free from political influence or organizational pressure, especially when using participatory methods, rigour must be defined broader than in purely statistical terms and also include quality thinking, sharp observation, engaging multiple perspectives and systematic cross-checking.

I agree with this widening of the span of meaning to include quality of thought and behaviour, and applying this to every step in an approach. Rigour for complexity has to be inclusive, with multiple dimensions and criteria, recognizing, weighing, and optimizing trade-offs between these, applicable at all stages of a process. This then raises questions of what counts as costs, benefits, and cost-effectiveness. A working definition of inclusive rigour for complexity can be:

> Cost-effectiveness in useful learning. This entails optimizing trade-offs and complementarities between validity, credibility, timeliness, relevance and range of data, and scale of applicability, these weighed against costs.

In elaboration,

- The cost side of cost-effectiveness includes opportunity costs of:
  o finance and other resources;
  o stakeholders' time;
  o professional and other capacity development and learning forgone;
  o inflexibility and irreversibility of methodological and other commitments.
- On the benefit side, useful learning includes:
  o learning with direct, probable, or potential value for policy or practice;
  o professional learning and other capacity development.
- Validity refers to accuracy, lack of bias, and representativeness.

- Credibility means being believable.
- Timeliness refers to activities and findings being timely in relation to practical relevance and need.
- Relevance and range of data refer to data with direct, probable, or potential utility.
- Scale of applicability refers to how widely relevant the anticipated findings and learning are likely to be.

Cost-effectiveness in this sense can be applied to all research and interventions, including those based on reductionist rigour, whose advocates and practitioners tend to downplay factors such as comparative costs and timeliness. Rigour can be sought through practices which are fitting to context, purpose, and resources. To meet the needs of complex conditions, such practices will be found not in routines from manuals but in source books that present repertoires of approaches and methods which can be combined and adapted creatively. Rigour for complexity has to be, in its genes, plural and inclusive.

The personal dimension

A personal dimension is fundamental to inclusive rigour. Creativity, judgement, and choice are entailed. There is no RCT routine to relieve one of responsibility for deciding what needs to be done and at what stage.

Two aspects are vital and are elaborated further later. The first is behavioural – creative adaptability. This refers to creativity in adopting, adapting, and combining methodologies and methods. It requires being creative in modifying, improvising, and inventing approaches and methods to fit context and purpose, and being open to adapting, evolving, or abandoning them in the light of experience. To do this well entails being open-minded, inquisitive, sensitive, alert, flexible, and nimble.

The second aspect is epistemological, and part of the rebuttal to cries of subjectivity. This is 'self-critical epistemological awareness' (Chambers, 1997: 32, 203). This refers to reflexivity and critical awareness of one's mindset, predilections, preferences, and biases, to offsetting these, and to continuous learning, unlearning, and changing. Beyond this it is concerned with critical observation and analysis of the processes of knowledge formation including distortions resulting from power relations (all power deceives), positionality, relationships, and interactions. For credible rigour, critical awareness must be transparent.

Canons for methodological rigour

Canons are principles to inform and determine action. Here I put forward eight canons for methodological rigour, separated for clarity and emphasis though in practice there are overlaps.

Eclectic methodological pluralism. This means in practice using any of the rapidly multiplying repertoire of methodologies and methods. Mixed methods are in this mode and have been used widely as in 'the combination of qualitative and quantitative approaches in a single evaluation' (White, 2009: 280). Their span can be much wider than just quantitative and qualitative as these are normally understood. They can include action research (Bradbury, 2015) and action learning. The explosion of participatory methodologies described in Chapter 5 offers a growing range of feasible combinations and adaptations. An increasing number of these combine information and communication technologies (ICTs) with other methods. Visualizations with maps and diagrams bring their own forms of rigour. Just as the purpose and context of each inquiry are unique, so are the combinations and sequences that are fitting. Methods can be transferred and even packages of methods, but rigour can be sought in scanning the range of possibilities and adapting, combining, and co-evolving these for the special conditions of each inquiry.

Seeking diversity and balance. This applies widely to offset biases (see Chapter 2). The most pervasive and pernicious biases come from power and wealth, on the part of those who are 'first', to the neglect of and failure to listen to and learn from those who are 'last'. Another is central tendency bias – the tendency for perceptions and conclusions to be dominated by averages, the 'typical' and 'the normal' (Todd, 2016). It can be offset by seeking positive and negative deviants and learning from outliers (Gladwell, 2008), those who are atypical, 'listening to angry people' (White, 2009) and visiting unvisited places. It extends to seeking diversity of experience, hoping for and expecting surprises, serendipity and Aha!s to generate new insights and questions. If there are no deviants or surprises, learning may not be inclusive and open enough and something significant may be being missed. If there are surprises, whatever else is found will gain in credibility.

Improvisation and innovation. Jazz provides an analogy, with improvisation around a basic theme or pattern. Creative and unpredictable innovation follows. Approach and methods are not a supermarket packaged meal for heating in a microwave: they are cooked from raw materials selected to fit the occasion. The huge and growing range and accessibility of ingredients gives scope for new recipes, for ingredients added in the course of cooking, for unique mixtures, and new combinations and inventions.

Adaptive iteration. Approaches and methods evolve. Repeated iterative review asks what has been learned, what problems encountered, and what needs to change in the learning process. Adaptive iteration can optimize the benefits from mixed methods. Iteration between qualitative and quantitative inquiry adds to each, with qualitative informing quantitative, and quantitative generating questions for qualitative, and each changing, evolving, and getting closer to significant reality as a result. If nothing is seen to need to change, something may be being missed.

Triangulation. Triangulation through comparisons enhances validity and credibility. It entails cross-checking and successive approximation. Wherever there are discrepancies it raises questions, probing into and answering, which adds to validity and credibility. Triangulation can be methodological between elements such as:

- types of evidence: secondary, primary, visual, oral;
- methods;
- professions, disciplines, specializations;
- locations;
- people and groups of people;
- domains of inquiry: organizations, communities, technologies, farms, farming systems;
- measurements;
- case studies (Rogers and Peersman, 2014: 94–6).

Inclusive participation for plural perspectives. Inclusive participation by diverse stakeholders is a means of triangulating plural perspectives (Befani et al., 2015). Complex conditions become a flat earth when seen through only one lens. Much is missed. Most obviously there are the different perspectives of:

- sorts of people: poor and wealthy, women, men, children, youth, age groups, occupations, sexualities, social and ethnic categories, key informants, those who are experts (local and professional), people with different past experiences and knowledges, and differences between people within each category and how they crosscut;
- team members;
- institutions: professions, disciplines, and those in different organizations and departments.

The articulation and sharing of plural and conflicting perspectives can iteratively lead to new insights and enhance validity and credibility.

Optimal ignorance and appropriate imprecision. These entail not finding out more than is needed.[2] Reductionist rigour with its set paths is vulnerable to data overkill, and waste of time and resources, by finding out, measuring, and analysing more and more precisely than is needed for practical and policy purposes. This requires judging when successive approximation and precision have gone far enough.

Interactive and experiential ground-truthing. This is as obviously important as it is frequently neglected. It is direct experiential learning by outsiders in participatory modes instead of relying only on secondary sources. Immersions and reality checks (Chapter 5) are one means.

Rigour from plural synergies

In synergy with these methodological canons and interwoven with them are three superordinate principles or meta-canons: participation, reflexivity, and responsible relevance. They are intimately intertwined and synergistic with each other. Together they are like a pervasive medium that everywhere embodies, expresses, and enhances inclusive rigour.

Rigour from participation

Participatory approaches cover an extensive range. Methodologies with participatory elements include action research (Bradbury, 2015) and action learning (Pedler and Burgoyne, 2015). There are relevant schools or approaches to evaluation such as Michael Quinn Patton's *Developmental Evaluation* (2011), subtitled *Applying Complexity Concepts to Enhance Innovation and Use*, and Ray Pawson's (2013) *The Science of Evaluation*. These and others, in all their rich diversity, are articulated in an extensive literature and are relevant.[3] In parallel, and perhaps not fully on their radar, the past three decades have witnessed the explosive flowering and diversification of participatory methodologies (PMs), reviewed in Chapter 5. These PMs have been less fully analysed and documented. Their approaches and methods resonate with and support rigour for complexity. Here PMs are a key element in eclectic methodological pluralism. Increasingly they are adopted, adapted, and combined in creative ways. Involving people, they belong in the complexity paradigm and what goes under the name of development has people at or near the centre. People's realities – their lives and livelihoods, the multifarious conditions they experience, their relationships, values, awareness, and aspirations – are idiosyncratic and in continuous flux. People's realities have been described as local, complex, dynamic, diverse, uncontrollable, and unpredictable.[4] Only people themselves have expert knowledge of the complexities they experience. If people come first, and those who are last come first of all, the answer to the question, whose complexity counts? has to be, *theirs*. Beyond this are innumerable other who? whose? questions (see Chapter 5), including who analyses?

In these seminal past three decades we have learned that local people, including those who are poor, isolated, excluded, vulnerable, weak, unable to read, even shy and withdrawing have a far greater capacity for inquiry – for research, appraisal, analysis, planning, monitoring, evaluating, mapping, diagramming, generating statistics, and more – into the many dimensions of their lives and conditions than outside professionals had supposed or widely still suppose. The Participatory Rural Appraisal (PRA) saying 'They can do it' means having confidence in people's abilities to do things we are inclined to think they cannot do. Local people have repeatedly revealed much that professionals did not and could not know. And unlike most outside professionals most of the time, they are by definition completely in touch and up to date with the conditions they are experiencing. For inclusive rigour for inquiry into the complexities of their realities, participatory methodologies are fundamental (for more on this theme see Chambers, 2008: Chapters 5, 6, and 7).

The rigour of inclusiveness is inherent not just in participatory methodologies, but in many participatory processes, not least those associated with PRA. Social mapping is an example: millions of social maps have been made since 1990 when they began to spread within and from India.[5] In social mapping anyone present and taking part can 'see what is being said' and correct it or add to it. There are dangers of domination, but these are visible to facilitators, and power relations are often reversed as those who get down and map are often women and youth, empowered by 'the democracy of the ground', while the more powerful people are relatively marginalized, often standing watching or not being present at all. In most cases outsiders are quickly ignored. And what people choose to show indicates what is significant for them.

With visual methods like mapping and diagramming the facilitated process can be described as *group-visual synergy* (Figure 4.4). This combines canons of inclusive rigour – triangulation with mutual correction and cumulative representation and successive approximation – in the group-visual process often rich in detail.

Often group-visual processes take off and the role of the facilitator becomes observation. It is typically transparent that people are continuously adding and correcting detail, with little eye contact and dominance. Rigour is in the observed motivation, visible inclusiveness, cross-checking, and cumulative visible representation of the complex reality on which participants are the pre-eminent experts. For inclusiveness, visual representation has many advantages (Chambers, 1997: 150) including semi-permanent visibility and detail difficult to represent in words. This is manifest not just in mapping but in other visible, tactile methods associated with PRA such as matrix scoring, Venn (chapati, tortilla, dumpling...) diagramming, and seasonal diagramming. All of these allow the observation and judgement which are part of the rigour of a facilitated participatory process.

Participatory approaches and methods that are well facilitated and conducted play a major part in inclusive rigour. For ground-truthing the unpredictable and emergent diversities and commonalities of local complexities, Reality Checks stand out (see Chapter 5). Researchers stay with families in different communities representative of a range of conditions, and wander around, observe, chat, and listen, to become in touch and up to date, and then meet and share notes.

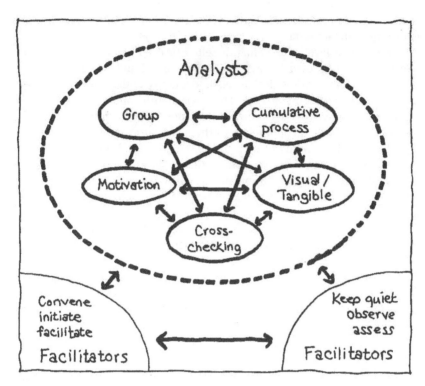

Figure 4.4 Group-visual synergy
Source: Chambers (1997: 160)

Rigour from reflexivity

The key phrase in the preceding paragraph is 'well facilitated and conducted'. Critics will say that a weakness of rigour from participation is the reliance on the fallibility and subjectivity of personal facilitation, observation, judgement, and action.

Appropriate personal behaviour and attitudes are pervasive priorities and cannot be taken for granted. The early stages of dissemination of any new participatory methodology which spreads fast are vulnerable to sloppy practice. This can come just when critical academics are beginning to take notice. This can lead to over-negative views and assertions of subjectivity, but bad practice in the early stages of spread has typically been reduced later. The response to the objection of subjective fallibility and bad practice has to be overt, transparent, and self-critical reflexivity to recognize and offset one's biases and the biases of research approaches and methods (see for example Camfield et al., 2014: 59), recognizing and learning from mistakes. Warts and all must be recognized and exposed: if no warts are shown, they may not have been recognized or if recognized, not revealed. For credibility as well as rigour, reflexivity is fundamental.

At a personal level, this demands self-critical epistemological awareness, reflecting on one's own behaviour, interactions, framings, categories, and mindset. At a methodological level, it demands critical examination and exposure of potential distortions. Those social anthropologists who tell stories against themselves,[6] recognizing their positionality and the distortions that result from how people relate to them, set an example. In all inquiries the validity and credibility of inclusive rigour could and should be enhanced by self-critical review of possible and actual errors and distortions. Arguably, this should include a description of the pathways followed by an inquiry, lessons learned and changes and adaptations made, together with an assessment of validity. One question to ask is whether any indicators have been altered in the course of an inquiry. For this can itself be an indicator of inclusive rigour through successive approximation and adaptation in a dynamic environment.

Reflecting critically on process, biases, perceptions, and how all power distorts and deceives, should be a key part of all research and evaluation. Its application with mechanistic methodologies such as RCTs has, however, been quite limited. An exception noted in Chapter 3 was a study that found the questionnaires used in an RCT had affected later behaviour and so introduced a bias (Zwane et al., 2011).[7] The potential for spurious correlations with questionnaire-based RCTs to result from uniformities in interview relationships and interactions remains a neglected area. Transparent critical reflexivity should be part of all rigour, reductionist as well as inclusive.

The rigour of responsible relevance

Reflexivity applies to the rigour of relevance, referring to usefulness or value added. In *Whose Reality Counts?* I saw the rigour of relevance in participatory approaches as combining:

> optimal ignorance and personal responsibility. This means that methods or processes are not facilitated for their own sake, but only if they make sense in the context. Judgement here is not simple. Facilitators often do not know what they do not know: the routine facilitation of a method may turn up a significant surprise. Participation in a method can be relevant to process by building confidence in a local person or group even if its direct output is irrelevant. What will be relevant may also be knowable only after the event, when priorities have been identified and actions planned. Good judgement may for these reasons mean facilitating a wide range of analysis in the early stages... The rigour of relevance... requires continuous reflection on the potential utility of process and analysis... (Chambers, 1997: 159–60)

In other words, the rigour of relevance is in cost-effectively optimizing useful-ness throughout a research or learning process. This requires critical reflection, triage, and iterative adaptation across all dimensions.

Now, in 2016, *responsible* can be added to *relevance*. Responsible relevance goes further than optimizing usefulness. It relates especially to research rela-tionships. It entails judgements and choices in order to optimize the benefits to all who participate; it means trying to avoid use of their time or resources on what will bring them no benefits. It means searching for activities from which all stand to gain. Imponderables about costs and benefits, both foreseen and unforeseen, and unpredictable serendipity, will remain. Fully responsible relevance demands continuous awareness, questioning, and reflexivity.

Pioneering rigour at scale

Complexity at scale raises the challenges of rigour to a new level. Fortunately, inspiring examples show what can be done by those who follow the canons of rigour and combine participation with reflexivity and responsible relevance.

PIALA in Ghana

PIALA (Participatory Impact Assessment and Learning Approach) began in pilot form first for an impact evaluation of the Doing Business with the Rural Poor Project in southern Vietnam (Van Hemelrijck and Kyei-Mensah, 2015; Van Hemelrijck, 2016a, b; Van Hemelrijck and Guijt, 2016). Lessons learned there were then incorporated in an evaluation of the Root and Tuber Improvement and Marketing Programme (RTIMP) in Ghana which is considered here. The RTIMP evaluation was conducted in 30 community clusters in 25 districts in Ghana and involved four products, each with its own supply chain. There were many domains and stakeholders: small farmer production, processing and market-linking, various funds and mechanisms including and mediated through district stakeholder forums, supply chain facilitation, farmer field forums, a micro-enterprise fund, information, education and communication, and good practice centres. The programme was implemented in many ways by many actors and in varied conditions from which a diversity of impacts over time could be expected. It was complex and diverse.

Eclectic methodological pluralism and creative adaptability were much in evidence. The team that evolved the approach was versatile, innovative, and experienced with participatory approaches and methods including PRA. Consider some of what they did. In a participatory process with stakehold-ers they developed a theory of change (ToC) diagram with 22 linked boxes, applicable separately to each of the four supply chains. Methods were selected specific to the causal links in the ToC and the evaluation questions. The meth-ods used combined a household questionnaire and conventional statistical analysis, key informant semi-structured interviews with many stakeholders including district officials and service providers, and focus groups and participatory approaches for generic change analysis, livelihood analysis, and constituent feedback.

Innovative methods were also employed in the analysis. Three of these embodying principles of rigour for complexity deserve special mention. The first was daily reflective practice and quality monitoring in the field (Van Hemelrijck and Kyei-Mensah, 2015: 39). For an average of two hours every evening, research teams reflected on research processes and outcomes during the day, guided by 'Were we able...?' and 'How well did we...?' questions, and reviewing conditions and power issues that could have influenced the data and generated biases.

The second was sense-making workshops. These were a two-stage process that engaged all stakeholders, including 'beneficiaries', in a collective analysis and discussion of the evidence. Twenty-three half-day workshops were conducted at local levels and a two-day workshop at national level. This sense-making took place not as is usual after the evaluation to make sense of findings, but during the evaluation itself with successive checking, triangulation, and learning contributing to the process. In the national sense-making workshop, focus groups reconstructed the causal flow of the theory of change with the evidence that had been obtained from the 25 districts as the basis for contribution scoring. The rigour of timeliness and relevant usefulness was sought by enabling stakeholders to engage with the evidence well before the final reporting and by a focus on practical policy, on what in the light of the findings should be done.

The third innovation was configurational analysis (Van Hemelrijck and Kyei-Mensah, 2015: 43–4). At the design stage, the idea of a counterfactual 'clean' (not treated, and not confounded or influenced) control met with no enthusiasm among a core learning group: a clean counterfactual would have been difficult or impossible to assure, and it was considered that resources would be better devoted to systemic inquiry into the four supply chains. The purpose of configurational analysis was to arrive at 'rigorous causal inference in the absence of clean control groups' (Van Hemelrijck and Kyei-Mensah, 2015: xvii). The counterfactual learning came not from predetermined controls (with all the risks and costs they would have incurred) but from areas where it was found that the programme had been relatively ineffective. Data from the districts were clustered and causal links analysed and scored in terms of contribution.

PIALA is an approach, not a specific methodology. In principle it could adopt any of a wide range of methods and adapt its building components, so long as it is consistent with its key principles of rigorous and systemic thinking and enabling voice. Its more or less standard pack of methods and tools has been expanded and adapted in an effectiveness review of Oxfam's work in Myanmar (Van Hemelrijck, 2016a). The creative methodological pluralism, sequences, iteration, reflection on data quality, facilitated participation, triangulation, successive approximation, and concern with learning for the future combine to make this evaluation rigorous and credible. On responsible relevance, learning was continuous with feedback to policy and practice especially through the sense-making workshops.

The Vietnam and Ghana evaluations cost about $483,000 of which $160,000 ($100,000 and $60,000 respectively) was for developing and pilot testing the methodology and documenting in great detail the processes and decisions affecting the quality of the evaluation, and $323,000 ($90,000 and $233,000 respectively) was for the two evaluations proper. The development and pilot testing costs were essential, as were patience, understanding, and support from the sponsors (the International Fund for Agricultural Development and the Bill & Melinda Gates Foundation). The total cost for this complicated multi-site evaluation was much less than for most rural RCTs which often cost more than $1 m (see Chapter 3). Moreover, through its inclusive rigour, the final PIALA report (van Hemelrijck and Kyei-Mensah, 2015) achieved a high level of validity, credibility, and relevance.

Additional benefits which may not have been fully foreseen were innovations in participatory methodologies of which the whole evaluation sector should be aware; insights into trade-offs between rigour, inclusiveness, and feasibility (Van Hemelrijck and Guijt, 2016); and an inspiring example of how the boundaries of evaluation practice and other inquiry can be pushed beyond what many would have considered the limits of the possible (Van Hemelrijck, 2016a, b).

A caveat is in order. The teams were exceptional in their experience, commitment, and ability to innovate. These qualities cannot be assumed. They point towards the worldwide shortage of such people and the need to multiply them, taken up in Chapter 6.

Rigour from systemic approaches

Inclusive rigour resonates with and is manifest in systemic action research (Burns, 2007; Burns and Worsley, 2015), which combines systems thinking and complexity science. Systems thinking has roots far back in cybernetics (Wiener, 1948) while complexity science has emerged mainly in the past three decades (Waldrop, 1994) and been articulated and related to international development only in the past 10 years or so, most definitively by Ben Ramalingam. His earlier explorations and reviews (e.g. Ramalingam et al., 2008) were followed by his *Aid on the Edge of Chaos: Rethinking International Cooperation in a Complex World* (2013), an accessible and magisterial overview. It is timely, if tardy, for systems thinking and complexity science to inform the mainstream of action inquiry, action, and evaluation in development to countervail Newtonian dominance.

Systemic action research has been a practical, embodied flag-bearer. In Danny Burns's words, systemic action research is:

> about achieving holistic change in complex social and organizational settings... complex issues cannot be adequately comprehended in

isolation from the wider system of which they are a part. Effective whole system change has to be underpinned by processes of in-depth inquiry, multi-stakeholder analysis, experimental action and experiential learning, enacted across a wide terrain. (Burns, 2007: 1)

This engages with the complexity of whole systems, involving an inclusive range of stakeholders, generating change, and locating inquiry-based learning at the heart of decision-making in an organization. Burns illustrates the variety of forms and trajectories and commonalities with four examples of participatory action inquiry. These are psychiatric care in Melbourne, a programme involving children in Bristol, UK, a national programme evaluation of a capacity-building initiative involving 142 programmes across Wales, and a whole organization inquiry into vulnerability with the British Red Cross. Besides system or organization-wide scale, these presented characteristics which, in Burns's words (2007: 85), need to be reflected in most systemic research designs, among which the most important were:

- an emergent research design;
- an exploratory inquiry phase;
- multiple inquiry streams operating at different levels;
- a structure for connecting organic inquiry to formal decision-making;
- a process for identifying cross-cutting links across inquiry streams;
- a commitment to open boundary inquiry;
- the active development of distributed leadership.

A more recent book, *Navigating Complexity in International Development: Facilitating Sustainable Change at Scale* (Burns and Worsley, 2015), relates practice more directly to complexity theory with the evidence of illuminating cases. Aspects emphasized include network development, power relations, ownership, systemic issue mapping, 'nurtured emergent development', participatory processes, and participation as action, drawing on cases as diverse as slavery and bonded labour in India, community radio and climate change in Ghana, a VSO programme on valuing volunteering, and girls' education in Afghanistan.

Parallel developments have taken place in evaluation practice (Befani et al., 2014, 2015) in an action research mode. In an evaluation, systemic approaches for complexity have come into focus and are being better articulated and explored (Befani et al., 2015). Inclusivity is repeatedly stressed in taking a complex systems perspective (see for instance Garcia and Zazueta, 2015, who contrast it with a theory-of-change only perspective), and with several authors arguing for a plurality of approaches – to identify multiple causality, to extend the boundaries of relevance, to identify unanticipated impacts, and so on.

Rigour is not a prominent explicit concern of these sources but they illustrate and support the canons of inclusive rigour. Rigour is a strange omission, perhaps even a blind spot. Except for *Development Evaluation* (Patton, 2011), it is not in the index of any of the books cited, nor others which I have consulted, nor in the title of any of the *IDS Bulletin* articles. To varying degrees these latter mention the superordinate canon of participation but do not stress reflexivity. That is, though, significantly recognized in PIALA, as part of what should be a wave of the future.

Rigour for wicked mess and gridlock

Interventions for change in complex conditions of wicked mess and gridlock on a scale broader than that of an organization, project or evaluation, pose related but different challenges. Gridlock makes their short-term futures predictable. They present formidable issues for policy and practice, compounded when the gridlock is reinforced by strong feedback forces which resist change and defy simple solutions. What principles or canons of rigour for complexity can apply in such cases? Evidence and experience point to continuous and sustained action learning with many interventions, and iteratively inquiring, engaging, taking action, reflecting, learning, and adapting, guided by the canons of inclusive rigour. Two contrasting examples shed light on this: the sugar industry in Kenya and rural sanitation in India.

The sugar industry in Kenya

Ashish Shah, working with ActionAid in western Kenya, struggled for over a decade to find ways of reforming the smallholder sugar industry. 'I don't know...and related thoughts' (Shah, 2013) is a moving story of his transition from confident diagnosis to questioning, doubt, gradually unravelling and acting on the elements and relationships of wickedly intertwined and complex problems, and making progress through acknowledging ignorance, sustained participatory commitment, and incremental changes.

The sugar industry was not viable economically; small farmers were not being paid regularly or anything like enough. To some the diagnosis and prescription were simple. In the words of a World Bank staff technocrat:

> Other reasons don't matter. The fact is that Kenya is an inefficient producer compared to most sugar producing countries. The markets need to be liberalized, and Kenya has to compete in the real world. If sugarcane farmers cannot produce and millers cannot mill sugar cheaply then they will have to switch to other crops where they have a comparative advantage. (Cited in Shah, 2013: 201)

Shah engaged with farmers. Challenged by them, he immersed himself in radical ground-truthing, physically in person farming a quarter of an acre of sugarcane. Through this and other engagement and inquiry over years he progressively uncovered and came to appreciate the interlocked complexity of the sugar industry and its stakeholders.

> Instead of my initial linear, static and simplified understanding of the 'problem facing the sugar industry', my understanding shifted (and

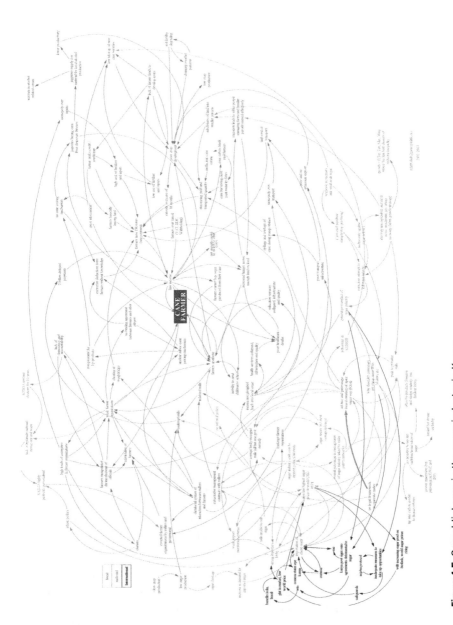

Figure 4.5 Causal linkages in the sugar industry in Kenya
Source: Ashish Shah, personal communication, 2015

continues to shift on a daily basis) to accept and embrace a much more complex and dynamic picture of the realities … (Shah, 2013: 205)

After listing 22 things he at first did not know, he added that there were far more than these which he did not detail because of space constraints for his chapter (Shah, 2013: 203–4). He came to appreciate more and more of the interwoven net of multiple disadvantages and obstacles faced by farmers, and the many problematic relationships in the sugar system. Eventually, he expressed these as a causal-linkage diagram (Figure 4.5). The practical wisdom that followed was that no one measure could begin to be adequate, and that many interventions were needed at many levels in the evolving conditions in numerous domains, sustained over time, through many means, and that the watchwords were participation, patience, and persistence. And for the record, during the 10 years he was most actively engaged, many reforms were achieved, farmers' conditions improved, and the sugar industry which once seemed doomed survived and does to this day.

Rural sanitation in India

Rural sanitation in India is one of the most intractable problems facing humankind in the first half of the 21st century.[8] In 2012 India had 60 per cent of the open defecation in the world, up from 55 per cent in 2000 and 51 per cent in 1990, and in 2016 probably well over 530 million people were defecating in the open in rural areas.[9] Open defecation and lack of hygiene are a huge health problem and a major reason why India has a third of the stunted children in the world. Over decades a succession of massive and costly programmes to provide subsidized toilets barely kept pace with population increase (and failed to do so from 2001 to 2011). Many of the toilets reported to have been constructed were not usable, used for other purposes, used only some of the time, not used at all, or most commonly until the census of 2011, simply non-existent (Hueso and Bell, 2013; Chambers and Myers, 2016; see also Chapter 1, pp 11–12). In August 2014 the new Prime Minister, Narendra Modi, launched a national campaign, the Swachh Bharat Mission (Gramin) (SBM-G) (Clean India Mission (Villages)) and declared October 2019 as a new target for rural India to be open defecation-free. Though not remotely possible, this target focused minds on action and sustained a vigorous campaign.

The wickedness of the mess is the way many political, cultural, and administrative forces have intertwined, interlocked, and trapped the system in the status quo. Consider some of them. The policy of individual household hardware subsidies has fed massive local-level corruption and political patronage; people have been reluctant to build toilets for themselves when if they waited they might get them free; many consider it polluting to have a toilet near their dwelling, and prefer open defecation, regarding that as more pleasant and healthier; if they were to have a toilet, they have wanted an expensive one with large underground storage to postpone having to empty it; many of those with toilets use them only some of the time in order to avoid filling them up (Chambers and Myers, 2016); and misleadingly inflated reports of successes in campaigns have been endemic in the administrative system.

In this gridlock, the way forward included decentralization, encouraging innovation and diversity, and rapid learning and sharing. A large number of parallel initiatives and campaigns were launched. District Collectors (the administrative heads of districts) of India's 643 rural districts were to run their own campaigns, drawing on a handbook of ideas for campaigns and themselves being creative. Rapid action learning was advocated and authorized in the guidelines for the SBM-G. The term 'action learning' was used in its commonsense meaning of learning from and through action, rather than in the classical and historical sense (Revans, 1982; Pedler and Burgoyne, 2015). Inclusive rigour was sought through rapid learning from district collectors who were positive deviants and through bringing them together to share their innovations and experiences in workshops. These confirmed that there was a cornucopia of promising practices that could be drawn on, developed, and spread.

Multiple initiatives and innovations with rapid action learning were conceived as a strategy for tackling messy, wicked problems on a vast scale. It was to be learning from action, reflection, and sharing. Inclusive rigour was to come from trawling for promising practical experiences and networking. Rapid action learning was slow to take off but by late 2016 was receiving new impetus.

Contrasts, commonalities, and concluding

Each messy, wicked problem at scale must be treated and tackled as unique. Moreover, external environments – political, economic, social, and so on – are complex and continuously change.

The two cases contrast in many ways such as location, nature, and scale, the forms of engagement and learning, the solutions sought and found, and the extent to which these have been effective. The understanding of the sugar industry in Kenya derives from intimate personal engagement, direct experiential learning, and reflexivity, sustained over 10 years. The understanding of rural sanitation in India derives from much indirect learning and research, and is less personal. The sugar industry is geographically localized while sanitation in rural India is country-wide with much local variation. Until 2015 more progress has been made with Kenyan sugar than with Indian rural sanitation. Other cases are needed and will differ yet again. We can expect to learn much more about how to know better and what to do in such contexts.

Some of what these two have in common may also be found in other situations of complex quagmire or gridlock. The problems both presented are wicked and messy: wicked in having been sustained over time by fiendishly interlocked forces of political patronage, corruption, misguided policy, and misinformation; and messy in presenting almost innumerable facets, defying simple linear solutions, and demanding multiple, parallel, patient, and resolute interventions, with learning and changing on many fronts. Both have presented many options and arenas for action. Both have been constrained by uncertainty about what could be made to work, where, and how. Four other commonalities which may hold more generally stand out.

No simple solutions. First, and most obviously, there are no simple solutions. When so many adverse forces interlock, the number of possible points or combinations of interventions multiplies. For the Kenyan sugar industry, using causal loop analysis (see Figure 4.5) Shah found that there were 'at least 33,000 strategies of action to dismantle the system of deprivation that trapped sugarcane farmers in Kenya and 56,000 if the problems facing women sugarcane farmers were factored in' (2013: 207). Single, simple, direct solutions could reinforce the gridlock as in India where successively raising the individual toilet hardware subsidy served to inhibit self-help and fuel corruption and malpractices. There is wisdom in the words attributed to the American wit H.L. Mencken, 'For every problem there is a solution that is simple, direct and wrong'.

Timescales and targets. Shah had hoped to make a mark in a matter of months. After 10 years he concluded,

> The sheer complexity of the systems that keep sugarcane farmers poor, excluded and marginalized in Kenya implies that for farmers and many of us involved in change processes, the time required to dismantle such systems of deprivation will be measured in decades, not in short project or programme cycles. (Shah, 2013: 207)

As for time-bound targets, those set for an open defecation-free rural India have been grotesquely unrealistic, not once, but again and again. The latest target is October 2019. Targets have their own pathologies and judgement is needed to optimize their level and timing.[10] With wicked mess, change is rarely rapid: comprehensive tipping points may be rare. It is enticing to think of nudges (Taylor and Sunstein, 2008) and other interventions leading to tipping points, as popularized by Malcolm Gladwell (2000). These would be like the phase transitions of complexity science (like ice becoming water). In an earlier draft I wrote, 'Tipping points may be elusive but could be key'. They can be sought. But reading, reflection, and evidence have made me now less hopeful. Liberation from quagmire treacle is more likely to be sticky and slow than apocalyptic. Or to change the imagery, it may entail a progressive weakening and loosening of strands in the constraining nets and painstaking gradual change. There will be exceptions, but usually it may be more a question of patient trial and error with incremental steps, spreading whatever works with vigilance to hold on to ground gained. A promising way forward may be long-term sustained commitments and networking by champions and other stakeholders in many domains and at many levels.

Ground-truthing and action learning. Here Ashish Shah's participatory immersions and learning from action by farming himself were exceptional and personally formative: they gave him insights and energy which he could scarcely have gained in any other way. I do not know of any equivalent in Indian rural sanitation: ground realities are selectively presented and perceived, with perceptions distorted by strategic ignorance and the biases noted in Chapter 2. In consequence, error, ignorance, and myth have been so widespread and deep that open-ended field visits avoiding more obvious biases could expose insights even in 2016. This points to the potential of rapid action learning from the innumerable initiatives in India's 643 rural districts. The essence sought is to be grounded, in touch, and up to date, with rapid feedback of field realities.

Action learning needs action. This means avoiding the excess of appraisal, analysis, and set plans that postponed much action in the 1960s and 1970s and has returned as a straitjacket in the 2000s and 2010s. We need the bias for action advocated by Peters and Waterman in their classic, *In Search of Excellence: Lessons from America's Best-run Companies* (1982), and expressed by the Cadbury executive whom they cite (p. 119) for his precept, 'Ready, fire, aim'. David Snowden's 'probe, sense, respond' for complex conditions applies (Wikipedia, 2017). The spirit expressed in the title of Peter Vaill's (1996) book, *Learning as a Way of Being: Strategies for Survival in a World of Permanent White Water,* is fitting, with stress on the long term and adaptive management.

Pluralism and inclusive rigour. This includes much that is in this chapter. Among the canons of inclusive rigour, eclectic methodological pluralism and mixed methods stand out: faced with wicked complexity, the methodological Taylorism of flat earth method research deserves history's dustbin. Ground-truthing, iterative learning, and adaptive management are key elements. There are lessons to learn from systemic approaches. Participation, reflexivity, and responsible relevance are fundamental. Par excellence, wicked mess and quagmire need the application of inclusive rigour. The way forward for gridlocks and quagmires is best sought through an eclectic plurality of interventions and approaches with engagement and action learning.

To conclude, this chapter has been an exploration with its own fallibilities. The critical reflexivity, pluralism, and behavioural precepts of inclusive rigour for complexity must be subject to their own principles: that is, assessed for cost-effectiveness, examined critically and iteratively, and tested against evidence, with successive approximation, triangulation, additions and subtractions, and modified as innovations and new insights lead to new repertoires and combinations. Applications of reductionist rigour should be subject to the same criteria and confined to conditions and applications where they are truly cost-effective compared with alternatives. Inclusive rigour for complexity requires a transformation of mindsets, values, and actions on the part of many or most development professionals whether in universities, governments, NGOs, or funding agencies. Transparent reflexivity and open-mindedness are among the fundamentals.

Agenda for reflection and action

Whether for appraisal, research, evaluation, informing policy, practical inter-ventions, or other purposes, this chapter raises issues about paradigms, rigour, cost-effectiveness, and choices of methodology and approach. For acting, reflecting, and learning in contexts of complexity, here is a short agenda of questions for reflection:

- Are you confronting complexity? How much of which paradigm applies?
- In choosing an approach and methods does the criterion of cost-effectiveness apply?
- Are powerful stakeholders predisposed to suboptimal methodologies? If so, what can you do about it?
- Do the canons of inclusive rigour apply? What scope do you see for:
  o eclectic methodological pluralism;
  o seeking diversity and balance;
  o improvisation and innovation;
  o sequential learning and adaptive iteration;
  o triangulation;
  o inclusive participation and plural perspectives;
  o optimal ignorance and appropriate imprecision;
  o interactive and experiential ground-truthing.
- What part can and should participation, reflexivity, and responsible rel-evance play?
- What trade-offs, complementarities, and synergies can you optimize for useful learning?

If you face wicked mess and gridlock:

- What can you learn from systemic approaches?
- Can system diagramming help in analysis?
- Is rapid action learning and sharing an option?
- What can be learnt from positive deviants?
- Can champions be found, inspired, and supported?
- Are there potential tipping points? Or nudges that might contribute?
- Can long-term engagement with learning, sharing, and changing be assured?

Notes

1. In earlier writing (Chambers, 2010) I characterized the two paradigms in terms of practice – one of Neo-Newtonian practice and one of adaptive pluralism. I now prefer Newtonian and Complexity as more inclusive

of the numerous dimensions of contrast without implying primacy to practice.

2. Optimal ignorance is not a new concept. See Ilchman and Uphoff (1971: 260–2) and Chambers (1974: 153).

3. In her encyclopaedic collection *The Sage Handbook of Action Research* (2015), Hilary Bradbury has brought together and edited 79 chapters in a volume of 806 pages.

4. For the local, complex, diverse, dynamic, and unpredictable characteristics of the realities of poor people see *Whose Reality Counts?* (Chambers, 1997: Chapter 8, pp. 162–87) and for a discussion of complexity and poverty see *Paradigms, Poverty and Adaptive Pluralism* (Chambers, 2010: 34–6).

5. *Millions* of social maps may seem an exaggeration. However, well over a million was my estimate some 10 years ago. They have for a long time been a standard part of international and national NGO practice, and many government programmes; are integral to methodologies such as Reflect and Community-Led Total Sanitation; and are widely used in programmes of natural resource management, health, agriculture, community development, forestry, irrigation, poverty, etc.

6. A classic example of social anthropologists telling stories against themselves is Evans-Pritchard in his study *The Nuer* (1940). See also McGee (2002).

7. I shall be grateful to any reader who can demonstrate my ignorance by bringing to my notice evidence of systematic bias from questionnaires, or evidence that it does not occur (r.chambers@ids.ac.uk).

8. In 2016, open defecation in India cannot compare in intensity of human suffering with the cataclysmic mayhem of the Middle East. I would argue, though, that it can compare in intractability. Indeed, precisely because it is less visible, is not an international priority, and does not affect other countries, it has received less attention.

9. This estimate, based on several sources, assumes that recent successes of the Swachh Bharat Mission (Gramin) campaign for an open defecation-free rural India will be offset by the widespread practice of only partial use of toilets (Chambers and Myers, 2016).

10. High but not totally impossible targets can improve performance, even if they are not achieved. However, wildly unrealistic targets can breed cynicism, inactivity, and misreporting. Commitment and motivation are key variables. Many variations, subtleties, and nuances make generalization perilous.

References

Befani, B., Barnett, C. and Stern, E. (2014) 'Introduction: rethinking impact evaluation for development', *IDS Bulletin* 45(6): 1–5, November.

Befani, B., Ramalingam, B. and Stern, E. (2015) 'Towards systemic approaches to evaluation and impact', *IDS Bulletin* 46(1): 1–6, January.

Bradbury, H. (ed.) (2015) *The Sage Handbook of Action Research*, 3rd edn, London: Sage Publications.

Burns, D. (2007) *Systemic Action Research: A Strategy for Whole System Change*, Bristol: The Policy Press, University of Bristol.

Burns, D. and Worsley, S. (2015) *Navigating Complexity in International Development: Facilitating Sustainable Change at Scale*, Rugby, UK: Practical Action Publishing.

Camfield, L., Duvendack, M. and Palmer-Jones, R. (2014) 'Things you wanted to know about bias in evaluations but never dared to think', *IDS Bulletin* 45(6): 49–64.

Chambers, R. (1974) *Managing Rural Development: Ideas and Experience from East Africa,* Uppsala: Scandinavian Institute of African Studies.

Chambers, R. (1997) *Whose Reality Counts? Putting the First Last,* Rugby, UK: Practical Action Publishing.

Chambers, R. (2008) *Revolutions in Development Inquiry,* London: Earthscan.

Chambers, R. (2010) *Paradigms, Poverty and Adaptive Pluralism*, Working Paper 344, Brighton, UK: IDS.

Chambers, R. and Myers, J. (2016) *Norms, Knowledge and Usage*, Frontiers in CLTS No 7, Brighton: CLTS Knowledge Hub, IDS.

Evans-Pritchard, E. (1940) *The Nuer,* New York: Oxford University Press.

Garcia, J.R. and Zazueta, A. (2015) 'Going beyond mixed methods to mixed approaches: a systems perspective for asking the right questions', *IDS Bulletin* 46(1) January: 30–43.

Gladwell, M. (2000) *The Tipping Point: How Little Things Can Make a Big Difference*, Boston, MA: Little, Brown.

Gladwell, M. (2008) *Outliers: The Story of Success*, London: Penguin Books.

Hueso, A. and Bell, B. (2013) 'An untold story of policy failure: the Total Sanitation Campaign in India', *Water Policy* 15(6): 1001–17 <http://dx.doi.org/10.2166/wp.2013.032>.

Ilchman, W. and Uphoff, N. (1971) *The Political Economy of Change*, Los Angeles: University of California Press.

Kuhn, T.S. (1962) *The Structure of Scientific Revolutions*, Chicago: Phoenix Books, The University of Chicago Press.

McGee, R. (2002) 'The self in participatory poverty research', in R. McGee and K. Brock (eds), *Knowing Poverty: Critical Reflections on Participatory Research and Policy*, pp. 14–43, Sterling, VA, and London: Earthscan.

Patton, M.Q. (2011) *Developmental Evaluation: Applying Complexity Concepts to Enhance Innovation and Use*, New York: The Guilford Press.

Pawson, R. (2013) *The Science of Evaluation: A Realist Manifesto*, London: Sage.

Pedler, M. and Burgoyne, J. (2015) 'Action learning', in H. Bradbury (ed.), *The Sage Handbook of Action Research*, pp. 179–87, London: Sage.

Peters, T.J. and Waterman, R.H. (1982) *In Search of Excellence: Lessons from America's Best-run Companies*, New York: Harper and Row.

Ramalingam, B. (2013) *Aid on the Edge of Chaos: Rethinking International Cooperation in a Complex World*, Oxford: Oxford University Press.

Ramalingam, B. and Jones, H. with Reba, T. and Young, J. (2008) *Exploring the Science of Complexity: Ideas and Implications for Development and Humanitarian Efforts*, Working Paper 285, London: ODI.

Revans, R. (1982) *The Origins and Growth of Action Learning*, Bromley, UK: Chartwell-Bratt.

Rogers, P. and Peersman, G. (2014) 'Developing a research agenda for impact evaluation in development', *IDS Bulletin* 45(6): 85–99.

Shah, A. (2013) 'I don't know…and related thoughts', in T. Wallace, F. Porter with M. Ralph-Bownman (eds), *Aid, NGOs and the Realities of Women's Lives*, pp. 199–211, Rugby, UK: Practical Action Publishing.

Taylor, R.H. and Sunstein, C.R. (2008) *Nudge: Improving Decisions about Health, Wealth and Happiness*, New Haven, CT: Yale University Press.

Todd, R. (2016) *The End of Average: How to Succeed in a World that Values Sameness*, London: Allen Lane.

Uphoff, N. (1992) *Learning from Gal Oya: Possibilities for Participatory Development and Post-Newtonian Social Science*, Ithaca, NY: Cornell University Press; London: IT Publications.

Vaill, P.B. (1996) *Learning as a Way of Being: Strategies for Survival in a World of Permanent White Water*, San Francisco: Jossey-Bass.

Van Hemelrick, A. (2016a) 'Local inclusive governance for building climate-resilient livelihoods: effectiveness review using PIALA (Participatory Impact Assessment and Learning Approach) of membership organisations in the Dry Zone of Myanmar', *Effectiveness Review Series* 2015/2016, Oxford: Oxfam GB.

Van Hemelrijck, A. (2016b) 'Stretching boundaries of evaluation practice with PIALA in Ghana' [blog], Evaluation for Africa, (posted 12 March 2016) <http://africaevaluation.org/Africa/2016/03/12/evaluation-practice-piala-ghana/> [accessed 16 December 2016].

Van Hemelrijck, A. and Guijt, I. (2016) *Balancing Inclusiveness, Rigour and Feasibility: Insights from Participatory Impact Evaluations in Ghana and Vietnam*, Centre for Development Impact Practice Paper 14, Brighton, UK: IDS.

Van Hemelrijck, A. and Kyei-Mensah, G. (2015) *Final Report on the participatory impact evaluation of the Root & Tuber Improvement & Marketing Program (RTIMP) conducted by PDA with support from the MOFA/GoG. Pilot Application of a Participatory Impact Assessment & Learning Approach (PIALA) developed with support from IFAD and the BMGF.* IFAD, Government of Ghana, and BMGF.

Waldrop, M.M. (1994) *Complexity*, London: Penguin Books.

White, H. (2009) 'Theory-based impact evaluation: principles and practice', *Journal of Development Effectiveness* 1(3): 271–84 <http://dx.doi.org/10.1080/19439340903114628>.

Wiener, N. (1948) *Cybernetics*, New York: John Wiley and Sons.

Wikipedia (2017) *Cynefin framework*, <https://en.wikipedia.org/wiki/Cynefin_framework> [accessed 2 January 2017].

Zwane, A.P., Zinman, J., Van Dusen, E., Pariente, W., Null, C., Miguel, E., Kremer, M., Karlan, D.S., Hornbeck, R., Gine, X., Duflo, E., Devoto, F., Crepon, B. and Banerjee, A. (2011) 'Being surveyed can change later behavior and related parameter estimates', *Proceedings of the National Academy of Sciences of the United States of America* 108(5): 1821–6 <http://dx.doi.org/10.1073/pnas.1000776108>.

CHAPTER 5
Power, participation, and knowledge: knowing better together

Abstract

Answering 'who?' and 'whose?' questions with 'theirs' can reverse power relations and open up almost limitless potentials for knowing better together through participatory methodologies (PMs). In the three decades preceding this book, much of the flowering and almost exponential proliferation of PMs has been below the mainstream professional radar. A phase of distinct names and brands for PMs has increasingly been complemented and superseded by eclectic pluralism and innovation to fit contextual needs. The natural history and morphology of PMs point to a future of ever more eclectic methodological pluralism through creative combinations and adaptations of visual, digital, and interactive methods and approaches. For embracing and expressing diversity and complexity three approaches have outstanding potential: participatory ICTs; participatory statistics; and Reality Checks with immersions. PMs have been used at scale to enable people living with poverty and marginalization to express their perspectives and priorities and to inform policy. For PMs to achieve their full empowering promise requires radical professional, institutional, and personal transformations at scale.

Keywords: power, knowledge, participation, methodologies, empowerment, realities, win–win, transformations

> All power deceives. (Chapter title in *Whose Reality Counts?* Chambers, 1997)
>
> Only the one who is sitting on the anthill knows that the ants are biting. (African proverb)
>
> They can do it. Ask them. Hand over the stick. (Precepts of participatory rural appraisal)

Springboard for this chapter

The theme of this chapter is that participatory methodologies (PMs) have an almost unlimited potential for knowing better together, and that in most cases they are 'win–win' because they bring gains in quality of data and insights while at the same time empowering those who generate them.

In *Revolutions in Development Inquiry* (Chambers, 2008) I traced some of the history of one stream of participatory methodologies, starting with the

http://dx.doi.org/10.3362/9781780449449.005

provocations of long, drawn-out questionnaire surveys and the biases of rural development tourism followed by chapters on observing the unobserved, RRA (rapid rural appraisal), which was explored and developed in the 1980s, and PRA (participatory rural appraisal) which followed in the 1990s. The final chapters were 'Who counts? Participation and numbers', 'Whose space? Mapping, power and ethics', 'Traps and liberations' and finally 'Participatory methodologies: drivers for change'. I am now taking that book as a springboard, not repeating it but updating it and taking the analysis further, with developments and reflections from the years which have followed. In this chapter I review the nature, relevance, and potential of PMs for our 21st century and present evidence that PMs can bridge paradigmatic binaries by generating inclusively rigorous findings, arguing that PMs provide means of navigating in the increasingly unpredictable and rapidly evolving world of knowing for development.

The abstract to the last chapter in the earlier book can be a springboard for this chapter now:

> With astonishing speed, the journey has brought us new modes of inquiry, most recently with the flowering, proliferation, and spread of participatory methodologies (PMs). With the pluralism and diversity of PMs we are in a new space: with a vastly enhanced repertoire; with a new eclectic creativity; and with a wealth of innovations specific to context and purpose.

This is confirmed and reinforced by developments in the eight years since that was written. This is in spite of the trend of many mindsets, practices, and methods to becoming more left hemisphere, reductionist, and Newtonian, as we saw in Chapter 3. The exponential multiplication of PMs presents ways of reversing the magnetic fields of dominant professionalism to a better balance and mix with less Newtonian practice and instead more adaptive pluralism and grounded realism.

Fundamentals: power, knowledge, and who? Whose?

Power and knowledge are inextricably intertwined (Gaventa and Cornwall, 2015). Most obvious is the power of purse strings: funders and sponsors of research, with whatever motives and priorities, determine much of what we come to study, how we study it, and so what we come to 'know'. And pervasively, across human relationships, 'All power deceives'. This simple assertion applies to many, perhaps even most, interactions between 'uppers' and 'lowers',[1] where what the upper knows or believes and what the lower conveys or shows to the upper, are often distorted, as we saw in Chapter 2. This can be on the lowers' side through deference, prudence, wishing to appear in a good light, wanting to please, and telling or showing the uppers what the uppers are believed to want to hear. In development, what lowers say, where they take uppers, what they show them, what they hide, who they arrange for them to meet, all these in subtle and not so subtle ways influence and distort what uppers experience and come to believe. At the same time uppers determine agendas, categories, questions, and priorities, and are often unaware of how their power handicaps their learning.[2] Or if they are aware, they may opt for strategic ignorance, not wanting to know or be known to know about how they are misled, or who they do not meet, what they are not shown, or where they do not go.

The consequence has often been the distortion or exclusion of the realities, priorities, and aspirations of those who live in poverty, of those who are variously vulnerable, marginalized, powerless, insecure, isolated, stigmatized, and physically weak, of those who are last and who for a fairer and more just world must be put first in both knowing and action. This is hardly an original thought! Again and again we hear that poor people are the experts on their lives, conditions, and experiences. Of course. Which makes it all the more remarkable that all of us professionals so repeatedly and self-uncritically impose our own categories and preconceptions on the realities of those who are last, those whom we are not to leave behind.

A first step towards putting the last first in knowing and action is to ask, not once but again and again and again, 'Who?' and 'Whose?' questions about realities and power. Anyone can compile a list of these. Here is a selection, some of the more obvious ones first: Whose reality counts? Whose knowledge? Whose priorities? Whose appraisal? Whose analysis? Whose planning? Whose action? Whose indicators? Whose monitoring and evaluation? Whose research? Whose voices? Whose language?...

And the list can go on: Whose convenience: time of day, ease of access, place, home territory? Whose facilitation? Whose relationships? Whose self-respect? Whose ego? Whose theory of change? Who participates in whose project? Whose adaptation? (Ramalingam, 2016). Who is empowered and who disempowered? And always, who gains and who loses?

Applying to all these questions, it has to be asked: if we are 'uppers' and they are 'lowers', is the answer 'ours' or 'theirs'? And if 'ours', whose among us? And if 'theirs', whose among them?

Answers to these questions are mediated by power embodied in contextual and personal, professional, institutional, and social dimensions and domains. These can be gender, class, caste, ethnicity, wealth, age, faith, specialization, professional status, and many others. To say this is to state the glaringly obvious. But what may seem obvious is not always visible or seen. It is, though, fundamental. If the realities of those who are last are to be justly and fairly recognized and acted on, reversals in power relations have to enable them to express themselves freely, gain confidence, take action, and claim their rights. And these reversals require many changes of behaviour and relationships with uppers using their power to empower lowers. This can take many forms such as convening, facilitating, listening, and other behaviours, and uppers finding ways to disempower themselves.

The mindsets, beliefs, experiences, behaviours, and learning of uppers are then key determinants. The PRA (participatory rural appraisal) injunctions all apply: *They can do it* – have confidence that lowers can do things; *Ask them* – repeatedly ask lowers their priorities and realities in response to 'theirs' in the Who? Whose? questions; *Sit down, listen, learn* – empower through behaviour and attitudes; and *Hand over the stick* – pass responsibility to lowers to do things themselves.[3]

Nor need these necessarily be lose–win equations where outsider uppers and facilitators have to lose. Zero-sum situations where confrontation is needed do occur in lowers' local contexts where uppers can at least initially lose or appear to lose. On the other hand, justice, peace, and harmony can be good for all stakeholders, while for facilitators empowering others can be profoundly fulfilling, enjoyable, even fun. Win–wins are to be sought not just because it is good to minimize losers but because win–wins are easier to achieve and more sustainable. And in terms of the meaning of rigour in this book, a theme of this chapter is that such reversals and win–wins tend to be rigorous – cost-effective in range and depth of insight and data, relevance, validity, timeliness, and credibility – in generating and sharing knowledge.

This is where participatory methodologies come into their own. Well facilitated, they produce knowledge which can be owned and used by, and which empowers, those lowers and local people who co-generate and articulate it. PMs and changes in power relations are a central means towards achieving the Sustainable Development Goals (SDGs). Without participatory approaches and methods, it is difficult to envisage how we can achieve the fairer and more secure and socially sustainable[4] world to which we aspire, in which no one is left behind.

Participatory methodologies

Participatory methodologies can be defined as combinations of approaches and methods through which people are facilitated to do things themselves. In the context of knowing, what they do may be appraisal, research, analysis, planning, action, monitoring, evaluation, facilitation, convening, organizing, or many other activities. Methodologies are systems of approaches and methods, and methods are distinct ways of doing things but the boundary between the two can be fuzzy, as for instance with participatory video.

PMs in this definition overlap with, and share values and interact with, other traditions: action research (Greenwood and Levin, 1998; Bradbury, 2015), action learning (Revans, 1982; Pedler and Burgoyne, 2015), and systemic action research (Burns, 2007; Burns and Worsley, 2015), among others. These are not watertight categories or compartments. And all have much to contribute to practical realism. They are part of a wider community of PMs with much in common with one another. I focus here on certain PMs which are often overlooked or little appreciated, not in any way to undervalue other traditions. The PMs concerned include PRA and methodologies which adopt and adapt PRA approaches and methods such as analysis by groups and visualizations. These PMs have commonalities which make them a useful and relatively manageable clustering for description and analysis. That said, the vast and exploding families of participatory approaches and methods are crying out for fuller understanding, and wider recognition, dissemination, and adoption.[5]

A brief history and overview

The recent history of PMs is remarkable. Precursors of current PMs can be found in the community development movement in colonial territories following the Second World War. Any history of PMs is likely to rediscover wheels. That said, in the four decades up to 2016 something unprecedented in its diversity, creativity, and spread has happened. In the late 1970s and 1980s, agriculture was a fertile field for participatory innovation. In the 1990s poverty and the community level were conspicuous. In the 2000s, applications in governance became more prominent. The last 10 years to the time of writing have been marked by an explosion of innovation through participatory information and communication technologies (ICTs).

Through these four decades one significant and fertile braided stream has been RRA, PRA, and PLA (participatory learning and action). In the 1980s, the mapping and visuals of agro-ecosystem analysis (Gypmantasiri et al., 1980; Conway, 1985) came together with the semi-structured interviewing of early RRA to provide more powerful and versatile ways for outsiders to appraise and analyse rural realities (Khon Kaen, 1987). In parallel, farmer participatory research in many manifestations, farmer field schools, and integrated pest management all took off. PRA (Chambers, 1997; Cornwall and Pratt, 2003; Mascarenhas et al, 1991) began in the late 1980s and its approach and methods exploded and diversified with innumerable applications. In the 1990s it spread to perhaps 100 countries with over 30 national networks. Materials were translated, mainly from English, into many languages. Common elements, taking many forms, were visual analytical mapping, diagramming, scoring, and ranking by small groups. This all happened with breathtaking speed.

Increasingly in the 1980s and 1990s, other named approaches and methodologies multiplied. The listing below is indicative not complete. The 1990s were marked by the spread and innovative adaptation of many of them. Among those that went to scale exponentially during the 1990s continuing to the present, each with spread and adoption in between 30 and 100 countries, and very extensively within some of these, were farmer participatory research, integrated pest management, farmer field schools (FFSs), participatory rural appraisal (PRA), participatory poverty assessments (PPAs), Reflect, participatory geographical information systems, participatory video, and community-led total sanitation (CLTS).

In the 1990s PMs flowered in a heyday of participation in which the World Bank under James Wolfensohn played a significant part. Then in the 2000s and to the present, innovation continued with many more methodologies, methods, and applications. How during this period these have multiplied is illustrated by the partial listing that follows. The proliferation of labels and acronyms can mislead: they can refer to a single quite integrated methodology, like CLTS, or to a whole family like popular theatre, or to a method like participatory video. With that caveat, an impression of what has happened can be given by listing some of the more prominent, widespread, or original PMs in rough chronological order of their introduction (the dates in brackets are of good sources, not when they originated) from the early 1980s to the present:

- popular theatre, forum theatre (Boal, 1992)
- farmer participatory research (Okali et al., 1994)
- immersions (Birch et al., 2007)
- participatory technology development (Haverkort et al., 1991)
- integrated pest management (Dent et al., 1995)
- farmer field schools (Braun et al., 2000)
- participatory seed breeding (Witcombe et al., 1996)
- positive deviance (Pascale and Sternin, 2010; Positive Deviance Initiative, 2010)
- participatory video (Shaw and Robertson, 1997)
- participatory statistics (Holland, 2013; see also later in this chapter)
- participatory monitoring and evaluation (Estrella et al., 2000; Cornwall, 2014)
- participatory rural appraisal (Mascarenhas et al., 1991; Chambers, 1997; Cornwall and Pratt, 2003)
- participatory natural resource management (forests, irrigation, wildlife management, etc.)
- Appreciative Inquiry (Cooperrider et al., 2008: pp 131-3)
- most significant change (Davies and Dart, 2004)
- outcome mapping (Earl et al., 2001)
- participatory poverty assessments (PPAs) (Norton et al., 2001; Robb, 2002)
- participatory learning and action (PLA, 1988–2013)
- Reflect[6] (Archer, 2007)
- Stepping Stones (Welbourn, 1995, 2013)
- report cards (Paul, 2002)
- citizens' juries (Pimbert and Wakeford, 2001)
- participatory budgeting (Cabannes, 2004)
- participatory approaches with ICTs (see later in this chapter)
- participatory geographic information systems[7]
- community-based development and community-driven development (Mansuri and Rao, 2003)
- participatory action learning system (Mayoux, 2007)

- participatory human rights analysis (Jupp, 2007: 108–9)
- participatory 3-D mapping (Rambaldi and Callosa-Tarr, 2002; CTA, 2016)
- participatory vulnerability analysis (ActionAid, 2002)
- ALPS (Accountability, Learning and Planning System) (David et al., 2006)
- Community-Led Total Sanitation[8] (Kar with Chambers, 2008)
- participatory social auditing (Auret and Barrientos, 2004)
- participatory approaches to local governance (Gaventa, 2004; Gaventa and Barrett, 2012; Rijal, 2013; Mathie and Gaventa, 2015)
- participatory value chain analysis (Nang'ole et al., 2011)
- Reality Check Approach[9] (Lewis, 2013: 121–4; and later in this chapter, pp 134–6)
- Constituency Voice (Keystone, 2014)
- visualizing sustainable landscapes (Boedhihartono, 2012)
- transformative story-telling (Lewin, 2011, 2012; Lewin et al., 2014)
- photo voice (Wang and Burris, 1997)
- PIALA (participatory impact and learning approach) (van Hemelrijck and Kyei-Mensah, 2015)
- sense-making workshops (van Hemelrijck and Guijt, 2016)

...and more.

The burgeoning and diversity of PMs is also illustrated by the periodical *PLA* (*Participatory Learning and Action*) and its predecessors *PLA Notes* and *RRA Notes*. These date back to 1988 and lasted until issue no. 66 in 2013 when *PLA* was tragically terminated.[10] This periodical provides a historical record of the proliferation of participatory methodologies and their applications, with issues dedicated to domains as diverse as children's participation (twice), performance and participation, animal healthcare, sexual and reproductive health, learning and teaching, local government, poverty reduction, literacy and empowerment, community water management, popular communications, immersions, community adaptation to climate change, and CLTS, to mention but some. So diverse are the contexts and so varied the combinations and inventions that it would seem there are few areas of human social activity where PMs have not been or could not be applied.

The nature and life cycles of participatory methodologies

Participatory methodologies have life cycles. The descriptions which follow draw on the experiences of PRA, Reflect, CLTS, and other PMs. Four phases or ages are typical.

First is the heroic age of birth and infancy, a time of rapid and intense development, innovation, learning, and excitement. As Wordsworth wrote about another revolution, 'Bliss was it in that dawn to be alive'.[11] Methods are invented, tried out, adopted, and developed or abandoned. PRA's heroic age in India from 1989 and into the 1990s was driven by passionate champion innovators who networked energetically. REFLECT, which at that stage had capital letters for Regenerated Freirian Literacy with Empowering

Community Techniques, was piloted in Uganda, Bangladesh, and El Salvador in 1993–1995. CLTS had a sudden birth in late 1999 and early 2000.

In this first age there were early pioneers. With PRA these were people in NGOs in South India, MYRADA and others, in Gujarat, the Aga Khan Rural Support Programme, and IIED in the UK. With Reflect, David Archer saw the potential of merging PRA with Freirian popular education, and in Action Aid had the support and freedom to be creative in combining them. CLTS was an innovation of Kamal Kar, a PRA practitioner and freelancer, in the course of an evaluation conducted for WaterAid in Bangladesh. In all cases there were supportive organizations. In all cases there was intense engagement in communities: the methodologies and methods were co-created interactively with local people, in the case of Reflect over months of innovation, and with CLTS interactively with one community first and then others.

The second age is childhood, with rapid growth. Attention is concentrated on promotion and spread. Publication and handbooks, and sharing and networking are priorities: with PRA there was a series of international South–South immersions of several days and nights in communities in India and the Philippines. Objectors and objections are experienced as growing pains. Reflect had few difficulties but PRA faced accusations of being romantic and old-fashioned with its beans and stones. The strongest opposition was to CLTS with its insistence on self-help instead of hardware subsidies for rural household toilets. The main activities are sharing and dissemination – through workshops, training, networking, advocacy, documentation, public presentations – all these linked with gaining funding and footholds and acceptance in organizations.

The third age is adolescence and early adulthood, confronting issues of scale, quality, and diversity. With rapid and extensive adoption which comes with success and publicity, bad practices proliferate. Donors demand superficial training. Manuals are written and interpreted by rote and without attention to attitudes and behaviour. The originators express concern. Training and quality assurance for facilitators become priorities. At the same time practices diversify. Some of these are positive and adaptations to context. PRA methods were adopted widely and at least 30 varieties of PRA were branded with their own names. Reflect took many different forms in different places but retained its core of facilitated small groups sustained over time. CLTS was renamed CATS (Community Approaches to Total Sanitation) by UNICEF but without any substantial difference apart from the name. CLTS was sufficiently distinct not to have conspicuous imitators and largely to maintain its integrity but with adaptations for India and for urban (Myers, 2015) contexts.

The fourth age is maturity. Issues of sustainability, quality of facilitation, training, and coverage persist. Often it is no longer mainly NGOs but governments that adopt and promote. The brand name is well recognized nationally and internationally. Questions are confronted of introduction into educational curricula. And here the analogy with human ages ends since none of the PMs considered has yet declined into dotage.

The proliferation of participatory methods

In parallel with and part of the proliferation of participatory *methodologies*, and as PMs have been passing through these phases, more and more participatory *methods* have been added to the repertoire. Many of these have proved to be versatile and adaptable for different purposes and contexts. Those which have been specific and focused in application, linked with clearly defined fixed routines, like visual diaries (Nagasundari, 2007; Narendranath, 2007; Noponen, 2007) have tended not to endure or spread.[12] Most others, especially those stemming from the original core PRA methods that are visual and tangible, have had a wide range of applications. Take the Ten Seed Technique, for instance. Ravi Jayakaran, one of the early innovators in the PRA tradition, has championed this method in which participants estimate, judge, value, or score by allocating 10 seeds between categories (Jayakaran, 2002). Applications of this one technique have been as varied as: patterns of distribution among a population for healthcare, incidence of diseases, HIV/AIDS, birth control practices, sanitation practices, education levels, and housing needs; water resources; rapid damage assessment in disasters; and analysis of trends, seasonality, livelihoods, expenditure, and changes in gender relations (for which see Table 5.1).

And Jayakaran has shown in 'Wholistic worldview analysis: understanding community realities' (2007) how the method can be applied to enable members of communities to distinguish issues of concern and the relative extents to which they are within the control of the community, depend on some help from outsiders, or are uncontrollable.

Table 5.1 Changes in gender responsibilities over 10 years

Area of work	Men (10 years ago)	Men (now)	Women (10 years ago)	Women (now)
Agriculture	10	6	0	4
Home-related	2	3	8	7
Credit-related	10	7	0	3
Cattle-related	10	5	0	5
Education	10	4	0	6
Purchase of assets	10	6	0	4
Marriage of children	5	6	5	4
Marketing/selling	10	7	0	3

Note: Men and women were facilitated in separate groups. They then met and with much discussion negotiated agreed scores. Matrices were developed on the ground using stones as counters, allowing successive approximation with easy adjustment of estimates.
Source: Chambers (1997: 174) from MYRADA South India

The diversity of PRA methods is striking. Both Neela Mukherjee (2002) and Josh Levene (International HIV/AIDS Alliance, 2006) have listed 100 tools, and Mukherjee (2009) published *Speaking to Power* which gives '27 Voice Tools for building bridges for participatory learning, action and policy-making'. Some of these, like the PRA methods of participatory mapping, matrix scoring, and trend diagramming, are applicable in many situations. Of these participatory mapping has probably been the most widely adopted and adapted. Applications since 1990 have been innumerable: social mapping to show households, people, and their characteristics; resource and land use mapping (in one case in Gujarat a participatory map of underground aqui-fers); facility mapping; and mapping of mobility, well-being, social networks, vulnerability, stigma, and drunken husbands, to name but a few. Starting with mapping on the ground and on paper, applications are now numerous also with geographic information systems (GIS), global positioning systems (GPS) and 3-D modelling (see Rambaldi et al., 2006; CTA, 2016). The number of participatory maps made since they began to spread in 1990 will run into millions.[13]

Visual and tactile media are a pervasive aspect of PRA and have shown the many strengths of visuals for ground-truthing and presenting and ana-lysing complex realities. An example is Andrea Cornwall's *Using Participatory Process Evaluation to Understand the Dynamics of Change in a Nutrition Education Programme* (Cornwall, 2014). Participants in an NGO programme were facili-tated to represent changes over time with string, showing ups and downs, so simple but richly informative. Not only did visuals enable them to represent their experience, but allowed evaluators through 'interviewing the diagram' to gain insights which could never have come from a purely verbal process. Various other PRA diagrams also gave a 'cloak of anonymity' which empow-ered participants to give honest feedback.

Contrasting characteristics of the verbal, visual, and digital, are shown in Table 5.2. In a PRA mode the strength of the visual includes being tangible, involving physical things – the ground or paper, chalks, pens or markers, counters, string, stones, and other improvised materials and symbols which can be moved around and altered. Digital refers mainly to democratic applica-tions of devices for citizens' participation and empowerment (see later).

Participatory visualizations have a versatility and range for presentation and analysis which are inaccessible verbally. It is strange that after kindergar-ten, perhaps, they feature so little in our educational systems.

Eclectic methodological pluralism: a new space

As the repertoire or suite of methods or tools has grown, so the scope for borrowing has been recognized and exploited. An example is combining the visual and tangible methods of PRA with new forms of diagramming and methods like card sorting. It also occurs in sequences and with complementar-ities adding depth and insights. This has been shown by mixes and sequences

Table 5.2 Verbal, visual, and digital compared

	Verbal	Visual	Digital
Medium	Words said and heard	Visuals made and seen	Messages sent and received
Typical context and interaction	Questionnaire Interview Bilateral	PRA focus group Multilateral	Individual with device
Common use	Survey data collection	Group or community appraisal and planning	Governance feedback from citizens
Frame and categories	Etic Standardized, preset	Emic Diverse, emergent	Etic Standardized, preset
Medium of expression and durability	Simple sentences Spoken, ephemeral	Complicated visuals Shown, cumulative	Simple, digital Transmitted, one-off
Selection of participants	By outsider	Joint by outsider and participants	Participants self-select
Outsider's role	Investigator Analyst	Convenor Facilitator	Moderator Analyst
Participant's role	Reactive Respondent	Interactive Co-creator	Mixed communicator
Eye contact, awareness of outsider	High	Medium to low	Very low or zero
Anonymity	Low	Often high 'cloak of anonymity'	High or low
Data distortions from interaction	High (prudence, deference, presenting self, etc.)	Low	Very low
Canons of rigour	Statistical	Iterative, visible triangulation, etc.	Level and quality of participation
Quality mainly assured by:	Outsiders' analysis	Participants and facilitation	Participants' motivation
Paradigmatically	Extractive Newtonian	Empowering Complex	Democratic Diverse

Note: These are general tendencies. In practice many crossovers and nuances can manifest.
Source: adapted from Chambers (1997: 150) with 'Digital' added

of popular and forum theatre and drama in their many forms, by drawings, diagramming, and story-telling.

So it has been that the proliferation of methods and the weakening of PM branding have seeded, enabled, and supported a new creative and eclectic methodological pluralism. As with ingredients in cooking, not everything can be combined with everything else[14] but every new method adds exponentially to the number of potential combinations. Intriguingly, this parallels developments in physical technology: Brian Arthur (2009) noted that more and more of the technological devices on the market were the product of combinations of many technical breakthroughs. Innovations have multiplier effects. A major part of this multiplication of possibilities has been ICTs. So it is that eclectic pluralism has been able to flower and become a gene of good PM practice. Creative, ad hoc pluralist adaptations, combinations, and sequences have become the stock in trade of leading facilitators.

Pluralism has also been evident in the range of applications of PMs. Reflect for instance has been adapted to meet local circumstances leading to a 'huge diversity of practice. In some places, the focus is on literacy and empowerment, as in the first pilot projects, but in many cases the focus is on social change without an explicit literacy element' (Sempere, 2009). Reflect has been used for teaching English for speakers of other languages (ESOL; Cardiff et al., n.d.), local planning in India, children's voice in Pakistan, mobilizing for basic rights in Nigeria, consolidating the landless movement in Brazil, opposing domestic violence in Peru, peace and reconciliation in Burundi, and a great variety of other purposes as described in the journal *Education Action*.

Pluralism has also taken the form of hybridization, when two or more PMs have merged. Reflect is a hybrid of the popular education of Paulo Freire and the visual methods and behaviour and attitudes of PRA. Stepping Stones evolved in parallel, and then Reflect and Stepping Stones came together as a further hybrid – STAR (STepping Stones And Reflect). Another example is Reflect with ESOL (Cardiff et al., n.d.). The participatory mapping and modelling of PRA formed a hybrid with GIS to become participatory GIS (Rambaldi et al., 2006) and participatory 3-D modelling (CTA, 2016). Reality Checks (see later) on primary healthcare and primary education in Bangladesh combined immersions (Birch et al., 2007) with participatory methods associated with RRA such as wandering around, key informants, listening, and observation.

All these developments make the repertoire and potentials of participatory approaches now far richer, and more versatile and varied, than most actors in international development recognize. This richness is both in methodologies which cohere, are labelled, and have basic principles, such as Reflect or CLTS, and also increasingly in individual methods which can be combined and adapted in sequences with others. The scope for ad hoc innovation and adaptation to context appears almost limitless, and of a new order of magnitude compared even with the recent past of 10 or 20 years ago. In good practice, creative improvisation and interactive innovation lead to processes which defy any reductionist, tidy classification, as with Andrea Cornwall, Charity Kabutha, and Tilly Sellers' participatory process evaluation to understand the dynamics of change in a nutrition education programme in Kenya (Cornwall, 2014). Facilitators know in advance their participatory approach and repertoire but not just what they are going to do. That evolves and emerges interactively and unpredictably. Each occasion is unique.

Participatory pluralism within organizations

Organizations can have their own core participatory procedures and at the same time allow and encourage creative diversity.

ActionAid International has shown what can be done. From 2000 onwards it made its participatory Accountability, Learning and Planning System (ALPS) (ActionAid, 2000; David and Mancini 2004; ActionAid International, 2006) central to how it operates and a means of expressing its values. Behaviour and attitudes are at the core of ALPS and annual Participatory Review and Reflection Processes (PRRPs) a key procedural element. PRRPs are designed to be inclusive, involving diverse stakeholders, and at all levels, allowing creative flexibility combined with critical review, assessing what has been done, what has been learned, and articulating what will be done differently in future. The participatory freedom within ActionAid International is reflected in a 2006 review of participatory approaches being used in 22 of its country programmes. No less than 14 of such approaches were listed. The numbers of country programmes using them were: PRA (22), Reflect (20), Participatory Vulnerability Analysis (16), Participatory Budget Analysis (16), Participatory Action Research (15), approaches with children (15), PPAs (14), Stepping Stones (14), STAR (12), Participatory Video (12), Social Audit (11), Immersions (10), Public Hearings (9), and Citizens' Juries (6). Participatory Review and Reflection Processes were so integral to the culture and practices of ActionAid International that they were not even listed.

Three methodologies for transformative revolutions

Three transformative revolutions are gathering momentum: participatory ICTs, participatory statistics and the Reality Check Approach.

Participatory ICTs

The rapid increase in momentum and scale of ICTs in recent decades has opened up a new world for participation, at the same time extending and blurring the boundaries of what can be described as participatory. To enumerate a few of the media and applications, we have participatory community radio, participatory video, participatory GIS and GPS, photo voice, digital storytelling, and innumerable participatory uses of mobile phones and tablets as well as text, instant messaging, and video conferencing apps. Applications of technologies may be either participatory or used for top-down, centre outwards, communication and control, or some alternation or mix of these as with webinars and conference calls. The range of applications of the variety of technologies is simply astonishing, leaving many including this participant-observer lagging in their learning. Consider what has happened with what can be seen as participatory applications, for instance: political mobilization as, famously, in the Arab Spring and elsewhere since; a referendum in Barcelona;

gaining support for causes and applying pressure on decision-makers (AVAAZ and others), sometimes accumulating millions of signatories to a letter, and with a record of substantial success; raising money for political campaigns from vast numbers of ordinary people, pioneered by Barack Obama and continued by Bernie Sanders; and many other applications including for participatory monitoring and evaluation (M&E).

New fields with new names emerge. Take Digital Citizen Engagement defined in a guide to its evaluation as: 'The use of new media/digital information and communication technologies to create or enhance the communication channels which facilitate the interaction between citizens and governments or the private sector' (Aptivate et al., 2016). The guide classifies and enumerates such interaction as being through media which are *low-tech* such as community radio, *medium-tech* such as SMS or call centres, or *high-tech* such as crowd-sourcing, interactive mapping, and web interfaces. And the many applications have included: social monitoring (public service delivery including beneficiary feedback, corruption reporting, and citizen-driven election monitoring); direct democracy (interaction with political representatives and participatory budgeting); and consultation, discussion, and deliberation. Cases on which the guide is grounded include online voting in participatory budgeting in Rio Grande do Sol, Brazil; U-Report, a 'long-standing and well-funded crowdsourcing platform' in Uganda; and MajiVoice, a service enabling Kenyans to give feedback to their water supply company using mobile phones or internet, and even pay for water when they draw it.

This is but a glimpse of part of the vast and growing field. There is a potent means here for empowering those with digital access and capabilities, though with the inevitable creation of a new group excluded and left behind. The multiplication of technologies, platforms, and channels has exponentially enhanced the range of PMs and the potential of eclectic and creative methodological pluralism.

These developments have given birth to a new voluntarism of those who process data. Two examples come from Kenya. One is Map Kibera, the participatory mapping of the largest slum in Africa, which was supported in its early stages by unpaid geeks. Another is Ushahidi, a software created in the disturbances after the Kenyan elections of 2008 to keep track of violence, and further developed and used worldwide for a whole range of emergencies: it relies on the voluntarism of geeks who receive information from people on the ground and relay it back again to those who need to know. A third Kenyan innovation has connected, liberated, and empowered the great majority of Kenyans. This is MPesa which enables them to use mobile phones to transfer money electronically, for instance remittances to relatives, without the delays and costs of going through banks.

Over the past two decades ICT PMs have added versatility and effectiveness to participatory methodologies through all sorts of adaptations and combinations.

Their many uses and applications include participatory monitoring. And as costs of hardware plummet and hardware capacities multiply, the scope for their use in PMs will grow in ways and for uses that cannot be foreseen.

Participatory statistics: a win–win

Participatory statistics span the Newtonian and Complexity paradigms. They are generated by those who live in conditions of complexity through facilitated processes which produce numbers that can be analysed with Newtonian statistical rigour without its reductionism.

Given their proven power and potential (see for example Holland, 2013), participatory statistics are puzzlingly under-recognized and neglected. The first dramatic demonstration of their power and potential was in Nepal in 1990 when Bimal Phnuyal led an ActionAid-Nepal study using participatory mapping in over 130 villages to generate insights and statistics on the extent to which services had reached people (ActionAid-Nepal, 1992). This was a form of participatory M&E. Aggregated, the results were presented in tables indistinguishable from those of a large-scale questionnaire survey. The population summed to 35,414. The difference was that arising as they did from collective cross-checked visualizations, the data were triangulated and more credible and probably much more accurate than anything that could have come from a questionnaire. Another example comes from Malawi where participatory census mapping identified a 35 per cent undercount in the national census (Barahona and Levy, 2003). Despite much pioneering with participatory statistics[15] they have nowhere to my knowledge been mainstreamed. Their quiet revolution remains under the radar of most development professionals and organizations.

No one to my knowledge has disputed that local people can count, calculate, measure, estimate, value, score, and make numerical comparisons. This includes experiences and knowledge which are not easily accessible by other means (Holland, 2013: 3–6). In a visual and tactile mode, they can do this with beans, counters, stones, or other objects, and this can be combined with other methods like mapping. Or statistics from focus groups can be aggregated. PMs are often thought to be only qualitative in their outputs. But in a participatory mode almost anything that is qualitative can be quantified and numbers aggregated from focus groups – for well-being (Rowley, 2014), relations with government (Narayan et al., 2000b), violence (Moser and McIlwaine, 2004), social norms, gender relations (see Table 5.1), and so on, and changes in these over time. These can then be analysed by a panoply of rigorous statistical methods, as demonstrated in *Participatory Impact Assessment: A Design Guide* (Catley et al., 2013 [2008]).

Who Counts? The Power of Participatory Statistics (Holland, 2013) makes the case with evidence. Its 12 chapters present examples where local people have been facilitated or have facilitated themselves to produce statistics. In

Bangladesh members of a social movement provided the basis for statistics on social change which they themselves monitored (Jupp with Ali, 2010, 2013). In Rwanda, there has been complete coverage of the nearly 15,000 rural villages, each of which has made its own cloth map showing households and ranked them into categories of wealth: these maps have been used nationally to identify students who qualify for bursaries for university, and those households that qualify for the national health insurance scheme[16] (Shah, 2013). Wealth and well-being ranking (Rowley, 2014) is another method generating categories and numbers which reflect detailed local knowledge, with information which tends not to be accessed when questionnaires are used, for instance about remittances or debts.

In the introduction to his book Holland (2013) writes:

> The book makes the following claims for a 'win-win' perspective on participatory statistics:
> - Participatory research can generate accurate and generalizable statistics in a timely, efficient (value for money) and effective way; and
> - Participatory statistics empower local people in a sphere of research that has traditionally been highly extractive and externally controlled.

Participatory statistics are usually a win–win: local people find the process and findings analysis interesting, learn from it, and are empowered by gaining evidence and confidence in their relations with authorities; outsiders are informed with a richness and relevance of detail not otherwise accessible; and the gap between the Newtonian and Complexity paradigms is bridged.

The slow uptake of participatory statistics means that the glass is far from even half full; it is only a fraction full. A vast empty space awaits explorers. One major part of this is through participatory and mixed method alternatives to randomized control trials (RCTs). Which makes this a wonderful time to be alive for innovative facilitators with freedom to open up this terrain. Look at what the PIALA team achieved (see Chapter 4). There is scope for much, much more of that.

The Reality Check Approach

In my view, the third methodological revolution, the Reality Check Approach (RCA) is the participatory innovation of the early 21st century with the greatest promise to transform knowing and action at scale (for useful resources see Lewis, 2013: 121–4; Reality Check Approach, 2016).[17] It can do this in the spirit of the SDGs by bringing the up-to-date realities of those who are not to be left behind credibly and persuasively to policy-makers, professionals, and the public. The Reality Check Approach can be used universally, in all countries, and has unique power to illuminate immediately the rapidly changing inequalities and the realities of poverty.

In RCAs, researchers are trained and orientated and then immersed in representative communities, spending days and nights, usually four, living as one of a family, taking part in chores and work, 'hanging out', wandering around and chatting, listening and observing, and having two-way, relaxed and informal conversations with many people. They may photograph but take no notes during the day. After their immersions they meet and compare experiences. The resulting reports are detailed, revealing, absorbing and, crucially, highly credible. They reveal realities and rates of social change of which capital city development professionals are typically unaware.

The first RCAs in Bangladesh in nine communities, one urban, one peri-urban, and one rural in each of three districts, were carried out in the same season for each of five consecutive years over 2007–11, with the same researchers revisiting the same families and communities. Sponsored by Sida, their focus was primary education and primary healthcare, but much else came to light. After it had run for five years, an evaluation of the RCA programme identified four key principles – depth, respect for voice, flexibility, and simplicity – and an orientation of learning rather than finding out (Pain et al., 2014).

Reality Checks have now been conducted in over nine countries, including Bangladesh, Indonesia, Mozambique, Nepal, Ethiopia, Cambodia, and Ghana. Realities have come to light which are missed, concealed, or distorted through the biases and superficiality of normal outside visits and power relationships. Surprising and important findings have always emerged. Here are a few plucked out of hundreds:

- When others conducted focus groups and participatory matrix scoring for an INGO, the chicken rearing it was promoting was highly valued; but a longitudinal RCA study found that chickens were the least valued of all domestic animals (GRM International, 2010a).
- In Nepal, road programmes designed for access to markets to sell produce and access to services were valued by people living in an area rather more for ease of leaving a remote area and consumer goods brought in (GRM International et al., 2013; Itad and FDM, 2015).
- In Bangladesh and Indonesia, education grants to poor students were almost entirely being spent on snacks sold by aggressive vendors outside schools (Jupp, 2010; Jupp et al., 2012).
- In Bangladesh salt was suddenly being consumed by children and adults in dangerous quantities (GRM International, 2010b).
- Boys in Bangladesh were not dropping out of school because of poverty but for other reasons (Jupp et al., 2012).
- In Nepal cultivation of the cash crop cardamom introduced by a farmer brought far more benefits than aid interventions (GRM International et al., 2013).
- In northern Ghana packets of bednets supplied by different organizations were lying in the homes of villagers unopened (Masset et al., 2013).

Where they take part, officials gain first-hand insights. In Malawi, for instance, DFID staff who took part in immersions experienced what lack of infrastructure meant, and learned that for rural people infrastructure was a higher priority than education (Ashish Shah, pers. comm.). Wherever they are conducted, then, Reality Checks can put outsiders in touch and bring them up to date: they provide credible instant insights across a wide (and to an extent unpredictable) range of aspects of life unlikely to be accessible in any other way.

For the 21st century and in the spirit of all the SDGs, Reality Checks could focus on inequality and poverty in all countries, whatever their level of 'development'. They have potential to illuminate and focus policies and practices to achieve the SDGs, most acutely SDG 1, 'End poverty in all its forms everywhere', and SDG 10, 'Reduce inequality within and among countries', by sparking and sustaining commitment to their achievement, and showing what would make most difference and be welcomed by those who would otherwise be left behind. The immediacy of Reality Checks, the relationships and interactions they allow, and their openness to whatever can be learned or observed, gives them an exceptionally inclusive rigour with credibility, freed from normal biases of courtesy and power relations. Through Reality Checks, the experiences and priorities of those left behind can regularly inform and confront policy-makers, practitioners, and the public. Let the RCA be a wave of the future. Those who are last in our world deserve nothing less.

These three methodologies have exceptional transformative potential. By analogy with HYVs (high-yielding varieties of crops) these can be described as HYMs (high-yielding methodologies) and, like other PMs, are global public goods.

Empowerment and the realities of those who are last

Many other PMs have also been used to enable those who are last to reflect and to articulate their realities and priorities and feed these 'upwards' to inform and influence policy and practice. The win–win in Box 5.1 is one example.

The Voices of the Poor project was designed to provide insights for the World Development Report 2000, *Attacking Poverty* (World Bank, 2000). One part of this was analysis of 81 participatory poverty assessments (Narayan et al., 2000a). The other entailed convening focus groups of poor, excluded, and vulnerable people in over 200 communities in 23 countries and facilitating their analysis and expression of their perspectives (Narayan et al., 2000b). These included their concepts of well-being and ill-being, their priorities, their relationships with institutions, and gender relations, and how these had changed over the previous 10 years.

The Participate Project (Burns et al., 2013; Leavy and Howard, 2013; Shahrokh and Wheeler, 2014; Burns et al., 2015) was undertaken to enable the priorities and perspectives of people who were living with extreme poverty and marginalization to inform and influence the SDG process and its high-level panel. This was in the SDG spirit of 'Leave no one behind'. Eighteen organizations in 30 countries that were already working with very diverse groups of marginalized people came together and enabled them to contribute their perspectives and priorities. Four ground-level panels of those people were convened and paralleled and informed the high-level panel. The 12 initial goals proposed by the high-level panel reflected sectoral thinking – education, water and sanitation, energy, poverty, and so on – while the 15 goals of the ground-level panel in India to a greater degree addressed causes and correlates of discrimination and disadvantage such as corruption, lack of recognition as citizens, and unsafe home environments (Narayanan et al., 2015). That ground-level panel went further and critiqued the high-level goals and listed in revealing detail what they thought was missing (Narayanan et al., 2015: 156–9).

Box 5.1 Monitoring and measuring empowerment and social change: the case of a social movement in Bangladesh

Sida as a funding agency wanted an evaluation of empowerment in a large social movement it supported in Bangladesh. Donors tried to impose logical frameworks and standard monitoring and evaluation approaches but the movement resisted. When outside design consultants were asked to suggest indicators for empowerment they came up with membership characteristics, leadership and group cohesion, collective action and wider networking, autonomy and maturity, and key benefits achieved. Then a team led by a consultant used an array of PRA tools, a listening study, and drama to generate value statements from members of the movement. The over 8,000 resulting key statements from groups and committees were 'peppered with perspectives which had never occurred to staff'. When grouped, the statements emerged and cohered as 132 indicators clustered under four headings: awareness; confidence and capability; effectiveness; and self-sustaining. A system of reflection sessions was then introduced in which groups assessed themselves against the criteria with either a happy or unhappy face, according to their satisfaction.

However, an outside review said 'in order to be a realistic monitoring tool it needs to be streamlined to reduce the number of indicators and the time taken to complete'. A donor consortium dismissed the approach with 'How can poor people engage in a process which takes three hours or more … they have mouths to feed'. When these comments were taken back to several member groups they were 'flabbergasted'.

We do this because it is important to us
Yes it takes a long time but it is time well spent
How could we review everything we do with only a few statements to describe it?
These people do not understand – we never talked about these things properly before – it has opened our eyes

The outsiders' concerns about time were based on sensitivity to the widespread experience with the extractive M&E of focus groups and questionnaire surveys. But this situation was different. The meetings mattered to the participants and were found valuable by them. They were even facilitated by members of the movement.

There were other paradigmatic differences – for example the way empowerment was a moving target, as groups changed the indicators, seeking to achieve more. Goals themselves can change in participatory processes; indeed, one indicator of a good process may be that the indicators do indeed change. If they do not, something may be wrong.

As social change took place, groups updated their indicators, gender relations within the household being one case. Statistics were derived and fed upwards, for instance one year that 79 per cent of the groups were able to access their full entitlements to primary education without payment of any bribes. As so often, the participatory processes were a win–win: people reviewed and reflected on their changing realities, their progress made, and what they now needed to do and funders were informed with unusually credible statistics.

Source: Jupp with Ali, 2010, 2013

For all these, good facilitation and rapport were vital. In Voices of the Poor this was achieved through exceptional training by Meera K. Shah and others; in Participate through organizations already working with those who were living with extreme poverty and marginalization; and in the movement in Bangladesh (Box 5.1) through horizontal facilitation by members of other groups. These remarkable initiatives have shown what can be done, and that progress can be made at scale in answering the question 'Whose reality counts?' with 'theirs', the realities of those left behind and kept out, amplifying their voices and making them count.

Co-generating and sharing knowledges

In writing this chapter it has been a struggle to keep up with developments. Innovations through combinations, sequences, and creativity, though rather scattered, are now incessant. They and their spread are often, even increasingly (Chapter 3) inhibited or prevented by the Newtonian methodologies demanded by those with money and power. In spite of this, it seems they multiply exponentially.

With PMs, as ever, there are the critical issues of Who? Whose? questions raised earlier in this chapter, and of power. Participatory approaches, by weakening or neutralizing the distortions of 'all power deceives', can be win–win. The participatory sense-making workshops of the PIALA project (see Chapter 4 pp 105–7) are an iconic example. The purpose of participatory sense-making is to enhance both the empowering value of impact evaluation or research, and the quality of insight. At community level this can be by instantly processing and sharing on site the data collected during fieldwork. At higher levels it goes beyond the traditional limited participation of checking out findings. It creates opportunities and facilitates processes in which programme stakeholders can challenge, strengthen, and add to evidence and findings. Co-generation of knowledges is then an integral part of processes of evaluation or research. And it is a win–win because the quality of findings are enhanced and stakeholders who take part themselves learn.

Contrasted with conventional research and evaluation, this is more than just validating. The participatory processes with multiple interactions mean that the knowledges generated are to a degree owned by all participant stakeholders. The answer to the question, Whose knowledges count? is 'everyone's' but most of all the knowledges of local stakeholders who are close to the realities.

A further frontier is co-generation of the approach, methods, and indicators themselves. 'Whose indicators count?' has indeed been answered (see for instance Box 5.1) by 'theirs': in the Centre for International Forestry Research's work on participatory monitoring in nine countries, characterized as 'Negotiated learning' (Guijt, 2007), it was 'verifiers' rather than other principles that made sense to local participants. Methods are less commonly entirely 'theirs' but can be and often should be co-evolved and negotiated: methods simply brought in from outside, however participatory they may be, will lack the added strength that can come from people's ideas and preferences for co-learning from which they will gain. Co-generation of a whole approach may be rare, but with local interest and commitment is an ultimate outcome of repeatedly following the PRA injunction: 'ask them'.

The future of participatory approaches and methods

Future historians may see the sudden flowering and spread of participatory approaches and methods in the past three decades only as a tiny blip, if at all. Compared with the explosion of ICTs they may seem insignificant. Most of us are more aware of how our lives and links with others have been transformed by email, Facebook, Twitter, YouTube, WhatsApp, and other astonishing wonders of the internet than we are of participatory methodologies which may have touched many of us little or not at all. Current generations have been mesmerized by television and computer screens, reducing face-to-face human interaction. Yet one may wonder whether, to live well, future generations will seek to strike a new balance; and whether the power of face-to-face participation to fulfil, to be fun, to co-generate valid and insightful knowledges, and above all to empower those who are left behind, those who are last, can become a countervailing wave.

The evidence and examples in this chapter make the case for making participatory methodologies and methods central in the agenda for knowing better. Their range and scope has expanded exponentially through combinations, sequences, improvisation, adaptation, and the creativity of facilitators. Well facilitated, they have almost limitless applications for empowering those who are most marginalized and last (see for instance Thomas and Narayanan, 2014). As with PIALA, they can present rigorous cost-effective alternatives to RCTs. There is no reason to suppose that the *potential* they offer will tail off. But whether that potential will be realized is another matter. For PMs to be a wave of the future requires radical changes in universities, colleges, and training institutes, textbooks, NGOs, governments, and funding agencies, and a multiplication of creative facilitators and champions with vision and courage. Ideas for how those personal, institutional, and professional transformations can be provoked, catalysed, supported, and sustained, are for the last chapter.

Agenda for reflection and action

These questions apply to all actors with powers of choice and management of methodology. For inclusive rigour, and to know better together:

- What scope and room for manoeuvre do you have to introduce and try out PMs?
- Do you need at the outset to build this into your budget?

- What combinations and adaptations are worth exploring to fit your needs?
- Can you ensure patience, flexibility, time, and resources for trials, piloting, and eclectic pluralism?
- Can you find, nurture, and support creative and committed facilitators?
- Can empowering ICTs have a role?
- Is there scope for participatory statistics?
- Can you promote or adapt the Reality Check Approach?
- Can you organize immersions for yourself and your colleagues?
- How can you share your experience, innovations, and methods with others?

Notes

1. Uppers are those who are superior or dominant, and lowers are those who are inferior or subordinate, in a situation or relationship.
2. When I worked for the Ford Foundation in India my warm glow at the sudden respect with which my work was regarded quickly gave way to cynicism. On two occasions I was nodding with approval at a conference speaker's surprisingly sound sentiments until I recognized my own prose.
3. Handing over the stick can be literal in some PRA visualization activities like mapping or diagramming on the ground, but it can also be, handing over the pen, the microphone, the megaphone, the conch shell (which gives authority to speak as in William Golding's *Lord of the Flies*), the knife (for cutting and apportioning a cake), and so on, and more generally is a metaphor for handing over initiative, control, and power.
4. *Socially* sustainable is an important qualification. Physical and biological sustainability are in future generations' interests. PMs may or may not contribute to these. Social sustainability refers to sustainability in society – in social, institutional, and political domains. This simplification avoids or evades the chapter or book-length discussion of dimensions of sustainability that it opens up.
5. It is a mysterious tragedy and missed opportunity that there is to my knowledge no fully fledged knowledge hub for participatory methodologies in the whole world. At IDS we have a website (www.participatorymethods.org) which, given the potential of this area, is tragically underfunded. It would be brazen of me to suggest to any wealthy philanthropists who read this that they might want to consider support.
6. www.reflect-action.org (Archer, 2007).
7. www.iapad.org and www.ppgis.net
8. www.communityledtotalsanitation.org
9. www.reality-check-approach.com
10. This is the second termination of an invaluable series on PMs. The first was produced by the rural development group at Cornell led by Norman Uphoff, and funded by USAID until it declined to renew its support. It is a mystery to me why donors and others are so blind to the importance of frontier periodicals like these. The *RRA Notes / PLA Notes / PLA* series is

available at www.iied.org/participatory-learning-action. Let me urge some donor with vision who reads this to revive the series.

11. In *The French Revolution, as it Appeared to Enthusiasts*. The next line is 'But to be young was very heaven'. Most of those involved in the early days of PRA were between 30 and 60 years old but it made them feel young.

12. The failure to survive of some PMs that require detailed fixed routines raises fascinating questions about paradigmatic incompatibilities. CLTS, Reflect, Stepping Stones and others that have flourished also have sequences but have stressed quality of facilitation and flexibility with space and encouragement for innovation.

13. This estimate is a personal guess based mainly on estimates for South and South-east Asia and sub-Saharan Africa. The nearly 15,000 collines (rural communities) in Rwanda have made their own cloth maps (personal communication with Sam Joseph) and these will have been based on earlier maps made by communities on the ground. All the communities in which the very large INGO, Plan International, works have been making participatory maps during at least the past decade. And many communities have made maps many times.

14. Incompatible mixtures, like salt in sweet, are at best unpalatable. There are paradigmatic issues here. Opinions differ on whether and how more didactic, sequential approaches (in the Newtonian mode) can be combined with more participatory (Complexity mode) approaches. PHAST (Participatory Hygiene and Sanitation Transformation), which has a thick manual and in its classic form entails many sessions with preset cards and is in more of a teaching mode, is reported to have been found incompatible with CLTS, which has a facilitating mode, a more flexible handbook, and encourages innovation.

15. There is a considerable literature, both grey and published in international journals (see e.g. Barahona and Levy, 2003; Chambers, 2008: 105–32; Holland, 2013).

16 Using participatory mapping to identify who will benefit can be fairer than cynics may suppose when it is well facilitated. But using it in the longer term without facilitation to identify who will, for instance, receive bursaries is bound to be open to abuse, as it proved to be in Rwanda.

17. I am grateful to Dee Jupp for advice and help with this section.

References

ActionAid-Nepal (1992) *Participatory Rural Appraisal Utilisation Survey Report Part 1*, Kathmandu: Monitoring and Evaluation Unit, ActionAid-Nepal.

ActionAid (2000) *Accountability, Learning and Planning System*, London: Action Aid.

ActionAid (2002) *Participatory Vulnerability Analysis: A Step-by-Step Guide for Field Staff* [pdf], London: ActionAid <https://www.actionaid.org.uk/sites/default/files/doc_lib/108_1_participatory_vulnerability_analysis_guide.pdf> [accessed 30 January 2017].

ActionAid International (2006) *ALPS: Accountability: Learning and Planning System*, Johannesburg: ActionAid International.

Aptivate, IDS and ica-uk (2016) *Evaluating Citizen Engagement: A Practical Guide,* Washington, DC: World Bank.

Archer, D. (2007) 'Seeds of success are seeds for potential failure: learning from the evolution of Reflect', in K. Brock and J. Pettit (eds) *Springs of Participation,* pp. 15–28, Rugby, UK: Practical Action Publishing.

Arthur, B. (2009) *The Nature of Technology: What It Is and How It Evolves,* New York: Free Press.

Auret, D. and Barrientos, S. (2004) *Participatory Social Auditing: A Practical Guide to a Gender-Sensitive Approach,* IDS Working Paper 237: Brighton, UK: IDS.

Barahona, C. and Levy, S. (2003) *How to Generate Statistics and Influence Policy Using Participatory Methods in Research: Reflections on Work in Malawi 1999–2002,* IDS Working Paper 212, Brighton, UK: IDS.

Birch, I., Catani, R. with Chambers, R. (eds) (2007) *Immersions: Learning about Poverty Face-to-Face,* PLA 57, London: IIED.

Boal, A. (1992) *Games For Actors and Non-Actors,* London: Routledge.

Boedhihartono, A.K. (2012) *Visualizing Sustainable Landscapes: Understanding and Negotiating Conservation and Development Trade-offs Using Visual Techniques,* Gland, Switzerland: IUCN.

Bradbury, H. (ed.) (2015) *The Sage Handbook of Action Research,* 3rd edn, London: Sage Reference.

Braun, A.R., Thiele, G. and Fernandez, A. (2000) *Farmer Field Schools and local Agricultural Research Committees: Complementary Platforms for Integrated Decision-making in Sustainable Agriculture,* Network Paper 105, London: ODI Agricultural Research and Extension Network.

Burns, D. (2007) *Systemic Action Research: A Strategy for Whole System Change,* Bristol, UK: The Policy Press.

Burns, D. and Worsley, S. (2015) *Navigating Complexity in International Development: Facilitating Sustainable Change at Scale,* Rugby, UK: Practical Action Publishing.

Burns, D., Howard, J. Lopez-Franco, E., Shahrokh, T. and Wheeler, J. (2013) *Work With Us: How People and Organisations Can Catalyse Sustainable Change,* Brighton, UK: IDS.

Burns, D., Ikita, P., Lopez-Franco, E., and Shahrokh, T. (2015) *Citizen Participation and for Sustainable Development,* Brighton, UK: IDS.

Cabannes, Y. (2004) 'Participatory budgeting: significant contribution to participatory democracy', *Environment and Urbanisation* 16(1): 27–46.

Cardiff, P., Newman, K. and Pearce, E. (n.d.) *Reflect for ESOL (English for Speakers of Other Languages), Resource Pack,* London: ActionAid <www.reflect-action.org/reflectesol> [accessed 4 September 2016].

Catley, A., Burns, J., Abebe, D. and Suji, O. (2013) [2008] *Participatory Impact Assessment: A Design Guide* [pdf], Medford, MA: Feinstein International Center, Tufts University <http://fic.tufts.edu/publication-item/participatory-impact-assessment-a-design-guide/> [accessed 18 December 2016].

Chambers, R. (1997) *Whose Reality Counts? Putting the First Last,* Rugby, UK: Practical Action Publishing.

Chambers, R. (2008) *Revolutions in Development Inquiry,* London: Earthscan.

Conway, G. (1985) 'Agro-ecosystem analysis', *Agricultural Administration* 20: 31–55.

Cooperrider, D.L., Whitney, D. and Stavros, J.M. (2008) *Appreciative Inquiry Handbook* (2nd edn), Brunswick, OH: Crown Custom Publishing.

Cornwall, A. (2014) *Using Participatory Process Evaluation to Understand the Dynamics of Change in a Nutrition Education Programme*, IDS Working Paper 437, Brighton, UK: IDS.

Cornwall, A. and Pratt, G. (eds) (2003) *Pathways to Participation: Reflections on PRA*, London: ITDG Publications.

CTA (2016) *The Power of Maps: Bringing the Third Dimension to the Negotiating Table*, Success Stories Series, Wageningen, The Netherlands: Technical Centre for Agricultural and Rural Cooperation.

David, R. and Mancini, A. (2004) *Going against the Flow: The Struggle to Make Organisational Systems Part of the Solution Rather Than Part of the Problem*, Lessons for Change No 7, Brighton, UK: IDS.

David, R., Mancini, A. and Guijt, I. (2006) 'Bringing systems into line with values: the practice of accountability, learning and planning system', in R. Eyben (ed.) *Relationships for Aid*, pp. 133–53, London: Earthscan.

Davies, R. and Dart, J. (2004) *The 'Most Significant Change' (MSC) Technique: A Guide to Its Use* [pdf] <www.mande.co.uk/docs/MSCGuide.pdf> [accessed 18 December 2016].

Dent, D. with Elliott, N.C., Farrell, J.A., Gutierrez, A.P. and van Lenteren, J.C. (1995) *Integrated Pest Management*, London: Chapman and Hall.

Earl, S., Carden, F. and Smutylo, T. (2001) *Outcome Mapping: Building Learning and Reflection into Development Programs*, Ottawa: International Development Research Centre.

Estrella, M. with Blauert, J., Campilan, D., Gaventa, J., Gonsalves, J., Guijt, I., Johnson, D. and Ricafort, R. (eds) (2000) *Learning from Change: Issues and Experiences in Participatory Monitoring and Evaluation*, London: Intermediate Technology Publications.

Gaventa, J. (2004) 'Strengthening participatory approaches to local governance: learning lessons from abroad', *National Civic Review* 93(4): 16–27 <http://dx.doi.org/10.1002/ncr.67>.

Gaventa, J. and Barrett, G. (2012) 'Mapping the outcomes of citizen's engagement', *World Development* 40(12): 2399–410 <http://dx.doi.org/10.1016/j.worlddev.2012.05.014>.

Gaventa, J. and Cornwall, A. (2015) 'Power and knowledge', in H. Bradbury (ed.), *The Sage Handbook of Action Research*, pp. 465–71, London: Sage.

Greenwood, D.J. and Levin, M. (1998) *Introduction to Action Research: Social Research for Social Change*, London: Sage Publications.

GRM International (2010a) *Reality Check – Mozambique (Year 1, 2010): Listening to the views of Households and Communities Living in the Newcastle Disease Control Programme Area* [pdf], Stockholm: GRM International <www.reality-check-approach.com/uploads/6/0/8/2/60824721/moz_ndc_report.pdf> [accessed 19 December 2016].

GRM International (2010b) *Reality Check Bangladesh 2009: Listening to Poor People's Realities about Primary Healthcare and Primary Education – Year 3* [pdf], Sida <www.sida.se/globalassets/publications/import/pdf/en/reality-check-bangladesh-2009.pdf> [accessed 19 December 2016].

GRM International with Effective Development Group and Foundation for Development Management (2013) *Research into the Long Term Impact of*

Development Interventions in the Koshi Hills of Nepal: Summary Report [pdf], Kathmandu: National Planning Commission, Government of Nepal <https://www.gov.uk/government/uploads/system/uploads/attachment_data/file/298721/Long-Term-Impact-Dev-Study-Report-Koshi-Hills-Nepal.pdf> [accessed 19 December 2016].

Guijt, I. (ed.) (2007) *Negotiated Learning: Collaborative Monitoring in Forest Resource Management*, Washington, DC: Resources for the Future.

Gypmantasiri et al. and Conway, G. (1980) *An Interdisciplinary Perspective of Cropping Systems in the Chiang Mai Valley: Key Questions for Research*, Multiple Cropping Project, Chiang Mai, Thailand: Faculty of Agriculture, University of Chiang Mai.

Haverkort, B., Kamp, J. and Waters-Bayer, A. (1991) *Joining Farmers' Experiments: Experiences in Participatory Technology Development*, Rugby, UK: Practical Action Publishing.

Holland, J. (ed.) (2013) *Who Counts? The Power of Participatory Statistics*, Rugby, UK: Practical Action Publishing.

IAPAD (2017) *Participatory avenues*, Integrated Approaches to Participatory Development [website], <http://www.iapad.org/> [accessed 28 February 2017].

International HIV/AIDS Alliance (2006) *Tools Together Now! 100 Participatory Tools to Mobilise Communities for HIV/AIDS*, Brighton, UK: International HIV/AIDS Alliance.

Itad with Foundation for Development Management (2015) *Nepal Rural Access Programme – Monitoring, Evaluation and Learning Component: Reality Check Approach Baseline Report* [pdf], Hove, UK: Itad <www.rapnepal.com/sites/default/files/report-publication/rca_baseline_report.pdf> [accessed 19 December 2016].

Jayakaran, R. (2002) *The Ten Seed Technique* [pdf], <we.riseup.net/assets/5575/Ten+seed+PLA.pdf> [accessed 4 September 2016].

Jayakaran, R. (2007) 'Wholistic worldview analysis: understanding community realities', *Participatory Learning and Action* 56: 41–8.

Jupp, D. (2007) 'Keeping the art of participation bubbling: some reflections on what stimulates creativity in using participatory methods', in K. Brock and J. Pettit (eds), *Springs of Participation*, pp. 107–22, Rugby, UK: Practical Action Publishing.

Jupp, D. (2010) *Indonesia Reality Check Main Study Findings: Listening to Poor People's Realities about Basic Education* [pdf], Australia Indonesia Partnership <www.participatorymethods.org/sites/participatorymethods.org/files/Indonesia-Reality-Check%20main%20findings-2010.pdf> [accessed 19 December 2016].

Jupp, D. with Ibn Ali, S. (2013) 'Accountability downwards, count-ability upwards: quantifying empowerment outcomes in Bangladesh', in J. Holland (ed.) *Who Counts? The Power of Participatory Statistics*, pp. 97–111, Rugby, UK: Practical Action Publishing.

Jupp, D. with Ibn Ali, S. and Barahona, C. (2010) *Measuring Empowerment? Ask Them: Quantifying Qualitative Outcomes from People's Own Analysis: Insights for Results-Based Management from the Experience of a Social Movement in Bangladesh* [pdf], Sida Studies in Evaluation, Stockholm <https://www.oecd.org/countries/bangladesh/46146440.pdf> [accessed 30 January 2017].

Jupp, D., Arvidson, M., Rukanuddin, S., Huda, E., Lewis, D., Jahan, N., Arif, R.H., Rahman, S., Afroz, D., Hossain, A., Kibria, G., Begum, N., Nayeem, M.H. and Verwilghen, J. (2012) *Reality Check Bangladesh 2011: Listening to Poor People's Realities about Primary Healthcare and Primary Education* – Year 5 [pdf], Sida <www.sida.se/globalassets/publications/import/pdf/en/reality-check-bangladesh-2011_3408.pdf> [accessed 19 December 2016].

Kar, K. with Chambers, R. (2008) *Handbook on Community-Led Total Sanitation* [pdf], Brighton: IDS and London: Plan <www.communityledtotalsanitation.org/resource/handbook-community-led-total-sanitation> [accessed 18 December 2016].

Keystone (2014) *Constituency Voice*, Technical Note 1, London: Keystone Accountability.

Khon Kaen University (1987) *Proceedings of the 1985 International Conference on Rapid Rural Appraisal*, Khon Kaen, Thailand: Rural Systems Research and Farming Systems Research Projects, KKU.

Leavy, J. and Howard, J. et al. (2013) *What Matters Most? Evidence from 84 Participatory Studies from Those Living with Extreme Poverty and Marginalisation*, Brighton, UK: IDS.

Lewin, T. (2011) 'Digital storytelling', *Participatory Learning and Action* 63: 54–62.

Lewin, T. (2012) 'Digital storytelling handbook' [online] <www.transformativestory.org/supporting-resources/> [accessed 18 December 2016].

Lewin, T., Pellizzer, V., Shahrokh, T., and Wheeler, J. (2014) 'Transformative storytelling for social change' [online], Participate and The Swiss Agency for Development and Cooperation <www.transformativestory.org> [accessed 18 December 2016].

Mansuri, G. and Rao, V. (2003) 'Evaluating Community-Based and Community-Driven Development: A Critical Review of the Evidence' [online], The World Bank <http://siteresources.worldbank.org/INTECAREGTOPCOMDRIDEV/Resources/DECstudy.pdf> [accessed 13 April 2017].

Mascarenhas, J., Shah, P., Joseph, S., Jayakaran, R., Devavaram, J., Ramachanran, V., Fernandez, A., Chambers, R. and Pretty, J. (eds) (1991) *Proceedings of the February 1991 PRA Workshop, Bangalore*, RRA Notes 13.

Masset, E., Jupp, D., Korboe, D., Dogbe, T. and Barnett, C. (2013) *Millennium Village Impact Evaluation Baseline Summary Report*, Hove, UK: Itad.

Mathie, A. and Gaventa, J. (eds) (2015) *Citizen-Led Innovation for a New Economy*, Rugby, UK: Practical Action Publishing.

Mayoux, L. (2007) 'Road to the foot of the mountain, but reaching for the sun: PALS adventures and challenges', in K. Brock and J. Pettit (eds), *Pathways to Participation*, pp. 93–106, Rugby, UK: Practical Action Publishing.

Moser, C. and McIlwaine, C. (2004) *Encounters with Violence in Latin America: Urban Poor Perceptions in Colombia and Guatemala*, London: Routledge.

Mukherjee, N. (2002) *Participatory Learning and Action with 100 Field Methods*, New Delhi: Concept Publishing Company.

Mukherjee, N. (2009) *Speaking to Power: 27 Voice Tools*, New Delhi: Concept Publishing Company.

Myers, J. (2015) 'An update of themes and trends in urban Community-Led Total Sanitation Projects', Briefing Paper 2104, *38th WEDC International Conference*, Loughborough University, UK.

Nagasundari, S. (2007) 'Evolution of the internal learning system: a case study of the new entity for social action', in K. Brock and J. Pettit (eds), *Springs of Participation*, pp. 81–91, Rugby, UK: Practical Action Publishing.

Nang'ole, E., Mithoefer, D. and Franzel, S. (2011) *Review of Guidelines and Manuals for Value Chain Analysis for Agricultural and Forestry Products*, ICRAF Occasional Paper 17, Nairobi: World Agroforestry Centre.

Narayan, D. with Patel, R., Schafft, K., Rademacher, A. and Koch-Schulte, S. (2000a) *Voices of the Poor: Can Anyone Hear Us?* New York: Oxford University Press for the World Bank.

Narayan, D., Chambers, R., Shah, M.K. and Petesch, P. (2000b) *Voices of the Poor: Crying out for Change*, New York: Oxford University Press for the World Bank.

Narayanan, P., Bharadwaj, S. and Chandrasekharan, A. (2015) 'Re-imagining development: marginalized people and the post-2015 agenda', in Thomas, T. and Narayanan, P. (eds), *Participation Pays: Pathways for Post-2015*, pp. 137–62, Rugby, UK: Practical Action Publishing.

Narendranath, D. (2007) 'Steering the boat of life with the Internal Learning System: the oar of learning', in K. Brock and J. Pettit (eds), *Springs of Participation*, pp. 67–79, Rugby, UK: Practical Action Publishing.

Noponen, H. (2007) 'It's not just about the pictures! It's also about principles, process and power: tensions in the development of the Internal Learning System', in K. Brock and J. Pettit (eds), *Springs of Participation*, pp. 53–65, Rugby, UK: Practical Action Publishing.

Norton, A., Bird, B., Brock, K., Kakande, M. and Turk, C. (2001) *A Rough Guide to PPAs: Participatory Poverty Assessment: An Introduction to Theory and Practice*, London: Overseas Development Institute.

Okali, C., Sumberg, J. and Farrington, J. (1994) *Farmer Participatory Research*, London: Intermediate Technology Publications.

Pain, A., Nycander, L., and Islam, K. (2014) *Evaluation of the Reality Check Approach in Bangladesh: Final Report* [pdf], Stockholm: Sida <www.sida.se/contentassets/57ac1b71f9014003aec0d0f3d4a2e4f5/evaluation-of-the-reality-check-approach-in-bangladesh---final-report_3739.pdf> [accessed 30 January 2017].

Pascale, R.T. and Sternin, J. (2010) *The Power of Positive Deviance: How Unlikely Innovators Solve the World's Toughest Problems*, Boston, MA: Harvard Business Review Press.

Paul, S. (2002) *Holding the State to Account: Citizen Monitoring in Action*, Bangalore: Books for Change.

Pedler, M. and Burgoyne, J. (2015) 'Action learning', in H. Bradbury (ed.), *The Sage Handbook of Action Research*, pp. 179–87, London: Sage.

Pimbert, M.P. and Wakeford, T. (eds) (2001) 'Deliberative democracy and citizen empowerment', *Special Issue of PLA Notes 40* [online], IIED <http://pubs.iied.org/6345IIED/?k=Deliberative+democracy+and+citizen+empowerment&s=PLA> [accessed 30 January 2017].

PLA Participatory Learning and Action (1988–2013) Numbers 1– 66, London: Institute for Environment and Development.

Positive Deviance Initiative (2010) *Basic Field Guide to the Positive Deviance Approach* [pdf], Tufts University <www.positivedeviance.org/resources/manuals_basicguide.html> [accessed 14 October 2016].

PPgis.net (no date) [website] <http://www.ppgis.net/> [accessed 28 February 2017].

Ramalingam, B. (2016) 'Learning to Adapt: Building adaptive management as a core competency in development practice' [online], USAID, IDS and mStar <www.globalinnovationexchange.org/learning-adapt> [accessed July 2016].

Rambaldi, G. and Callosa-Tarr, J. (2002) *Participatory 3-Dimensional Modelling: Guiding Principles and Applications*, Los Banos, the Philippines: ASEAN Regional Centre for Biodiversity Conservation.

Rambaldi, G., Corbett, J., McCall, M., Olson, R., Muchemi, J., Kwaku Kyem, P.A., Wiener, D. and Chambers, R. (eds) (2006) *Mapping for Change: Practice, Technologies and Communication*, PLA 54, London: IIED.

Reality Check Approach (2016) [website], <http://www.reality-check-approach.com/> [accessed 28 February 2017].

Revans, R. (1982) *The Origins and Growth of Action Learning*, Bromley, UK: Chartwell-Bratt.

Rijal, M. (ed.) (2013) *Participatory Democracy: Issues and reflections*, Kathmandu: ActionAid International Nepal and Institute for Local Governance and Development.

Robb, C. (2002) *Can the Poor Influence Policy? Participatory Poverty Assessments in the Developing World* (2nd edn), Washington, DC: World Bank 'Directions in Development'.

Rowley, J. (ed.) (2014) *Wellbeing Ranking: Developments in Applied Community-level Poverty Research*, Rugby, UK: Practical Action Publishing.

Sempere, K. (2009) 'The Reflect evaluation framework is published', *EducationAction* 23: 27–8 <www.actionaid.org/sites/files/actionaid/education_action_23_-_english.pdf> [accessed 10 October 2016].

Shah, A. (2013) 'Participatory statistics, local decision-making, and national policy design: *Ubudehe* community planning in Rwanda', in J. Holland (ed.) *Who Counts? The Power of Participatory Statistics*, pp. 49–63, Rugby, UK: Practical Action Publishing.

Shahrokh, T. and Wheeler, J. (eds) (2014) *Knowledge from the Margins: An Anthology from a Global Network on Participatory Practice and Policy Influence*, Brighton, UK: IDS.

Shaw, J. and Robertson, C. (1997) *Participatory Video: A Practical Guide to Using Video Creatively in Group Development Work*, London: Routledge.

Thomas, T. and Narayanan, P. (eds) (2015) *Participation Pays: Pathways for post-2015*, Rugby, UK: Practical Action Publishing.

Van Hemelrijck, A., and Guijt, I. (2016) *Balancing Inclusiveness, Rigour and Feasibility; Insights from Participatory Impact Evaluations in Ghana and Vietnam*, Centre for Development Impact Practice Paper 14, Brighton, UK: IDS.

Van Hemelrijck, A. and Kyei-Mensah, G. (2015) *Final Report on the participatory impact evaluation of the Root & Tuber Improvement & Marketing Program (RTIMP) conducted by PDA with support from the MOFA/GoG. Pilot Application of a Participatory Impact Assessment & Learning Approach (PIALA) developed with support from IFAD and the BMGF*, IFAD, Government of Ghana and BMGF.

Wang, C. and Burris, M.A. (1997) 'Photovoice: concept, methodology, and use for participatory needs assessment', *Health Education Behaviour* 24(3): 369–87.

Welbourn, A. (1995) *Stepping Stones: A Training Package on Gender, HIV, Communication and Relationship Skills*, Strategies for Hope, London: ActionAid.

Welbourn, A. (2013) 'From local to global and back again – learning from Stepping Stones', in T. Wallace, F. Porter, and M. Ralph-Bowman (eds), *Aid, NGOs and the Realities of Women's Lives*, pp. 175–88, Rugby, UK: Practical Action Publishing.

Witcombe, J.R., Joshi, A. and Joshi, K.D. (1996) 'Farmer participatory crop improvement. 1. Varietal selection and breeding methods and their impact on biodiversity', *Experimental Agriculture* 32(4): 445–60.

World Bank (2000) *World Development Report 2000/2001: Attacking Poverty*, New York: Oxford University Press for the World Bank.

CHAPTER 6
Knowing for a better future

Abstract

To minimize errors, myths, and biases, open up blind spots, liberate from lock-ins and know better in a 21st century of universalism and accelerating unforeseeable change demands a new and revolutionary professionalism. This entails epistemological, behavioural, and experiential transformations through synergies: of vocabulary and concepts; participatory ground-truthing; the behaviours, attitudes, and relationships of good facilitation; critical reflection and reflexivity; and principles, values, commitment, and energy. Facilitators and creative champions of participatory approaches and methods are central as agents of adaptive pluralism, innovation, and transformation. Arenas for radical action are professional – challenging and changing convention; institutional – upending procedures and cultures; personal – engaging with a passion for knowing better and doing better; and collective – forming alliances of the like-minded. Radical rethinking and transformations are required in the procedures, relationships, and cultures of government departments, NGOs, funding agencies, and other development organizations and in the teaching, training, and textbooks of universities, colleges, and training institutes. To overcome inertia, conservatism, and the comfort zones of business as usual, and to do this sustainably and at scale, are enthralling challenges. In facing and overcoming these, funding agencies and those who work in them have pivotal parts to play. For those passionate for a better world, the 21st century promises exhilaration and fulfilment. Better knowing and doing will come from the sum and synergies of innumerable personal choices and actions. The adventure of our human efforts to know better and do better will have no end.

Keywords: professionalism, revolutionary, reflexivity, facilitation, relationships, personal, passion, commitment, love, truth

> You can't cross the sea merely by standing and staring at the water. (Rabindranath Tagore)

> No great improvements in the lot of mankind are possible, until a great change takes place in the fundamental constitution of their modes of thought. (John Stuart Mill, *Autobiography*)

> It is not that we should simply seek new and better ways for managing society, the economy and the world. The point is that we should fundamentally change how we behave. (Vaclav Havel)

> The philosophers have *interpreted* the world in various ways; the point however is to *change* it. (Karl Marx, 1845)

http://dx.doi.org/10.3362/9781780449449.006

> Change requires knowing that 'we don't know'. (Ashish Shah, 2013: 210)

> You see things; and you say 'Why?' But I dream things and say 'Why not?' (George Bernard Shaw, *Back to Methuselah*)

The agendas for knowing better at the end of each chapter challenge and provoke.[1] They are not about marginal improvements to business as usual. They imply revolutionary change. I hope others like me will be thrilled by the scope they open up. They take us beyond knowing better to doing better, and learning and knowing through doing. Knowing and doing are inextricably intertwined, not least in a participatory mode.[2] Participatory approaches also take us further, through explorations and creative initiatives promising to make our own lives more fulfilling and rewarding. Can those agendas inform and inspire a passion for action for transformative change? And synergize with other drivers for good change? In all countries? For those who can act, the opportunities for innovation and making a difference look limitless. The many bad forces and trends in our world and the dead hand of inertia can be confronted. They are all the more reason for exploring and exploiting ways of knowing and acting better, and doing this with energy and passion. In this final chapter, trying to combine vision and realism, I build on earlier chapters to propose elements in a revolutionary professionalism for knowing and action in development.

Knowing better in our unforeseeable 21st century

Seeking to know better in our 21st century promises to be exciting, enthralling, and fun. To avoid errors, myths, and biases, to look for and shed light on blind spots, to become aware of our professional lenses, to liberate from the lock-ins of mechanistic methodologies – these offer adventures and almost boundless opportunities for knowing more and knowing better. When we add exploring complexity and recognize the explosion of participatory methodologies, the future beckons with invitations to be bold, adventurous, and innovative, and to enjoy. We can dream of and bring about a new and revolutionary professionalism of knowing.

What then does this demand? Let us start by setting the context with three salient reflections.

Accelerating social change

That change is accelerating is a truism. People may have been saying this for millennia. But that does not mean that it is not true or relevant for development and for us today. Accelerating change intensifies unpredictability. We are in a new space. Innovations in ICTs in their many manifestations are unprecedented in their spectacular speed, scale, and effects on those of us who are connected. The World Wide Web was only invented by Tim Berners-Lee in 1989.[3] Now there are new social networks and apps almost every month. For those of us who were around before they existed, and who are now habituated to and hooked on email, internet, and social media, it needs an effort of imagination to think ourselves back into that earlier but so recent time without digital interconnectivity, and to recognize how spectacularly different our world has now become. And to realize that more and more of the younger among us have known nothing else.

But 'we' here are only the more connected and better off two-thirds of humankind. What about the other third, and most of all those who are last – those who are poor, sick, disabled, aged, insecure and vulnerable, powerless, marginalized, discriminated against, stigmatized, isolated, imprisoned, enslaved...who are unseen and turned away from? Bear in mind that there is often a gender dimension. Are earlier moving accounts of their realities, like those of Harsh Mander (2001, 2015) for India and Parasuraman et al. (2003) for several Asian countries, now out of date? Answers come from Mander's deeply disturbing *Looking Away: Inequality, Prejudice and Indifference in New India* (2015) and from the Participate Project (Shahrokh and Wheeler, 2014) in many countries which fed the realities of those who are last into the Sustainable Development Goal (SDG) process. Much has changed and many have moved up the ladder but many have been left behind or have become excluded, discriminated against, and unseen.

From the perspective of the last, there is so much that needs to be better known and acted on. Context and conditions change fast. For many millions, war, civil war, and insecurities make life suddenly and dramatically worse. Many inequalities have been widening (ISSC et al., 2016), too often masked by average improvements in indicators of well-being. At the same time, the awareness, aspirations, and priorities of those who are last have been changing ever faster.[4] The imperative is stronger than ever for better ground-truthing and knowing, to know and understand their realities, and to be in touch and up to date, so that knowledge can inform and enable better action. But knowing is not enough unless it leads to doing. Informed action has to follow knowledge. And that demands focused energy from passion and commitment.

Redefining development

In parallel with other changes, the past three decades have witnessed a deep and continuing shift in professional understandings of development. Three significant shifts away from reductionist economic definitions of development were the launch of the annual Human Development Report in 1990 and its introduction of the Human Development Index; the Copenhagen Social Summit and the Beijing World Conference on Women, both in 1995; and the World Development Report, *Attacking Poverty* (World Bank, 2000). The latest major step, an affirmation and coming of age of a long trend, has been the evolution, content, and universalism of the SDGs. The process of formulating them, in contrast with their predecessors, the Millennium Development Goals (MDGs), was inclusive, participatory, and transparent to an unprecedented degree. It included expressions of the priorities and aspirations of many of those who are last, including four ground-level panels to inform and complement the high-level panel. Further, the scope and orientation of the 17 goals are broader than the MDGs. They include global goals. SDG 13, for instance, is to take urgent action to combat climate change and its impacts. The words *sustainable* and *sustainably* are used 13 times. At country, social, and individual levels, the universalism of the SDGs, applying to all countries, and endorsed by all, opens up promising potential for advocacy and impact on policy and practice. SDG 1, 'End poverty in all its forms everywhere', and SDG 10, 'Reduce inequality within and among countries', are frontal challenges to richer countries, such as the United States and the United Kingdom, where it is a matter of national shame that economic and other inequalities are so extreme and continue to widen.

The SDGs reinforce the massive shift in thinking and orientation that has been taking place, from vertical to horizontal, from the wealthier world thinking and acting in a North–South, 'us'–'them' way, towards new mindsets, behaviours, and relationships which are 'all of us equally together'. It was a landmark, a historic achievement, when member countries of the UN accepted all the SDGs as applying equally to all.[5] The shift in relationships which had been gradual over decades was publicly recognized and affirmed. A new stage in the journey was recognized, with much for wealthier countries to learn from others. This is a new world where we can celebrate and all gain from interconnected reciprocities.

It is a world for which 'development' must continue to be rethought and applied everywhere. Redefining it as 'good change' (see Chambers, 2005: 185–6) provokes reflection and debate which can be transformative. Like a Trojan horse it can smuggle the Who? Whose? questions into the citadels of past and current top-down development thinking and practice. Who knows better? Who defines what is good? What change matters? Whose values count? Whose realities are relevant? In the spirit of universalism the questions are for all nations and all people. In the spirit of equality and justice the answers point first to those who have least voice, those to whom the SDGs' 'leave no one behind' applies, those who are last. And they are to be found in every country.

To know better in the new context

Development as good change can then be to put first those who are last, their aspirations, and priorities, and do this everywhere. This means that knowing better also applies everywhere. Chapters 4 and 5 should have universal relevance. Complexity is everywhere. Participatory methodologies (PMs) are for all. That so many PMs have evolved and continue to evolve in developing countries provides the richer world with opportunities to learn. The transfer of knowledge, insight, and technology is multi-directional. Learning is mutual. We are in a more level, more interconnected, more egalitarian space. The 'international' of 'international development' has a new sense of universalism. Thrilling opportunities open up; the scope for knowing better is dramatically amplified when it becomes 'everyone knowing better' and 'knowing better together'.

At the same time the future becomes ever harder to foresee. As an American economist reportedly said: 'The only thing I can be sure about the future is that it will surprise me'.[6] To keep up to date and in touch with those left out and left behind in our ever faster future demands key qualities to a new degree. More and more, to know better means to be alert, versatile, sensitive, nimble, and innovative. It means to collaborate more in partnerships co-constructing and co-generating knowledge, co-innovating, co-learning, co-evolving, and co-improvising approaches and methods, and co-owning the outcomes. It is not just social change that accelerates; to keep in touch and up to date, approaches to knowing must also accelerate through innovation and adaptation if they are to fit and meet rapidly emerging conditions and needs. More and more we have to think, live, work, and learn in and through the paradigm of complexity, adopting and adapting its words and concepts, values and principles, methods and procedures, behaviours and attitudes, relationships and mindsets. This means countering and transcending much current practice. The new professionalism of practice this demands has to combine knowing better with doing better.

For a new professionalism of knowing: five fundamentals

For this new professionalism I propose five fundamentals. These are guided by principles and values that inform and support continuous learning, creativity and innovation, and keeping grounded in keeping in touch and up to date. More and more professionals are pioneering in this space. Let us first ask and explore what formative elements and strands there may be in their thinking and practice.

The two paradigms – of Newtonian practice for controllable things and of adaptive pluralism for social complexity (see Chapter 4) – provide some of the frames and categories to apply in this analysis. Let me stress once again that this is not either-or between the paradigms, but a question of what combination and balance of which elements fit best for each purpose and context. However, as I argued in Chapters 3 and 4, there is an imbalance in much development, the Newtonian paradigm, propagated by power and demands for upward accountability, having invaded, overridden, distorted, repressed, and subverted elements of adaptive pluralism. Often the left hemisphere of the brain has come to dominate the right.[7]

Without excluding elements of the Newtonian paradigm according to context, the five fundamentals for a new professionalism of knowing and doing that follow are nested in and resonate with adaptive pluralism for social complexity. The five are: words and concepts that express and shape our mindsets and influence our actions; ground-truthing as basic to a rigour of realism; facilitation and behaviour, attitudes, and relationships as a way of living and being; reflexivity, aka self-critical epistemological awareness; and principles, values, and passion.

Words and concepts

Studying how the lexicon of development has shifted in its content and emphasis can be fascinating.[8] It is also seriously significant, a source of both concern and opportunity. In Chapter 3 I discussed the insidious creep and infiltration of vocabulary and with it procedures, values, mindsets, relationships, and behaviours from the private sector.[9] Dropping old words and concepts and introducing new is often so slow and incremental that it is barely noticed.[10] Over the past three decades the neoliberal language and mindsets of money and the market have permeated and eroded the more social and ethical language that preceded it. New lexicons have reinforced dominant relationships, with a paradigmatic shift from complexity, participation, and emergence to a simpler linearity of preset targets and upwards accountability. These are now widely adopted and accepted in some governments and widely in aid without serious question. Actors and organizations have become iron filings in an intensifying magnetic field of which they seem largely unconscious, or if conscious, do not publicly challenge. For my part, I have to pinch myself and question my malleable memory (see Chapter 1). I have to offset the tendency for older people to see the past as a golden age. But the 1990s, led by Wolfensohn at the World Bank and social development champions, really were very different. The visions and vocabulary of that time have been overridden, buried, and forgotten. Since then much development discourse has descended into a dysfunctional linguistic trap. The words speak for themselves (Table 6.1).

This shift of words and concepts, and the ways of thinking, values, principles, behaviours, roles, and relationships that go with them, can be portrayed by composite and emblematic sentences:

> Mid-1990s. *In good development practice, donors assess proposals and plans from applicants, stating goals and how they will be reached, and value participation and responsible commitment to achieving benefits for poor people.*

> Mid-2010s. *In best development practice, commissioners assess competitive bids and business cases from suppliers designed to deliver results, and reward compliance and accountability for achieving measurable targets.*

Finally, if I may be excused serious whimsy, the classically Newtonian acronym SMART refers to targets being Specific, Measurable, Achievable, Relevant, and Time-bound. This can be revised for conditions of complexity as in Table 6.2, with the middle columns representing how they may regard each other.

Table 6.1 Contrasting lexicons of the mid-1990s and mid-2010s

Mid-1990s progressive development speak	Mid-2010s DFID linear and market speak
Donor	Commissioner
Recipient	Supplier
Proposal	Bid
Plan	Business case
Funding	Procurement
Vision	Target
Achieve	Deliver
Commitment	Compliance
Inspire	Incentivize
Responsibility	Accountability
Participation	Feedback
Assess	Measure
Benefits	Results
Good practice	Best practice

All linguistic trends are not negative, however. Organizations' own vocabularies express and reinforce their cultures and provide some insulation. A study of the large Christian INGO World Vision found eight vocabularies of practice being used. These related to project management, facilitation, community, bureaucracy and doing things 'by the book', enterprise, religion, friendship, and finally science and academic (Kontinen, 2016).

More significant on the positive side, some key words, categories, and orientations introduced and established in earlier decades have survived and flourished, and, for all the ways they are misused, appear irreversibly embedded: gender equality, sustainability, empowerment, transparency, and accountability, for instance. Others have expanded in their applications as well as frequency of use. *Power* is now part of the accepted language of development, even if those who wield it tend to apply it to others rather than reflexively to

Table 6.2 What is SMART?

Newtonian, as used in practice	Newtonian SMART seen through a complexity lens	SMART for complexity and adaptive pluralism seen through a Newtonian lens	SMART for complexity and adaptive pluralism
Specific	Simplistic	Subjective	Systemic
Measurable	Mechanical	Muddled	Manageable
Achievable	Artificial	Anecdotal	Adaptable
Relevant	Rigid	Rigourless	Realistic
Time-bound	Target-fixated	Transient	Timely

themselves. *Justice* is widely applied as in social justice, climate justice, tax justice, environmental justice, and intergenerational justice. *Inequality,* in decline since the 1990s and 2000s, is bouncing back.[11] *Reflexivity* and even *passion* are heard more often. And other words, concepts, and categories have become more prominent: participatory M&E, learning, creativity, adaptation, pluralism, resilience, responsibility, complexity itself, and many co-words such as co-convening, co-constructing, and co-learning.

Ground-truthing: a participatory rigour of realism

By ground-truthing I mean being in touch and up to date with ground realities, often through direct, face-to-face interaction, listening, and learning with people, especially those who are last, in their living environments.[12]

Critical here is the ground-truthing of immersions (Birch et al., 2007) where outsiders stay and live with families in communities, not as important people but as human beings, take part in activities, have conversations, wander around, observe, and listen. Immersions are easier said than done. They can be challenging to organize and require resolution to carry out. But they are immensely rewarding as experiential learning and ideally should be integral to the professionalism of all who work in development. Yet hardly any do them. A second-best and default mode is to learn from the immersions of others. The participatory research and learning of the Reality Check Approach (RCA) (see Chapter 5 pp 134–6) opens a window which simply was not there in the early 2000s. I cannot overemphasize how important this breakthrough is and its universal transformative potential in the spirit of the SDGs. Ground-truthing can take many forms with many complementary methodologies, but for rigorous, open-ended, up-to-date insights into the realities of those who are last, the RCA is unrivalled.

Facilitation: behaviours, attitudes, relationships, and being

Facilitation and facilitators and the roles, attitudes, behaviours, and personal qualities that go with good facilitation are at the core of the new professionalism. The shortage of good and creative facilitators is acute and worldwide. Those celebrated in this book are exceptional. Ways have to be found to multiply them and their qualities on a vast scale, to trust them, to empower them with discretion, freedom, and resources, and to spread their influence.

Facilitation and facilitators are key to taking PMs to scale. They have been at the core of the remarkable spread of integrated pest management, Reflect, and CLTS, to mention but three. Whatever the shortcomings and losses of quality, these have been taken to scale with almost spectacular speed. In all three cases high-priority and substantial resources have been devoted to selecting, training, and mentoring facilitators. Creative facilitators will also be vital for scaling up, adapting, and further evolving other PMs especially participatory statistics, the RCA, and some participatory applications of ICTs.

This priority can only be achieved through supporters and sponsors in agencies especially funders, governments, NGOs, universities and colleges, and government training institutions. Ideally, those who can commission PMs need to be confident that there is an adequate and reliable pool of good facilitators with fitting experience and commitment; and almost everywhere the pool is smaller than needed. There is a hen-egg problem. The danger is that all but the most visionary and bold will continue to follow the default mode of traditional questionnaire surveys for which an army of trained investigators can be mustered in most places. For taking the new professionalism to scale, filling the facilitator gap is fundamental.

Facilitation can transform power relations. Beyond the four forms of power often described – power over (common usage), power to (agency), power with (collective power), and power within (self-confidence) – there is a fifth power, essential in the new professionalism: power to empower, the power of 'uppers' to empower 'lowers' (Chambers, 1997: 58–60) through convening, encouraging, listening, supporting, and in PRA-speak, 'handing over the stick' or passing the baton. For many, conditioned by didactic interaction, this is revolutionary; but a personal and behavioural revolution, from teaching to empowering, is basic to the new professionalism. The vision can be for all development professionals[13] to be socialized into seeing themselves and acting as facilitators in situations where they have power over and power to, supporting and nurturing power with and power within among 'lowers'.

What is good facilitation varies by context, personalities, purpose, and other dimensions, and can take many forms. People who have been trained to facilitate are not necessarily good at it: they may behave with a formulaic lack of spontaneity which comes over as an insincere application of techniques.[15] Facilitators are all different and must be themselves and do their own thing based on who they are and how they relate to others, and be human, not robotic. Much depends on what a person is like as a person.

Paradigmatically, facilitating and empowering contrast with supervising and controlling. At its best facilitation is creative, with improvisation. It can go as far as co-evolving agenda and process with participants and even knowing 'when not to be there'. Facilitation has a huge literature and folklore (see Chambers, 2002; KM4D, 2015; IDS, n.d.). For all its variety, it often entails enabling others to express their views, do their own analysis, and interact creatively. Here is a recent articulation:

> The facilitators' central task is to create an environment of trust, respect and tolerance. The participants need to feel secure and confident to share their perspectives, feelings and interpretations without fear or shame in order to make learning and understanding possible. (Herout and Schmid, 2015: 64)

Tilly Sellers (1995) wrote that facilitators should establish rapport, show respect, abandon preconceptions, hand over the stick, watch, listen, learn and learn from mistakes, be self-critical and self-aware, be flexible, support and share, and be honest. Her list invites all of us to write our own.[15]

Shifting to and consolidating this way of being, working, and relating presents another point of entry for moving from Newtonian practices to adaptive pluralism, with changes in roles, behaviours, and relationships. There is less supervising, instructing, and auditing and more mentoring, coaching, and facilitating. Conforming and complying evolve towards responsible autonomy and performance. Top-down quality control becomes participatory quality assurance. Relationships are less hierarchical, more democratic, and less punitive and more supportive, especially when things do not work out well. Trust and transparency synergize with more collaborative and collegial learning, and grounded realism and truth.

Good facilitation and facilitators and the attitudes and behaviours that go with them are then at the core of good change, not just for PMs but universally, in the bloodstream of all development practice – in development organizations, governments, projects and relationships, in schools, universities and colleges, and in communities and families. For the transformative revolution of a new professionalism, facilitative attitudes and behaviours have to become so universal that they permeate all relevant[16] domains and relationships.

Reflexivity

Reflexivity is another term for self-critical epistemological awareness (Chambers, 1997: 32), critical reflection on how we form and frame our knowledges. It entails striving to be aware of personal biases, predilections and mental frames, and mental categories and pigeonholes for interpreting the world, and how power and relationships can distort what we know. It means reviewing and reflecting on these and trying to offset the distortions and misjudgements to which they give rise.

Rapid change demands rapid learning and adaptation and, as noted earlier, being alert, nimble, in touch, and up to date. There is more to this than just learning. Rapid change also implies rapid unlearning and learning from what does not work. Three decades ago David Korten (1984) called this 'embracing error'. Nowadays it is expressed as 'learning from failure', 'lessons learned', or 'failing forwards' and famously Engineers Without Borders (Canada) have an annual Failure Report which celebrates learning from what has not worked. We can be warned by Eric Hoffer's aphorism: 'In times of change learners inherit the earth; while the learned find themselves beautifully equipped to deal with a world that no longer exists'.

But it is now more than just learning that is imperative. It is knowing what to learn, and what to pay attention to, and how to do this. The digital age allows those who are connected to be instantly learned across an astronomical range of topics. Erudition is accessible on the internet at the touch of a button.

But instant communications also disable, becoming an addictive impediment to critical reflection and forms of learning that need sustained attention, like reading books. Reading retreats for professionals are now a rarity. And I have been alarmed at my own withdrawal symptoms when I cannot access emails. I have become one of the new addicts, hooked on the instant and the latest, not wishing to admit that this postpones and avoids any sort of in-depth introspection. Time for reflexivity is rarely ring-fenced.

In relation to knowing, reflexivity has external and internal dimensions. Externally, there is being aware of continuous influences of context, positionality, relationships, power, and behaviour. These include how we are seen and treated, where we are taken and not taken, what we are shown and not shown, what we are told and not told, and incentive systems and rewards. The first three chapters considered these and other aspects, and how they have to be recognized, mitigated, and offset.

The internal dimensions of reflexivity are more problematic. This is where we hold up a mirror to our minds and emotions and seek to recognize and explore how we construe the world, and how this has been moulded by our life experiences of upbringing, education, disciplinary training, and the influence of faiths, family, relationships, emotions, and vocabulary, and questioning how these structure our views of the world and may misrepresent realities.

Full and honest internal reflexivity is not easy. In the preface I mentioned some aspects of my own mindset. I have touched on this elsewhere in this book and more can be found in the first chapter of *Into the Unknown* (Chambers, 2014). Reflecting on and challenging one's mindset can be threatening or liberating, frightening, or fun. And we all have embedded beliefs especially of faith (religious, atheist, agnostic, scientific)[17] which are often put socially or personally out of bounds for examination or questioning. In a spirit of epistemic relativism, one can ask what parts of one's mindset one allows to be questioned and what are out of bounds and why, and consider how different other people are, and what can be learned from them. My appeal is that we can be animated and inspired by two sayings:

> He who knows only his own side of the case knows little of that. (John Stuart Mill)

> You may be right and I may be wrong and by an effort together we may get closer to the truth. (attributed to Karl Popper)

Social, institutional, professional, and political milieus can inhibit or prevent reflexivity. The fascinating World Development Report 2015, *Mind, Society, and Behavior*, provides an illustration. I challenged the authors to conclude with a short chapter reflecting critically on their own mindsets and behaviour in framing and preparing the report. This, I thought, would set a wonderful and prominent example to other development professionals. The team went as far as to commission a study to compare the views of poor people in Jakarta, Lima, and Nairobi with what a random sample of World Bank staff thought those views would be. This found that 'development professionals may assume that poor individuals may be less autonomous, less responsible, less hopeful, and less knowledgeable than they in fact are' (World Bank, 2015: 18).

That they did not go further and rise to the challenge to reflect on themselves illustrates the constraints many face. Context and pressures of time would have made this difficult to do even if they wished. Consider the situation. Towards the end of any big, time-bound, and intellectually demanding work like the World Development Report (it has 214 double-column, tightly written pages), physical and mental exhaustion take their toll, and deadlines tyrannize. Team agreement on such a controversial step would have been time-consuming and difficult. They might have thought that such reflexivity could undermine the report, or be unacceptable within the World Bank. These same inhibitors may apply in other cases of group and institutional writing, especially with deadlines demanded by imperious power. And consultants who are the main eyes, ears, and sources of insight for many funders may think critical reflection would be shooting themselves in the foot, losing not just credibility but future contracts.

A contrary case can be made that transparent and perceptive reflexivity enhances credibility. Authors who note their biases and limitations make what they do say all the more believable. Paradoxically, this may be the more so when conclusions are controversial. Virginia Woolf's admonition applies:

> when any subject is highly controversial...one cannot hope to tell the truth. One can only show how one came to hold the opinion one does hold. One can only give the audience the chance of drawing their own conclusions as they observe the limitations, the prejudices, the idiosyncrasies of the speaker. (Virginia Woolf, *A Room of One's Own*, 1928)

Finally, I cannot hide when I reflect on my own mindset which I have brought to this discussion. I find it attractive once again to make a distinction between reductionist and inclusive. A reductionist mindset is associated with the paradigm of things and Newtonian practices and an inclusive mindset with that of people, adaptive pluralism, and complexity. I complacently (and virtuously in my own eyes) associate myself with inclusiveness. This distinction also exposes once again my predilection for binary contrasts. Whatever my protests that it is not either-or but both-and or a balance and mixture to fit need and context, binary contrasts remain for me a favourite frame for analysis and exposition. It is a deeply embedded part of how I try to make sense of the world.

Without the corrective discipline of reflexivity, the new professionalism would be vulnerable to superficiality and error. Reflective practice cannot on its own guarantee depth of insight or realism. But it is, pervasively, one vital ingredient for knowing and doing better.

Principles, values, and passion

Much, but not all, research and knowledge, particularly in the natural and physical sciences, aspires to be rigorous according to scientific canons and thus objective. Objectivity, scientific rigour, evidence, and results are often considered incompatible with feeling, emotion, empathy, and passion. *Dispassionate* is, after all, close to being a synonym for objective, for not allowing emotion to cloud one's view. *Subjective* is a disparaging put-down: research should strive for its opposite, the objectivity of rigorous and accurate elucidation and presentation of facts uninfluenced by the subjectivity of the researcher. Emotion has no place: it is personal and subjective and leads to unreliability. Certainly those who are passionate about causes or hold deep-rooted beliefs are vulnerable to distorted views, selecting and distorting evidence, and exhibiting tendencies towards myth and error. But so, too, are scientists as we saw from numerous examples discussed in Chapter 1. For challenges of knowing and conditions of complexity, an alternative view can be based on principles and values, and the human drivers of commitment and passion for truth.

First, principles and values are analogous to simple rules for edge-of-chaos emergence. They can guide adaptive behaviour in social and other conditions which are complex, uncontrollable, and unpredictable. In organizations, non-negotiable principles can be an enabling frame for decisions and action.[18] The behavioural and attitudinal principles and values associated with participatory approaches and good facilitation can generate and support democratic and empowering relationships. And the quality of what is learned, for instance through ground-truthing, is related to the quality of the relationships involved.

Principles and values are both personal and collective. They can be evolved from personal to collective through participatory processes leading to convergent consensus on a mission statement for an organization, as they have done, for instance, in ActionAid International. Principles and values can be internalized personally, institutionally, and professionally and guide behaviour across activities as widely varied as management, advocacy, job descriptions and recruitment, negotiations and innovations, not to mention everyday work and living.

Critical reflection is the more important because unlike physical science with its usually stable subject matter, social realities are in constant flux. Notably, as the realities, values, aspirations, and priorities of the people who are left out and behind change, so what they perceive as better for themselves will change. At a meta-level, values and principles may be robust and non-negotiable. At levels of detail, as circumstances and people change, so the expression of those higher level values and principles changes.

Second, passion for truth is fundamental. Passion and knowing better are synergistic. Energy is needed to drive adaptive agents in edge-of-chaos emergence.[19] Passionate commitment to finding out the truth has to be a core and key source of energy and driver. A deep commitment to finding out the truth countervails against biases and makes it easier to acknowledge personal and professional error, recognizing that we are all on trajectories of learning and unlearning. One can be passionately committed to achieving gender equality, justice, sustainability, or peace and at the same time passionate about finding out 'the truth' and respecting evidence which challenges one's beliefs. Passionate commitment is a great driving force and source of energy to make good change happen. When candidates for posts in 'tech firms' have been asked to submit statements of passion instead of conventional résumés, many have been selected who would otherwise have been overlooked, with good results (Rose, 2016: 91–4). Those who are passionate and care work hard and usually well. Values, principles, commitment, and passion are a powerful combination and potent force for driving revolutionary change.

Each of these five fundamentals presents a focus for action and analysis. Each reinforces the others. All five are formative for mindsets, behaviours, and relationships. Each is a domain for intervention and action to know better and through knowing better, seeing how to do better. They face many obstacles, and present many points of entry.

Practical transformations

The new professionalism is revolutionary. To make these five fundamentals living realities and to do this at scale requires radical transformations in four domains: professional, institutional, personal, and collective. Each presents promising points of entry and synergizes with the others.

Revolutionary professionalism

Values, norms, and methods are integral to the new professionalism. Those prevailing in professions across the board cry out for root-and-branch questioning and revision. Many need to be stood on their heads. Again and again this is a question of recognizing complexity and its paradigm, and offsetting, neutralizing, and reversing top-down Newtonian magnetism, materialism, and reductionism. This is most salient in the teaching, training, and application of the social sciences but applies too to all professions because all involve people, power, and relationships. The pervasive imperative of asking the Who? Whose? questions and exploring and acting on the implications of answering with 'theirs' has force in almost every social context.

Putting the last first opens up exhilarating realms for professional innovation. It stands many values, norms, and methods on their heads. Much appears in a new light, challenging convention. Eclectic methodological pluralism, developing, applying, and combining participatory methodologies, comes into its own. There is a vast territory presented by PMs waiting to be explored. And with exploration more will open up. To see this needs vision. Acting on that vision calls for a courageous spirit of adventure and a willingness to take risks. Beyond this, many points of entry to trigger and support the transformative professional changes for knowing and doing better can be suggested. Readers will have their own ideas. Some of the more vital and potentially transformative concern teaching and training, especially at tertiary level:

- *Academic values and incentives.* These manifest in a conservative form in many ways. Editors of journals, the referees they select, the high status of some hard international journals and low status of others have discouraged and deterred publications on participatory approaches and methods. The values and criteria for academic assessments and appointments and promotion boards in universities and colleges all too often almost mindlessly reinforce convention, an irony when practised by those regarded as highly intelligent.
- *Textbooks.* Commissioning the rewriting of textbooks is crucial. Recycled from generation to generation of students and familiar to teachers, they perpetuate the past, misfit our world of accelerating change, and rarely include participatory approaches and methods.
- *Critical reflection.* Reflexivity is rarely part of university and college courses. Yet arguably every course should include critical reflection by every student to realize how teaching and the discipline concerned have provided lenses, vocabulary, and categories for seeing and understanding the world, and how different these are in other disciplines. It remains a bizarre blind spot that universities and training colleges, and their staff, rarely recognize or practise, let alone facilitate, reflexivity among their students.
- *Teaching and training.* Most teaching and training worldwide is rooted in a didactic, top-down mode. This then imprints top-down relationships in students who reproduce them in their subsequent lives.

In a revolutionary professionalism all these are reversed and stood on their heads. Academic values and incentives, journal editors and referees, appointments boards and academic assessment procedures reorient to appreciate and reward pluralism, diversity, participation, and participatory approaches. Textbooks are continuously rewritten to keep up with accelerating change and understanding. Reflexivity is introduced in all courses. Teaching and training become less didactic and more facilitative in primary and secondary as well as tertiary education. Facilitation and its behaviour, attitudes, repertoire, and skills become a cornerstone of tertiary education, laying the ground for students after university, college, or training institute to have facilitation as part of their equipment for later life.

Professional transformations apply far more extensively than just in schools, colleges, universities, and training institutes. But what happens in these is formative and upstream in many careers. At tertiary level, many of those emerging with diplomas and degrees perpetuate the problems when they should be embodying solutions. Instead of needing rehabilitation, as at present, graduates must go forth as seeds and drivers of change. The dream is to form and nurture generations who will see the world and act and relate to others in it in a more participatory, democratic, and sensitive manner.

Participatory management and institutions

The vision here is of decentralized and democratic institutions, using that word to mean both organizations and norms and procedures within organizations, with multi-directional free flows of information. Organizations with top-down command structures and practices and which stress accountability upwards inhibit and distort learning. Participatory management, with countervailing accountabilities 'downwards' to those who are lower and those who are deprived in the wider society, is the way forward. Participatory organizations like Praxis and ActionAid International, and their dynamics, vulnerabilities, and sustainability, inspire by showing what can be done. The private sector presents many examples of the profitability of decentralized participatory approaches, often based on combinations of freedom and trust. Surprisingly, the modern military has similar features.

These are not new insights. There is a vast business management literature on these lines. *Participation Pays* is the title of a remarkable book from civil society (Thomas and Narayanan, 2015). Participation is also the profit-making practice of innumerable firms. One example shows what is possible.

Kyocera is a multinational of 229 companies with high-tech products such as fine ceramic components, semi-conductors, telecoms, microelectronic packages, and fibre-optic components.[20] Its Amoeba management system is built around cells that expand, divide, and disband. What energizes all this and holds it together? The Kyocera philosophy has as its most essential criterion 'what is the right thing to do as a human being?' Its success is attributed to managers devoting their lives to earning the trust of their employees, and its commitment to 'the most fundamental human ethical and social norms' (Kyocera, n.d.). Its vision is to 'Preserve the spirit to work fairly and honourably, respect people, our work, our company and our global community'. The corporate motto is 'Respect the divine and love people'. Respect and love have been a high-tech win–win. In showing the way to the new professionalism some of the private sector, as in this case, are ahead of the game. In contrast, large government bureaucracies, together with their political masters, are often among the worst laggards.

Points of entry for transforming organizations are many, including some of those indicated earlier for education and training. The four below follow from earlier parts of this book. They are synergistic and widely applicable:

- *Learning and unlearning*. Minimizing error and myth by applauding and rewarding learning and adaptation, with reporting 'lessons learned' to give staff and colleagues confidence that they will not be penalized but recognized and rewarded for rapid learning and adaptation.

- *Procedures and methods.* Introducing participatory approaches at all levels. Pushing back against the constraints of top-down power. Bringing to light hidden transaction and motivation costs. Introducing principles and canons which trust and empower in place of the mechanistic Newtonian procedures discussed in Chapter 3 which confine and control.
- *Facilitation.* Training and reorientation to democratic and empowering facilitation. Introducing facilitation as a way of enabling interactions, managing meetings, and changing organizational cultures and behaviour. Using power to empower, the power of 'uppers' to empower 'lowers' (Chambers, 1997: 58–60) through convening, encouraging, listening, supporting, and in PRA-speak, handing over the stick or passing the baton.
- *Words, values, and culture.* Introducing and living transformative words and values. Replacing market-speak with a vocabulary of complexity and relationships and making the rhetoric real with words already accepted like *empowerment, transparency, partnership,* and (on its way) *trust.* And adopting and living a transformative corporate motto, inspired by Kyocera's, of respect and love.

Which brings us to the third and utterly and universally basic domain which informs and drives all others – the personal.

The primacy of the personal

The personal is primary. Change starts with individual people. The revolutionary changes of a new professionalism need the inspiration and drive of champions to become mass movements in which everyone's actions matter and contribute. Transformations occur through individual decisions and acts and accumulations of innumerable quiet, small steps in the same direction. Many are unseen and unsung whose lives exemplify Wordsworth's 'best portion of a good man's life, his little, nameless, unremembered acts of kindness and of love'.[21] Besides kindness and love are vision, commitment, passion, and courage to face and tackle the realities of poverty, oppression, discrimination, intolerance, stigma, and the terrible insecurities and suffering of war and civil disorder. The many unseen and unheard who act to reduce and overcome these deserve to be celebrated, for mass movements need not just champions but multitudes of foot soldiers.

Who we are and where we are in immediate terms show us what we can do. The agendas at the end of earlier chapters raise questions designed to help. Key personal aspects stand out: behaviour, attitudes, facilitation, avoiding errors, questioning beliefs, offsetting biases, and throughout reflexivity or self-critical epistemological awareness. These need to be lived and embedded in the genes of the new professionalism.

Much hinges too on how we relate and interact. Learning to listen sounds simplistic but is basic, applying to all of us especially when we are interpersonally powerful and dominant. It applies most with multiple 'uppers' such as older, white, educated, patriarchal men who enjoy talking (mea culpa). Listening matters in the family, in work, in schools, universities and colleges, and in all upper-lower contexts. The Listening Project (Anderson et al., 2012) is a striking example of the revelations that can come from simply asking and listening, as was done in a more structured way in the *Voices of the Poor* (Narayan et al., 2000).

Nor is there any substitute for personal ground-truthing. Doing this through immersions (Birch et al., 2007) promises powerful, sometimes scales-from-the-eyes, personal experiences. Direct, personal, unconstrained meetings and having conversations with others without being important or treated specially can have a lasting impact. In development, immersions have immense transformative potential. They are key to the revealing and often unexpected findings that come from Reality Checks.[22] Personally they can be hugely rewarding in insights and in provoking and energizing action. They demand careful organizing but that should not prevent them becoming an integral part of the training of development professionals and of development practice. They will repay major investment.

Ground-truthing is exemplified outstandingly in the work of Harsh Mander. Too many of us, including myself, follow the easy path of, to borrow the title of his 2015 book, *Looking Away*. We need many more who do not look away but engage directly in the causes of justice, decency, and common humanity. All this amounts to each of us doing what we can, striving to keep in touch and up to date. Beyond just knowing better, this is then a question of individual and collective commitment and action.

Collective: passionate communities

Whether professionally or institutionally, alliances and collective action are almost always more effective than action that is only individual. Coming together, sharing ideas, having a common vision, deciding who will do what, taking joint action, and the solidarity and mutual support which follow from these are drivers for transformation. Participatory methodologies have shown this again and again. Margaret Mead's famous remark, 'Never doubt that a small group of thoughtful, committed citizens can change the world: indeed, it's the only thing that ever has', is an encouragement. Repeatedly in my own experience there have been groups of us drawn together by enthusiastic commitment to exploring, developing, and disseminating an approach or methodology, each doing what he or she was best placed to do, sharing resources, contacts, materials, and co-convening meetings, workshops, and conferences of like-minded and like-committed others. There have been passionate communities for rapid rural appraisal, participatory rural appraisal, Farmer First, participatory statistics, and now for CLTS. I think all involved looked forward eagerly, as I did, to our meetings. In all cases the excitement was in sharing what we had done and learned, innovations we had discovered, successes, and the spread of the approach and methodology. The same has happened repeatedly with other participatory approaches and methods – Reflect and Stepping Stones, for instance. Energy is generated and intensified by common commitment and sense of purpose.[23]

Then there are passionate communities focused on more than methodologies and approaches to include institutional change. ILAC (Institutional Learning and Change), which was born at the CGIAR Conference in Costa Rica in 2002 (where an earlier version of Chapter 1 originated), had the International Agricultural Centres as its field and faced institutional resistances but over a decade left its mark.

On a larger scale are transformative movements driven by passion for particular causes and for justice, often fuelled by anger at exploitation and suffering. Such communities, self-forming, driven, energized, and united by outrage and focused by common purpose are potent collective ways forward on broader stages.

The new professionalism resonates with and supports all these. It is paradigmatic and pervasive and, as we have seen, has professional, institutional, personal, and collective dimensions. Many who struggle for good change working in the spirit of this new professionalism can show others the way. There is much to learn from them. As champions and pioneers they can enable the rest of us to perceive and explore pathways to new and better ways of knowing, better practices, and better relationships. It needs not a few but a multiplicity of communities of passion, of allies with like minds and like emotions. They may not think of themselves as communities. What matters is solidarity to confront, overcome and transform convention, inertia, mechanistic practices, comfortable habit, and power. Taking these on can be experienced as a thrilling collective challenge and opportunity. A future can be envisaged with innumerable such communities of passion committed to knowing better and doing better, to ideals like truth, trust, and transparency, to equality and justice, and to secure and sustainable living for everyone on our planet.

The transformative power of funding

For better or for worse, most of what we come to know and do depends on research which in turn is determined by funding and funders. These include foundations, bilateral and multilateral donor agencies, governments and government funding bodies, grants committees, and smaller actors like NGOs, private individuals, and in a big way the private sector, which has its own interests. For the rest, many factors determine or influence research priorities and methodologies: political priorities, changing realities, fashions, and, as noted in Chapters 2 and 3, professional training and mindsets together with measurability, researchability, convenience, preference for the reductionist rigour which has privileged randomized control trials (RCTs), and professional incentives.

The power of funding is overarching. The scope for those in funding agencies to determine research priorities and approaches is enormous. Many of them are enlightened.[24] Many, unseen and unsung, work hard to simplify procedural requirements, to be in touch with ground realities, and to identify priorities. All the same, as we saw in Chapter 3, choice and flexibility are constrained by researchers' need for support and income, by competitive bidding, and by straitjackets of upwards accountability. As the IDS toilet graffiti had it: *Let's speak truth to power,* provoking the repost, *Yes, if someone will fund us.* What we research into, how we research, and so what we find out and come to believe we know, depends largely on what can be funded, which is largely determined by funding agencies.

The experience, again and again, has been that funding agencies withdraw support too early with promising participatory approaches. They lack the vision and patience needed for the necessary sustained support over years, or prefer less participatory, more Newtonian and positivist approaches, or move champions to other posts to be replaced by others with other agendas. The CGIAR has several times terminated support for innovative staff or programmes. These are most vulnerable when there is a financial crunch, becoming the first to go. When staff had to be cut at ICRISAT in the 1980s, it was the social anthropologist who was not renewed. With economies sought in recent years, it was all the 'systems' programmes with a participatory element that were closed down, including the remarkable and promising Aquatic Agricultural Systems project which was trying out an original, open-ended participatory approach (Douthwaite et al., forthcoming; Marina Apgar, pers. comm.). The conservative retreat to normal comfort zones is an easy reflex. The switch of mindset and vision, from the classic linear approach of breeding high-yielding varieties (HYVs) of crops to also evolving high-yielding methodologies (HYMs), did not occur or could not be maintained. Yet HYMs, like HYVs, are global public goods.

Knowing better requires funders of research and all others to be reflexive and know better what we need to know and how, as part of the professionalism of knowing. More than ever, now in the second decade of the 21st century, those with the purse strings hold the power. Take methodologies. Preferences of funding agencies have supported a sharp shift towards what can be termed Newtonian research. If one research methodology like RCTs receives massive funding, it will dominate, as it has done. And because all power deceives, negative feedback and the learning it would bring are muted and delayed, as they have been with RCTs. To my knowledge, the cost of RCTs has not been compared with participatory approaches, but the PIALA evaluation in Vietnam (see Chapter 4), including time and resources for methodological innovation, cost a small fraction of the average cost for rural sanitation RCT in India.

The secrets of the success of PIALA were creative and committed facilitators and donors (BMGF and IFAD) who provided resources for methodological innovation and were patient. However, they did not have to wait as long as they would have had to with an RCT. For a future new professionalism with participatory methodologies, those who fund research must learn the lessons: find creative and committed facilitators and allow them time to pilot and evolve appropriate methodologies. If donors will do this, the results over a few years should be richly rewarding and cost effective.

From a paradigmatic perspective, relationships are significant. A repeated complaint in the Listening Project (Anderson et al., 2012) was that recipients did not meet their donors face-to-face and that the funders with whom they dealt were transferred after only short periods in post. The importance of relationships was stressed again and again. To shift from relationships which are distant, impersonal, auditing, and controlling to become more face-to-face, personal, trusting, and empowering takes time. It also needs staff and motivation. Instead of continually reducing staff and the ratio of staff to finance, as so many funders have done, value for money will come from augmenting staff and encouraging them to get closer, face-to-face with their partners, and more in touch with the ground and the action.

The bottom line is that funders can push, encourage, and enable those they support to be transformative – professionally, institutionally, personally, and collectively – and to put the last first. In the mode of eclectic pluralism this can be through applications and innovations of participatory methodologies to fit complex social realities. Those who are last today and in the future deserve no less. At the same time, funders need to observe practice in the field. More than ever the impact of the research and approaches they commission will gain from their personal ground-truthing and critical reflection. They can be powerful champions. They can lead as new professionals.

To make it happen: vision, guts, and passion

Knowing better does not assure action; and action may or may not be good. Here Martin Luther King can inspire us with his commitment, courage, and insights. He showed the transformative power of vision, guts, and passion combined with realism and how these could win against deeply entrenched resistance. In his words: 'Power without love is reckless and abusive, and love without power is sentimental and anaemic. Power at its best is love implementing the demands of justice, and justice at its best is power correcting everything that stands against love.'[25]

Love has had no part in mainstream development discourse. But with *relationships* now accepted and *empathy* heard more often, *love* should not be far behind. *Love* was used at an IDS conference in July 2016. It is in Kyocera's motto. In IDS workshops where participants brainstorm words they would like to be used and acted on in development, *love* now comes up more often. It has no obvious part in the Newtonian paradigm: it cannot be measured. It is at home, though, with the attitudes, behaviours, and relationships of social complexity. We can take a cue from Martin Luther King and reflect on love whenever power is discussed. Empathy and love can transform how we see power, how we use it, and how we think and act.

For good change, love and power need to be informed and inspired by grounded realism and direct experiential learning and feeling. This means having the vision and guts to face the realities of poverty, inequality, oppression, discrimination, intolerance, stigma, and the terrible insecurities and suffering of war and civil disorder. Most of us, not least myself, do not often if ever manage to do that face-to-face. We must celebrate and multiply those who do not look away but engage directly on the side of justice, decency, common humanity, and peace, fired and driven by outrage. This is about much more than mindsets and knowing. It is about feeling as well. It is about champions with vision, guts, and passion.[26]

Values are fundamental. The great religions of Baha'i, Buddhism, Christianity, Confucianism, Hinduism, Islam, Jainism, Judaism, Sikhism and other faiths, together with humanism, all enjoin inclusiveness and generosity (Tyndale, 2006). As Mahatma Gandhi saw them: 'the different religions are beautiful flowers from the same garden, or they are branches of the same majestic tree. Therefore they are equally true, though being received and interpreted through human instruments, equally imperfect'.

The values of love and loving one's neighbour are universal. The SDG consensus resonates with loving our neighbours by directing us to leave no one behind. This gives priority to those of our global neighbours wherever they are who are last. Knowing their realities better and the experience of that knowing can provoke passion and outrage, generating commitment and energy and actions, big and small, to make our world a better place.

The future of knowing better, of learning and unlearning, of practical and inclusive realism, of ground-truthing, facilitation and reflexivity, should continue for the rest of this century to present the thrill and fulfilment of unfolding experiences, insights, and opportunities. We face a future of continuous change, innovation, new technologies, and proliferating combinations and inventiveness from eclectic methodological pluralism. The challenge will be to see and seize opportunities, to push back against Newtonian rigidities, to make, protect, and use space for adaptive flexibility and creativity. There will be more and more to know and more to strive to know better. For all those with freedom to act and who are committed to good change and to evolving and embodying a new professionalism for complexity, putting the last first and leaving no one behind, our 21st century opens up for proactive engagement. For innovators, activists, and those passionate for a better world, it holds out promise of an exhilarating time to be alive. There will be so much to explore, so much to discover, so much to know, and so much to do.

What we can do depends on who we are and where we are. Innumerable small acts mount up and reinforce one another. From whatever we and others do, large or small, we can strive to learn and find better ways of knowing and doing. Ideals like equality, justice, well-being for all, and putting the last first, will always be there for us to strive towards. As our unforeseeable 21st century unfolds, it is a privilege to be explorers looking for good ways forward. The enthralling adventures of our human struggle to know better and do better should have no end.

Notes

1. If you are coming straight to this last chapter you may wish first to read or scan the abstracts of the five earlier chapters to give you background.

2. To keep this book manageable I am not considering the vast literature, numerous schools, and rich experiences of action research and participatory action research. For an authoritative coverage of these see Hilary Bradbury's *The Sage Handbook of Action Research* (2015), which has 79 chapters and (this is no disparagement) weighs 1.4 kilos on our family scales.

3. For more on accelerating change see *Into the Unknown* (Chambers, 2014), 'The future is faster' (pp. 124–6) and 'New exclusions, inclusions and impacts' (pp. 126–7).

4. For nearly two decades I have been asking participants in workshops whether the awareness, aspirations, and priorities of 'poor people' (a shorthand label) were changing slower, at about the same rate, or faster, than 10 to 15 years earlier. The overwhelming view throughout has been that the rate had become faster.

5. Readers inclined to critical, perhaps cynical, realism may see my enthusiasm for the SDGs as yet another manifestation of naïve optimism. Wealthier countries can simply ignore their commitments. My view is that steps in good directions do matter and can make a difference. Change first the language and the public commitments, and then make these the foundations for monitoring, exposing, comparing, and shaming, raising public awareness, changing mindsets, and campaigning for good change.

6. Economists bear out the uncertainties of economic futures by the extent to which they disagree (Chambers, 1997: 51–3). An exception was the prediction of some nine out of 10 economists that Brexit would have bad economic effects. One might have thought that this almost unprecedented agreement would have been a deciding factor in the popular vote. It was not. It is also conceivable, though in my view unlikely, that it will prove to have been wrong.

7. For a brilliant, erudite, and fascinating analysis of right and left hemispheres of the brain in Western history I recommend Iain McGilchrist (2009) *The Master and his Emissary*. The left hemisphere of the brain is paradigmatically Newtonian. McGilchrist's conclusion, 'The master betrayed' (pp. 428 ff.), illuminates the pathological nature of the constraints of recently required development procedures. He writes that the left hemisphere is 'a wonderful servant, but a very poor master' and that 'we have already fallen for the left hemisphere's propaganda' (p. 437). One comes to recognize that governments and donors have indeed fallen into that trap.

8. For extended and mischievous fun with words and concepts in development see *Provocations for Development,* part 1, 'Word play' (Chambers, 2012: 3–34). For wonderful sources of insight and entertainment, which I enthusiastically recommend, see Andrea Cornwall and Deborah Eade's *Deconstructing Development Discourse* (2010). For a nuanced and detailed understanding of the complexities of the evolution of mainstream vocabulary in the 1990s see Andrea Cornwall's *Beneficiary, Consumer, Citizen* (2000).

9. As trustees of ActionAid, Barbara Harriss-White and I fought a battle to stop words from the private sector infiltrating ActionAid-speak and thinking. We lost. They were a tide overwhelming the whole sector. So ActionAid began to talk and think about its *market* and its *brand.* I have been acculturated to these words which no longer sound so discordant. But in early 2016 I could still be shocked when one of the senior staff of another large, well-known, British-based INGO referred to it as 'this company'. One wonders how far this can go. Will the tide ever turn?

10. Word changes in repetitive public announcements are, however, very noticeable. An example is when privatized rail companies in the UK started calling us customers instead of passengers (a change which still grates with me).

11. Wilkinson and Pickett (2009) have shown that inequality, not income, explains differences in indicators of human well-being above about $25,000 per capita. The World Social Science Report 2016 is *Challenging Inequalities: Pathways to a Just World* (ISSC et al., 2016).

12. My laptop tells me that groundtruthing, ground-truthing and ground truthing are not legitimate expressions or spellings. So much the worse for the laptop programmers.

13. Arguably, facilitation and empowerment should permeate behaviour and attitudes in all formative upper–lower relationships, in the family, in schools and colleges, and within organizations. Were that so we would be living in a very different world.

14. I recollect a workshop in Washington, DC, where a group I was in was enjoying a preliminary brainstorm only to be repeatedly interrupted by a facilitator asking us whether we were clear about our objectives. The facilitator probably felt he had to do something to justify his fee, but having to deal with him was an irritating distraction. Paradoxically, he succeeded in uniting the group – against him.

15. This is not the place to share a personal list of dos and don'ts of facilitation. Participants in workshops over the years have listed well over a hundred. 'Listen' often scores highest. Respect can be elaborated to include respecting the right of those who are shy or feel threatened not to participate and offer strategies they can adopt in self-protection (See '21 tips for surviving participatory workshops' in Chambers, 2002: 188–94).

16. Facilitation is less relevant in crisis logistics and relationships. Facilitative approaches have been shown to have many applications with people in emergencies, but when it comes to logistics for ordering and supply of things like equipment or food a short-term command and control approach may be needed. Unfortunately, the top-down approaches to

short-term logistics with things tend to persist too long and permeate other emergency activities with people.

17. Materialist scientists have a faith, though they may not wish to acknowledge this. Like other faiths it is marked by what is rejected out of hand.

18. For a fuller treatment of non-negotiable principles, expressed as values, objectives, and behaviours, see *Ideas for Development* (Chambers, 2005: 74–6).

19. Energy and where it comes from is a strangely neglected aspect of complexity theory. It is, however, needed for all adaptive behaviour. An adaptive agent or adaptive system cannot adapt without energy. See Uphoff's (1992) seminal chapter, 'Social energy as an offset to equilibrium and entropy', and my paper *Paradigms, Poverty and Adaptive Pluralism* (Chambers, 2010: 48).

20. For the example of Kyocera I am grateful to James Allen, who also introduced the word *love* in the discourse at the 50th Anniversary Conference at IDS.

21. The source is William Wordsworth's *Tintern Abbey* (1798).

22. I recommend a visit to www.reality-check-approach.com where much readable and insightful material on RCA can be found.

23. For a fuller discussion and illustration of passionate communities see Chambers (2014: 122–4).

24. Many in funding agencies are enlightened but constrained by procedures. Helping them change the institutional systems in which they are enmeshed is a largely unrecognized opportunity for those of us on the outside.

25. I am grateful to James Allen for the quotation from Martin Luther King.

26. I am embarrassed to write this, being aware of my own life of looking away, living comfortably, avoiding conflict, and habitually seeking win–win ways forward. I write this because I believe it is right, not because I live it.

References

Anderson, M., Brown, D. and Jean, I. (2012) *Time to Listen: Hearing People on the Receiving End of International Aid*, Cambridge, MA: CDA Collaborative Learning Projects.

Birch, I., Catani, F. and Chambers, R. (2007) *Immersions: Learning about Poverty Face-to-Face* [pdf], PLA 57, London: IIED <www.iied.org/pla-57-immersions-learning-about-poverty-face-face> [accessed 13 October 2016].

Bradbury, H. (ed.) (2015) *The Sage Handbook of Action Research*, 3rd edn, London: Sage Reference.

Chambers, R. (1997) *Whose Reality Counts? Putting the First Last*, Rugby, UK: Practical Action Publishing.

Chambers, R. (2002) *Participatory Workshops: A Sourcebook 21 Sets of Ideas and Activities*, London and Sterling, VA: Earthscan.

Chambers, R. (2005) *Ideas for Development*, London: Earthscan.

Chambers, R. (2010) *Paradigms, Poverty and Adaptive Pluralism*, Working Paper 344, Brighton, UK: IDS.

Chambers, R. (2012) *Provocations for Development*, Rugby, UK: Practical Action Publishing.

Chambers, R. (2014) *Into the Unknown: Explorations in Development Practice*, Rugby, UK: Practical Action Publishing.

Cornwall, A. (2000) *Beneficiary, Consumer, Citizen: Perspectives on Participation for Poverty Reduction*, Sida Studies No 2, Stockholm: Sida.

Cornwall, A. and Eade, D. (eds) (2010) *Deconstructing Development Discourse: Buzzwords and Fuzzwords*, Rugby, UK: Practical Action Publishing in association with Oxfam GB.

Douthwaite, B., Apgar, J. M., Schwarz, A., Attwood, S., Seranatra Sellamutu, S. (forthcoming) *A new professionalism for agricultural research for development*. International Journal of Agricultural Sustainability.

Gandhi, M. (n.d.) *AZQuotes.com*, <www.azquotes.com/quote/593345> [accessed 4 January 2017].

Hayman, R., King, S., Kontinen, T. and Narayanaswamy, L. (eds) (2016) *Negotiating Knowledge: Evidence and Experience in Development NGOs*, Rugby, UK: Practical Action Publishing.

Herout, P. and Schmid, E. (2015) 'Doing, knowing, learning: systematization of experiences based on the knowledge management of HORIZONT3000' *Knowledge Management for Development Journal* 11(1): 64–76.

IDS (no date) *Facilitate*, Participatory Methods [website], Institute of Development Studies, <http://www.participatorymethods.org/task/facilitate> [accessed 28 February 2017].

ISSC, IDS and UNESCO (2016) *World Social Science Report 2016: Challenging Inequalities: Pathways to a Just World* [pdf], Paris: International Social Science Council, the Institute of Development Studies (IDS) and UNESCO <http://unesdoc.unesco.org/images/0024/002458/245825e.pdf> [accessed 31 January 2017].

KM4D (2015) 'Facilitation for development', *Knowledge Management for Development Journal* 11(1).

Kontinen, T. (2016) 'What sense does it make? Vocabularies of practice and knowledge creation in a development NGO', in R. Hayman, S. King, T. Kontinen, and L. Narayanaswamy (eds), *Negotiating Knowledge*, pp. 29–45, Rugby, UK: Practical Action Publishing.

Korten, D. (1984) 'Rural development programming: the learning process approach', in D. Korten and R. Klaus (eds), *People-centred Development: Contributions towards Theory and Planning Frameworks*, pp. 176–88, West Hartford, CT: Kumarian Press.

Kyocera (no date) *Corporate motto / management rationale* [online], <http://global.kyocera.com/company/philosophy/> [accessed 28 February 2017].

McGilchrist, I. (2009) *The Master and his Emissary: The Divided Brain and the Making of the Western World*, New Haven, CT and London: Yale University Press.

Mander, H. (2001) *Unheard Voices: Stories of Forgotten Lives*, New Delhi: Penguin Books.

Mander, H. (2015) *Looking Away: Inequality, Prejudice and Indifference in New India* [online], New Delhi: Speaking Tiger <http://speakingtigerbooks.com/books/looking-away-inequality-prejudice-and-indifference-in-new-india/> [accessed 13 October 2016].

Narayan, D., Chambers, R., Shah, M. and Petesch, P. (2000) *Voices of the Poor: Crying Out for Change*, New York: Oxford University Press for the World Bank.

Parasuraman, S., Gomathy, K. and Fernandez, B. (2003) *Listening to People Living in Poverty*, Bangalore: Books for Change.

Reality Check Approach (2016) [website], <http://www.reality-check-approach.com/> [accessed 28 February 2017].

Rose, T. (2016) *The End of Average: How to Succeed in a World that Values Sameness*, London: Allen Lane, Penguin Random House.

Sellers, T. (1995) *Participatory Appraisal Workshop Proceedings*, Hull, UK: Department of Public Health Medicine, University of Hull and East Riding.

Shah, A. (2013) 'I don't know … and related thoughts' in T. Wallace, F. Porter, with M. Ralph-Bowman (eds), *Aid, NGOs and the Realities of Women's Lives*, pp. 199–211, Rugby, UK: Practical Action Publishing.

Shahrokh, T. and Wheeler, J. (eds) (2014) *Knowledge from the Margins: An Anthology From a Global Network on Participatory Practice and Policy Influence*, Brighton, UK: IDS.

Thomas, T. and Narayanan, P. (eds) (2015) *Participation Pays: Pathways for Post-2015*, Rugby, UK: Practical Action Publishing.

Tyndale, W. (ed.) (2006) *Visions of Development: Faith-based Initiatives*, Aldershot, UK: Ashgate.

Uphoff, N. (1992) *Learning from Gal Oya: Possibilities for Participatory Development and Post-Newtonian Social Science*, Ithaca, NY: Cornell University Press.

Wilkinson, R. and Pickett, K. (2009) *The Spirit Level: Why More Equal Societies Almost Always Do Better*, London: Allen Lane, Penguin Random House.

World Bank (2000) *World Development Report 2000: Attacking Poverty*, Washington, DC: World Bank.

World Bank (2015) *World Development Report 2015: Mind, Society, and Behavior*, Washington, DC: World Bank.

Glossary of meanings

This glossary presents the meanings I try to be consistent in giving to words in this book. I am not saying that this is what they *should* mean. Others may wish to give some of them other meanings.

Agenda	is used not like a list of topics to be covered in a meeting but in its original more normative and operational Latin sense of 'things that ought to be done'
Approach	an orientation to action or process, especially related to a choice of methodology. An approach can, for instance, be participatory, qualitative, quantitative, statistical, reductionist or inclusive
Appropriate imprecision	not investing in more precise measurement than needed. Aka proportionate accuracy. See also *Optimal ignorance*
Biases	(among professionals) preferences for and tendencies towards behaviours, choices, locations, people, priorities, topics, qualities and/or methods which give an unbalanced, distorted and/or incomplete view of realities (Chapter 2)
Blind spots	domains, locations, topics, factors, aspects, dimensions, approaches and/or methods which are systemically not recognized, and/or neglected; and little or not at all researched or acted on (Chapter 2)
Canon	a principle to inform and guide action (Chapter 4)
Complex	exhibiting non-linearity, unpredictability and emergence, as with people and social processes
Complexity	a system condition characterised by many interacting parts, linkages dimensions and processes, and exhibiting non-linearity, unpredictability and emergence (Chapter 4)
Confirmation bias	the tendency to search for, favour, recall, and repeat information that confirms what one believes or wants to believe, with the corollary of discounting, dismissing or denying whatever is contradictory
Coprophilia	an abnormal interest in faeces and their evacuation

Cost-effective	having a high benefit to cost ratio, with benefits assessed by actual and potential effects and impact including stakeholders' learning and capacity, costs assessed to include transaction costs and opportunity costs of finance, professional capacity, and people's time, and both benefits and costs assessed inclusively to embrace quality and utility of data, insights, motivation, and morale
Development	good change
Discomfort zone	a concern, topic, relationship or activity which makes an individual, group, organisation, profession or discipline feel discomfort, including embarrassment for reasons such as lack of competence or confidence, threat whether physical, psychological, social, financial, political, professional or to status, personal comfort or convenience, or difficulty of conducting research
Eclectic methodological pluralism	being open to using any methodology, method or combination of methodologies and methods. This pluralism is broader than 'mixed methods' when that refers only to a combination of quantitative and qualitative
Emic	expressing the knowledge, concepts, categories, and values of insiders, within a social group
Entomophagy	eating insects, larvae, pupae, centipedes, millipedes or spiders
Epistemic relativism	the concept of there being many knowledges, both shared and personal, variously influenced by social and physical context, methodologies, discipline, ideology and personality
Epistemological	to do with knowing and the nature of knowledge(s)
Etic	expressing the knowledge, concepts, categories and values of outsiders to a social group
Ground-truthing	observing local conditions directly and having face-to-face, listening, and learning interaction with local people, and especially with those who are last (see *Last*), or being credibly informed by others who do this, as with Reality Checks (Chapter 5)
Harijans	Children of God, Gandhi's name for Untouchables (India), now Dalits
Heuristic	*adj.* of practical value for learning, especially for oneself

Inclusive rigour	rigour for complexity sought through inclusiveness, and the canons of eclectic methodological pluralism, seeking diversity and balance, improvisation and innovation, adaptive iteration, triangulation, inclusive participation and plural perspectives, optimal ignorance and appropriate imprecision, and interactive and experiential ground-truthing (Chapter 4)
Last, as in 'the last'	those who are, or in various combinations are, poor, vulnerable, marginalized, weak, disabled, displaced, insecure, discriminated against, stigmatized, oppressed, excluded, powerless, or otherwise disadvantaged, including all those left out and left behind
Linear	in a line, following or intended to follow a straight and predictable path
Lock-in	a procedure in which early actions and decisions commit to a fixed sequence of required actions and/or targets, such as RCTs, systematic reviews, logframes, and payment by results (Chapter 3)
Logical framework (logframe)	a project design, management, and monitoring tool in matrix form typically specifying objective, purpose, outputs and activities, together with assumptions, indicators, and means of verification
Method	a way of doing something. As methods become more elaborate with longer processes they sometimes merge into methodologies e.g. participatory video can be considered both method and methodology
Methodology	a system of methods
Mindset	predispositions, ideologies, values, beliefs, words, categories and constructs, values and emotions which frame and influence how a person sees, learns about, and interprets the world
Myth	misguided belief. I do not use it in its other sense of a traditional or legendary story
Neglected tropical disease (NTD)	one of 17 diseases predominantly found between the tropics of Cancer and Capricorn which has historically been neglected, for instance soil-transmitted helminths such as ascaris and hookworm, schistosomiasis, trachoma, and filariasis
Newtonian	exhibiting linearity, following rules or laws with set patterns and predictable outcomes as with many physical things

Non-linear	not in a straight line, following an irregular and often unpredictable path
Ontological	to do with the nature of things and of being
Optimal ignorance	not finding out more than needed, especially for practical purposes. Requires knowing what it is not worth knowing. See also *Appropriate imprecision*
Paradigm	a coherent and mutually supporting pattern or system of concepts and ontological assumptions, values and principles, methods and procedures, roles and behaviours, relationships, and mindsets, orientations and dispositions.
Payment by results	an arrangement where a contractor is paid in whole only after satisfactory completion of a contract, sometimes with part payment in tranches depending on reaching agreed stages
Pluralism	having, using or being open to different approaches, methods, criteria, canons or other aspects or dimensions
Positionality	a person's social situation, context, and relationships
Positivism	a form of empiricism which holds to experimental method and observation as means of establishing objective reality
Professionalism	concepts, values, methods, behaviours, and mindsets dominant in a profession or discipline
Randomized Control Trial	a type of scientific, often medical, experiment or investigation where the similar entities being studied (such as people, households or communities) are randomly allocated between one or more treatments and a control, with baselines measured in all these before treatment and then repeated later
Randomista	a person committed to Randomised Control Trials and similar approaches. Often used in a light-hearted, mildly pejorative sense
Reality Check	direct, face-to-face, unconstrained, and open-ended interaction, listening, and learning between an outsider(s) and those living at the grass roots, especially those who are 'last'. See Reality Check Approach in Chapter 5
Reductionism	reducing the multiple, diverse, and complex to the unitary, standard, and/or simple for purposes of measurement, research, and/or analysis, or studying part of a system separately from the whole, or seeking to understand a complex whole as the sum of its separated component parts
Reductionist rigour	rigour sought through the canons of sampling, measurement, and statistics

Reflexivity, self-critical	being critically aware of one's personal biases, predilections, preferences, frames, and categories for interpreting the world. Aka self-critical epistemological awareness
Relevant	having practical utility for learning and acting. Responsible relevance in research includes relationships and costs and benefits to research participants.
Results-Based Management	management strategies which focus on achieving outputs, outcomes, and impacts, and measuring and monitoring quantitative indicators as key tools for assessing performance against targets
Rigour	cost-effectiveness in useful learning, with trade-offs between scale of applicability, range of relevant data, validity, timeliness and credibility, these set against costs which include opportunity costs of people's time and other resources (Chapter 4)
Theory of change	a theory of means and pathways to achieve desired results. In common usage a theory of change charts pathways from needs to activities, outcomes, and impacts, and articulates the assumptions underlying the reasoning
Triangulation	using two or more methods, approaches, sources, informants, perspectives, and/or contexts for finding out about and understanding something, with cross-checking and often successive approximation
Universe	the range of phenomena of concern and under study
Validity	the quality and degree of correspondence with reality

Index

accountability 66, 73, 74, 75,
  76*box*, 77
Accountability, Learning and
  Planning System *see* ALPS
Action Aid 74, 85n29, 109, 131
action learning 99, 101, 109,
  112, 114
adaptive iteration 99, 100
adaptive pluralism paradigm 95*fig*,
  153
Africa
  anthropological particularism 61
  deforestation 5, 14
  desertification 10, 11, 17
  extrapolation 13
  historical evidence 14
  Integrated Rural Development
    Projects 3
  masculinities 32
  Michigan State University
    and 8, 9
  participatory mapping 132
  payment by results 76*box*
  power relations 9
  project bias 30
  socialism 11
  Training and Visit System 4
  undernutrition 42
  woodfuel gap theory 4
  see also Kenya
  agenda 177*gl*
agriculture, designing tests that will
  fail 29
ALPS (Accountability, Learning and
  Planning System) 85n28,
  125, 131

American Medical Association 6
Ananthpur, K. et al.(2014) 67
Anderson, M.B. et al. (2012), *Time to
  Listen* 74, 75, 79, 81
  anthropological particularism 61
Appreciative Inquiry 124
  approach 177*gl*
  appropriate imprecision 100,
    177*gl*
Aptivate et al. (2016) 132
Archer, David 126
Arlen, Michael 57
artefacts of methodology, findings
  as 62–3
arteriosclerosis 5, 6
Arthur, Brian 130
Asia
  Training and Visit System 4
  undernutrition and stunting 42
  see also Bangladesh; China;
    India
Asian Development Bank report
  1991 15

Banerjee, A. and Duflo, E. 64, 65
Bangladesh
  Flood Action Plan 14
  logframes 74
  monitoring and
    measuring 137*box*, 138
  Reality Checks 135
  rickets 6
  statistics 134
  behaviour and attitudes 103, 104,
    122, 130, 131
behavioural–creative adaptability 98

Beijing World Conference on
  Women 1995 151
beliefs 4, 5, 12, 14–17, 20
Bennett, Arnold 57
Berners-Lee, Tim 151
biases 27–8, 50, 177*gl*
  airport bias 30
  child sex abuse 33
  entomophagy 35
  development tourism 30–1
  diarrhoea and environmental
    enteric dysfunction 40
  diplomatic bias 31
  faecally transmitted
    infections 41–2
  gender bias 31–2
  harmful traditional practices 32
  infant faeces 37
  masculinities and men 32
  past blind spots 31–3
  personal bias 30, 43, 47*t*, 48*t*
  professional bias 31, 47*t*, 48*t*
  project bias 30
  reliability of research 44, 45
  and rigour 94, 99
  seasonal bias 30, 31
  security 31
  sexuality 33
  spatial bias 30
  tarmac bias 30
  unpaid care 32
  urban slum bias 31
  water bias 41
'The Big Push Back' 81
Bill & Melinda Gates
  Foundation 78, 107
Blair, Tony 10
blind spots 177*gl*
  climate change and ocean
    ecology 36
  cookstove air pollution 35
  corruption 33, 34
  diarrhoea and environmental
    enteric dysfunction 39, 40
  entomophagy 34, 35

faecal sludge management 38
faecally transmitted infections 38,
  39, 41–2
incontinence 38
infant faeces 37
neglected tropical diseases 35
open defecation 37
personal and psychological
  preferences 43
recurrent dimensions 43–5
rural sanitation programme 41
shame, taboos, privacy, and
  power 43
water bias 41
Booth, Charles 60
Bradbury, Hilary, *The Sage Handbook
  of Action Research* 116
Brundtland Report 1987 5, 17
Bulletin of the American Soil Science
  Society 13
Burns, Danny 107, 108
Burns, D. and Worsley, S., *Navigating
  Complexity in International
  Development: Facilitating
  Sustainable Change at Scale* 108
Bush, George W. 10

canon 177*gl*
Carroll, Lewis xi
Carter, Jimmy 15
Catholic Church 33
Catley, A. et al., *Participatory Impact
  Assessment: A Design Guide* 133
Centre for International Forestry
  Research 138
CGIAR (Consultative Group for
  International Agricultural
  Research) 167, 168
Challenger disaster 19
Chambers, Robert
  Into the Unknown 159
  Putting the Last First 46
  *Revolutions in Development
    Inquiry* 119, 120
  Whose Reality Counts? 104

Chilcot Inquiry (Iraq Inquiry) 2016 10
child sex abuse 33, 43, 48
China 7, 62, 63
citizens' juries 124
CLTS (community-led total
   sanitation) 12, 18, 65, 69, 125,
   126, 141n14, 156
Cochrane Collaboration 69
Cochrane Systematic Review 39
collective action 166–7
commitment 154, 157, 161–2,
   166–7, 169
community-based/driven
   development 124
community-led total sanitation *see*
   CLTS
comparative analysis 71
competitive bidding 76, 77, 78
complex 177*gl*
complex systems perspective 108
complexity 177*gl*
complexity paradigm 92, 94–8, 101,
   105–8, 113–15
confidentiality and secrecy 9
configurational analysis 106
confirmation bias 18, 50, 177*gl*
Constituency Voice 125
constructivist memory 19
Consultative Group for International
   Agricultural Research *see* CGIAR
Copenhagen Social Summit
   1995 151
copropholia 177*gl*
Cornwall, Andrea, *Using Participatory
   Process Evaluation to Understand the
   Dynamics of Change in a Nutrition
   Education Programme* 128, 130
corruption
   and blind spots 33, 34, 44, 48
   logframes 74
   strategic ignorance 28, 29
   subsidies and 111, 113
cost-effectiveness 178*gl*
   and accountability 75, 76*box*
   alternatives to RCTs 71, 72, 139

randomized control trials 64, 71,
   80, 81
reduction in staff 74
and rigour for complexity 97–8,
   105
costs, hidden 76, 77, 78–80, 81
cotton 11
counter incentives 45
creative adaptability 105
cross-sectional studies 72
Curtis, Valerie 43
   *Don't Look, Don't Touch, Don't Eat:
   The Science behind Revulsion* 37

Dangour, A.D. et al. (2013) 39, 70
data 11–14
Deaton, Angus 64, 66, 83n12
debt 3, 4
deforestation 5, 14, 15
demotivation 79, 80
Department for International
   Development, UK *see* DFID
desertification 5, 9, 10, 11, 17
development 151, 152, 178*gl*
DFID (Department for International
   Development, UK) 74, 75, 78
diarrhoea 12, 13*t*, 18, 38, 39–40,
   70–1, 72
Digital Citizen Engagement 132
disciplinary convergence 61, 62
discomfort zone 178*gl*
disgust 37, 43
distance and insulation 15
Doing Business with the Rural Poor
   Project, Vietnam 105

Education Action (journal) 130
EED (environmental enteric
   dysfunction) 38, 39, 40, 41–2,
   52n16, 68
ego 11, 19
Einstein, Albert 57
emic 178*gl*
empowerment 119, 122, 128, 130,
   132, 136–9

entomophagy 178*gl*
epistemic relativism 58, 59, 60, 80,
    159, 178*gl*
epistemological 178*gl*
epistemology 98, 104, 158
errors 1–5, 27
    behavioural and experiential 14,
        15–19
    data-related 11, 12–14
    relational and personal 9, 10–11
    sources of 9–19
    etic 178*gl*
Ethiopia 8, 15, 16
European Evaluation Society 80
Evans-Pritchard, E., *The Nuer* 116n6
evidence-based policy 73
Eyben, Rosalind 32, 81, 83n6
Eyben, Rosalind et al., *The Politics
    of Evidence and Results in
    International Development:
    Playing the Game to Change the
    Rules?* 81

facilitation 156, 157–8
faecally transmitted infections
    see FTIs
Fairhead, J. and Leach, M. 14
farmer field schools 123, 124
farmer participatory
    research 123, 124
Fleming, Alexander 23n28
Ford Foundation 72
Freire, Paulo 130
Freud, Sigmund 33
frustration 74, 79
FTIs (faecally transmitted
    infections) 8, 39, 41–2
funding
    and accountability 73, 74
    blind spots 34, 35, 36, 44, 49
    counter incentives 45
    and dissonance 8
    error and myth 10
    mechanistic procedures 72
    and power 77, 78, 80–1

randomized control trials 65, 68,
    69, 78, 79
relationships 79, 80
transformative 167, 168–9

Gambia 40
Gandhi, Mahatma 170
gender 32, 37, 38, 43, 127t
Gender and Development
    Network 32
geographic information system
    see GIS
Ghana 105–7
Giles-Hansen, C. 51n11
Gill, Gerry 14, 15
Gladwell, Malcolm 113
Gough, Kathleen 14
Green, Duncan 84n21
    How Change Happens xiv
gridlock 109–14
ground-truthing 11, 100, 101, 102,
    114, 128, 156, 166, 178*gl*
group-visual synergy 102, 103*fig*
The Guardian 70
Guinea 5

harmful traditional practices *see*
    HTPs
Harriss, John 14, 16
Hartigan, Pamela 85n25
Harijans 178*gl*
Haslam, Nick 37
    Psychology in the Bathroom 43
Haswell, Margaret 61
Havel, Vaclav 149
Hawthorne effect 23n27
Hayman, R. et al., *Negotiating
    Knowledge* 81
Helicobacter pylori 5
Hellden, U. 13, 14
heresies 5–7, 8
Herout, P. and Schmid, E. 157
heuristic 178*gl*
Higgs, Marietta 33
Hill, Polly 61

history, overlooking 6, 14
history, rewriting 19
Hoffer, Eric 158
Holland, J., ed., *Who Counts? The Power of Participatory Statistics* 133, 134
homocysteine 5, 6
  HTPs (harmful traditional practices) 32, 43
Hueso, Andres 37
Hulme, David, *Should Rich Nations Help the Poor?* xiv
Human Development Index 61, 151
Humphrey, Jean
  'Child undernutrition, tropical enteropathy, toilets and handwashing' 40, 45
Huppert, Walter 28, 34
hybridization 130

Ibbott, Ralph 16
ICDDR, B *see* International Centre for Diarrhoeal Disease Research, Bangladesh
ICRISAT (International Crops Research Centre for the Semi-Arid Tropics) 17, 21n12, 186
ICTs (information and communication technologies) 99, 123, 130, 131–2, 133, 150, 151
IDS Bulletin 42
Ikeda, Kikunae 6
ILAC (Institutional Learning and Change) 167
illegality 10, 28, 43, 44, 48
immersions 114, 124, 126, 130, 135
improvisation 99, 130, 157
incentives 38, 39, 44–5
income-poverty concept 60, 61
incontinence 38
India 38, 43
  agricultural research 45
  corruption 33, 34
  Five-Year Plan 4

Ford Foundation 72
open defecation 13, 62, 72, 111, 112, 113
payment by results 84n19
Participatory Rural Appraisals 125
randomized control trials 67
rural sanitation programme 4, 111, 112, 113
social mapping 102
special projects 15
Total Sanitation Campaign 4, 11, 12
tree harvesting 6
undernutrition 42
warabandi irrigation 4
infant faeces 37, 43
information and communication technologies *see* ICTs
innovation 29, 78, 99, 112, 123–6, 130
irreversibility 68, 80, 81, 155
irrigation 4
Institutional Learning and Change *see* ILAC
interests 10
integrated pest management 123, 124, 156
Integrated Rural Development Projects 3
Intergovernmental Panel on Climate Change (IPCC) 36
interlocking factors 41, 109, 112, 113
International Agricultural Research Centres 10
International Centre for Diarrhoeal Disease Research, Bangladesh (ICDDR,B) 39
International Continence Society 38
International Crops Research Centre for the Semi-Arid Tropics *see* ICRISAT
International Fund for Agricultural Development 107

International Rice Research Institute
see IRRI
International Water Management
Institute *see* IWMI
intersex people 33
Intergovernmental Panel on Climate
Change *see* IPCC
Iraq, invasion of 10
IRRI (International Rice Research
Institute) 4, 7, 8, 17
IWMI (International Water
Management Institute) 28, 29

Jayakaran, Ravi, 'Wholistic
worldview analysis:
understanding community
realities' 127
Jolly, Richard 15, 61
Jolly, S. et al. (2006) 33

Kabutha, Charity 130
Kanbur, Ravi 61
Keeley, J. and Scoones, I. 13, 16
Kenya
historical aspect 14
nutrition education
programme 130
participatory ICTs 132
sugar industry 109–10, 111*fig*,
112, 113
water, sanitation, and hygiene 72
Kilvenmani incident 14, 16, 17
King, Martin Luther 169
Klenner, Frederick 6, 8
knowledges 57–83
co-generation and sharing 138, 139
epistemic relativism 58, 59, 60,
80, 159
local 58, 101, 102
mechanistic methodologies 64–9
mechanistic procedures 73–7, 78
methodological paradigms 58, 59t
and new professionalism 153–62
participatory methodologies 152,
153

plurality of 58
Korten, David 2, 158
Kuhn, Thomas, *The Structure of
Scientific Revolutions* 92
Kyocera 164

Lamprey, Hugh 9, 13
The Lancet 39, 40, 45
'the last' 179*gl*
Laulanié, Henri de 7
Leach, Gerald and Mearns,
Robin 11, 14
Leach, Melissa 85n26
Leach, Melissa and Mearns, Robin,
*The Lie of the Land: Challenging
Received Wisdom on the African
Environment* 9
Lehrer, J. 6
lenses 57, 59–63
Levene, Josh 128
LGBT (lesbian, gay, bisexual,
transgender) 33, 43
linear 179*gl*
Listening Project 166, 169
literature overviews 72
local governance, participatory
approaches to 125
local knowledge 58, 101, 102
lock-in 179*gl*
Loevinsohn, M. et al. (2014) 39, 71
logframes 73, 74, 78, 179*gl*
Lu, Caizhen, *Poverty and Development
in China: Alternative Approaches to
Poverty Assessment* 62, 63

MacNeice, Louis 91
Madagascar 7
Malawi 133, 135
Mali 65, 67
Mander, Harsh, *Looking Away:
Inequality, Prejudice and
Indifference in New India* 151, 166
Map Kibera 132
marginality, institutional and
professional 44

Marshall, Barry 5, 8
Marx, Karl 149
Mbioni (journal) 16
McCully, Kilmer 5, 6, 8
McGilchrist, Iain, *The Master and his Emissary* xi, 171n7
MDGs (Millennium Development Goals) 41, 46, 61, 152
MDI (multi-dimensional poverty index) 62, 63
Mead, Margaret 166
measurability 36, 39
mechanistic methodologies 63, 64, 72, 80, 81
media 128, 129t, 131–2
memory, malleable 19, 63
Mencken, H.L. 113
menstruation 43
method 179gl
methodology 179gl
methodological paradigms 58, 59t
methodological pluralism, eclectic 99, 105, 128, 129, 130, 178gl
methodological rigour 98, 99–100, 101
Michigan State University *see* MSU
Mill, John Stuart 149, 159
Millennium Development Goals *see* MDGs
Millennium Development Villages 30
Millinga, Ntimbanjao 16
mindset 10–11, 179gl
modernism 10
Modi, Narendra 111
most significant change 124
Mozambique 9
MPesa 132
MSU (Michigan State University) 8, 9
Mukherjee, Neela, *Speaking to Power* 128
multi-dimensional poverty index *see* MDI
Myrdal, Gunnar 61

myths 3, 27, 30, 164, 179gl
  sources of 9–19

Naitsios, Andrew 57
Narayan, D. et al., *Voices of the Poor* 136, 166
narratives 5, 9–11, 13, 14, 15, 16, 17
national debt 3
neglected topics 28, 31, 32–6, 38, 46
neglected tropical diseases *see* NTDs
neo-Malthusian vicious circle 16
neo-Marxism 10
Nepal 14, 15, 73, 74, 133
New Scientist 58
Newton, Isaac 91
Newtonian paradigm 92, 94fig, 96t, 138, 153, 179gl
non-linear 180gl
Norman, David 11
NTDs (neglected tropical diseases) 35, 44, 51n6, 179gl
Nyerere, Julius 11, 16

ontological 180gl
open defecation, India 111, 112
  blind spots 37, 43
  misleading data 12, 13, 29
  and stunting 45
  and taboo 43
  targets 11, 113
  underestimation of 62
  and undernutrition 42, 71, 72
optimal ignorance 100, 104, 180gl
outcome mapping 124
Orza, Luisa 84n22

Padfield, Harland 29
paradigms 58, 59t, 180gl
Parasuraman, S. et al. (2003) 151
Participate Project 136, 151
participatory action learning system 124
participatory approaches with ICTs 124, 131, 132, 133
participatory budgeting 124, 132

participatory census mapping 133

participatory geographic information systems 124, 128, 130

participatory human rights analysis 125

Participatory Hygiene and Sanitation Transformation *see* PHAST

Participatory Impact Assessment and Learning Approach *see* PIALA

participatory learning and action *see* PLA

participatory management and institutions 164–5

participatory mapping 18, 128, 130–3

participatory methodologies *see* PMs

participatory monitoring and evaluation 124, 132

participatory natural resource management 124

participatory pluralism 131

participatory poverty assessment *see* PPA

Participatory Review and Reflection Processes *see* PRRPs

Participatory Rural Appraisal *see* PRA

participatory seed breeding 124

participatory social auditing 125

participatory statistics 124, 133–4

participatory technology development 124

participatory 3-D mapping 125

participatory value chain analysis 125

participatory video 122, 123, 124, 131

participatory vulnerability analysis 125

passion 166, 167, 169–70

patriarchy and taboos 43

Patton, M.Q. *Development Evaluation* 108

Pawson, Ray, *The Science of Evaluation* 101

PbR (payment by results) 73, 75, 76*box*, 78, 180*gl*

personal, primacy of 165–6

Peters, T.J. and Waterman, R.H., *In Search of Excellence: Lessons from America's Best-run Companies* 114

PHAST (Participatory Hygiene and Sanitation Transformation) 141n14

phone hacking scandals 28

photo voice 125, 131

PIALA (Participatory Impact Assessment and Learning Approach) 97, 105–7, 125, 138, 168, 169

PLA (participatory learning and action) 123, 124, 125

PLA Notes 125

PLOS Neglected Tropical Diseases (journal) 35

pluralism 95*fig*, 114, 180*gl*

PMs (participatory methodologies) 101, 119–40
 history and overview 123–5
 life cycles 125, 126, 127
 participatory methods 127–8
 policies and programmes 3–4

polio research 6, 8

Poonam, S.K. and Petri, W.A. 41

Popper, Karl 159

positionality 180*gl*

positive deviance 112, 124

positivism 180*gl*

post-harvest losses of crops 4

Poverty Action Laboratory, MIT 65, 66, 67, 80

power 9, 10, 120, 121–2, 169

PPA (participatory poverty assessment) 62, 63, 123, 124, 136

PRA (Participatory Rural Appraisal) 101, 102, 123, 124, 125, 127–8

Prendergast, A. and Kelly, P. 42

Pretty, Jules 18

procedures 63, 72–5, 79–81, 92, 96*t*, 165
PRRPs (Participatory Review and Reflection Processes) 131
principles, values, and passion 161–2
priorities 35, 44, 49
proceduralization 74, 75
professional and personal preferences 43, 46, 47*t*, 48*t*
professionalism, new 150, 153–70, 180*gl*
  fundamentals of 153–62
public relations 18, 19

questionnaire surveys 60, 62, 67
Quinn Patton, Michael, *Developmental Evaluation* 101

Ramalingam, Ben, *Aid on the Edge of Chaos: Rethinking International Cooperation in a Complex World* 107
Randomista 180*gl*
randomized control trials *see* RCTs
Rao, V.K.R.V., *Food, Nutrition and Poverty in India* 42
rapid action learning 112
rapid rural appraisal *see* RRA
Rashomon effect 63, 64
RBM (results-based management) 73, 79, 181*gl*
RCA *see* Reality Check Approach
RCTs (randomized control trials) 64, 65–9, 180*gl*
  alternatives to 139
  and conformity 78
  before-after comparability 66
  causality 66
  choice of topics 66
  contamination 65
  costs 68
  funding 65, 68, 69, 78, 79
  irreversibility 68
  limitations of 80

opportunity costs 79
privileging of 69, 70
questionnaire survey 104
realities 121, 122, 127
Reality Check 180*gl*
Reality Check Approach (RCA) 102, 125, 134, 135–6, 156
reductionism 39, 59, 61, 64, 70, 80, 95
reductionist rigour 95, 98, 100, 114, 168, 180*gl*
REFLECT (Regenerated Freirian Literacy with Empowering Community Techniques) 74, 124, 125, 126, 130
reflexivity, self-critical xii–xiii, xiv, 103, 104, 106, 158–60, 181*gl*
Rehfuss, E. and Bartram, J. 69, 70
relationships 16, 79, 80, 81, 96*t*, 105
relevant 181*gl*
repetition 15, 16, 17
repetitive confirmation bias 18
report cards 124
results-based management *see* RBM
revolutionary professionalism 162, 163, 164
Rhodesia 29
Richardson, Anthony and Poloczanska, Elvira, 'Ocean science, under-researched and under threat' 45
rickets 6
rigour 91–115, 181*gl*
  group-visual synergy 102
  inclusive 94, 95–102, 104, 107–9, 112, 114, 136, 179*gl*
  maps and diagrams 99
  meanings and forms 94, 95–8
  from participation 101
  pluralism and 114
  reductionist 95, 98, 100, 114, 168, 180*gl*
  reflexivity 103, 104
  responsible relevance 104, 105
  systemic action research 107–8, 109

rigour (*cont.*)
  triangulation and 100
  wicked mess and gridlock 109–14, 115
RNA, non-genetic changes in 6
Root and Tuber Improvement and Marketing Programme *see* RTIMP
Rowntree, Seebohm 60
Rozin, P. 43
RRA (rapid rural appraisal) 120, 123, 130
RRA Notes 125
RTIMP (Root and Tuber Improvement and Marketing Programme) 97, 105
Rumsfeld, Donald 27
'rural development tourism' 15
rural sanitation programme 4, 29, 30, 41, 111, 112, 113
Rwanda 134

Sahara desert 5
Santa Fe Institute 49
Sasakawa Global 2000 programme 8, 15, 16
Saxena, N,C. 6
Schultz, Kathyrn, *Being Wrong: Adventures in the Margin of Error* 19
Science 45
Schmidt, W. 70
Scott, James, *Seeing Like a State* 83n8
SDGs (Sustainable Development Goals) xi, 2, 46, 62, 136, 152
selective experiences 15, 16
'self-critical epistemological awareness' 98
self-delusion 19
Sellers, Tilly 130, 157, 158
Sempere, K. 130
Sen, Amartya 2, 61
sense-making workshops 106, 107, 125, 138
sex workers 33
sexuality 33, 43

Shaffer, Paul 64, 71
Shah, Ashish 109–10, 113, 114
Sharma, S. and Atero, A., *Empowering Women through Better Healthcare and Nutrition in Developing Countries* 42
Sida (Swedish International Development Cooperation Agency) 135, 137*box*
Sijbesma, Christine et al. (2011) 68
silos 8, 44
Smaling, E. et al. (1997) 13
SMART (Specific, Measurable, Achievable, Relevant, and Time-bound) 154, 155*t*
Snowden, David 114
social change, acceleration of 150, 151
social mapping 102
soundbites 18–19
South Asia Conference on Sanitation 2013 18
Spears, Dean 42, 45, 71
Spicker, P. 60
SQUAT survey, North India 67
SR (systematic reviews) 64, 69, 70–1, 78, 79, 108
SRI (System of Rice Intensification) 7, 8, 10, 29
Starkey, P. 17
statistics
  misleading 11–14
  participatory 79, 124, 133–4
  and poverty 60
  and repetition 18, 20
  and research 39, 40*t*, 45, 70, 71
  sticky 17
Stepping Stones 124, 130
Stevenson, Jacqui 77
strategic ignorance 8, 28–9, 30
structural adjustment 3
stunting 41, 42, 45, 65, 68, 70
Sudan 13, 14

sugar industry 109–10, 111*fig*, 112, 113
Sumner, Andy and Tribe, Michael, *International Development Studies: theories and methods in research and practice* xiv
Sustainable Development Goals *see* SDGs
Swedish International Development Cooperation Agency *see* Sida
Swift, J. 10, 11, 14, 20
System of Rice Intensification *see* SRI
systematic reviews *see* SRs

T and V (Training and Visit) System of Agricultural Extension 3, 4, 10
taboos 37, 43, 44
Tagore, Rabindranath 149
Tanzania 4, 11, 16
Temin, Howard 6
Ten Seed Technique 127
theatre 124, 129
theory of change (ToC) 73, 105, 181*gl*
Thomas, T. and Narayanan, P., eds., *Participation Pays* 164
timescales and targets 113
TSC (Total Sanitation Campaign) 4
Training and Visit System of Agricultural Extension *see* T and V
transformations 131–6
transformative story-telling 125
trends 80–2
triangulation 63, 100, 102, 133, 181*gl*
truth 5, 8, 14, 17, 58, 159–62

Ujamaa programme 4, 11, 16
Umami, the fifth taste 6
UN Trust Fund for Women 77
undernutrition 40–5, 71, 72
UNICEF 2, 72
United Nations Environment Programme 17

universal 181*gl*
University of Dar es Salaam 4
Uphoff, N. 8, 92, 140n10
Uphoff, N. and Coombs, J. 6
Ushahidi (software) 132

Vaill, Peter, *Learning as a Way of Being: Strategies for Survival in a World of Permanent White Water* 114
validity 181*gl*
values, professional 47*t*
van Es, M. and Guijt, I. 72
Van Hemelrijck, A. and Guijt, I. 97
Van Hemelrijck, A. and Kyei-Mensah, G. 97, 106
Venkataraman, V., *Testing CLTS Approaches for Scalability* 72
Vietnam 105, 107
visual representation 99, 102, 103*fig*, 123, 127–9, 133
visualizing sustainable landscapes 125
Voices of the Poor project 136–8, 139

Wade, Robert 33, 34
Waller, John, *Fabulous Science: Fact and Fiction in the History of Scientific Discovery* 19
Waller, Richard, *Pastoral Poverty in Historical Perspective* 61
warabandi system irrigation 4, 10
WARDA (West African Rice Development Association) 29
Warren, J.R. 5
WASH (water, sanitation, and hygiene)
  blind spots 37–42, 44
  Evidence Gap Map 39
  literature reviews 72
  randomized control trials 67, 72
  systematic reviews 70
  and undernutrition 66, 71
Waddington, H. et al. (2009) 71

wealth and well-being ranking 134
Wegener, Alfred 5, 8
West African Rice Development
  Association *see* WARDA
White, H. 99
wicked mess 109, 113, 114, 138, 164
Wilkinson, R. and Pickett, K. 172n11
win-win 122, 133–4, 136, 137*box*,
Wolfensohn, James 124, 154
woodfuel gap theory 4, 11
Woolf, Virginia, *A Room of One's
  Own* 160
words and concepts 154–5, 156
Wordsworth, William 125, 165
World Bank 27
  Attacking Poverty 49, 136, 151
  gender equality 32
  Human Development Reports 32,
    49, 60

  Integrated Rural Development
    Projects 3
  Mind, Society and Behavior 28, 50,
    69, 159, 160
  payment by results 75
  and participation 124
  Training and Visit System 3, 4
  Water and Sanitation project 12
World Social Summit of 1995 60
World Water Week 41
World Vision 155

young males and violence 49

Zenawi, Meles 15
Zimbabwe 68

www.ingramcontent.com/pod-product-compliance
Lightning Source LLC
Jackson TN
JSHW011929131224
75386JS00035B/1133